UNDER THE SHADOW OF THE SWASTIKA

Under the Shadow of the Swastika

The Moral Dilemmas of Resistance and Collaboration in Hitler's Europe

Rab Bennett
Senior Lecturer in Politics
Manchester Metropolitan University

First published 1999 by
MACMILLAN PRESS LTD
Houndmills, Basingstoke, Hampshire RG21 6XS
and London
Companies and representatives
throughout the world

ISBN 0–333–65602–4

A catalogue record for this book is available
from the British Library.

This book is printed on paper suitable for recycling and
made from fully managed and sustained forest sources.

10   9   8   7   6   5   4   3   2   1
08   07   06   05   04   03   02   01   00   99

Printed and bound in Great Britain by
Antony Rowe Ltd, Chippenham, Wiltshire

To Carol
and to
Thomas and Rebecca

Contents

Acknowledgements

I wish to record my thanks to Ralph White for the invitation to attend the University of Salford postgraduate seminars during the academic years 1992–94 on the subject of Resistance and Collaboration, and for allowing me to try out some of the ideas developed in this book. The works of Primo Levi and Elie Wiesel have had a profound influence on the development of my ideas. I must also express a general intellectual indebtedness to Michael Walzer and Lawrence Langer. Their excellent works in the areas of the ethics of war and the Holocaust have had a lasting influence on my ideas, as is evident throughout this book. I am grateful to Lawrence Langer for his encouraging comments on my outline.

Thanks also to Mike Garner and Bob Auld for reading various drafts, and for stimulating discussions. Their pointed questioning prompted much-needed clarification of key issues.

I should also like to record a special thanks to Dr David Edward Williams of Sett Valley Medical Centre for his professional excellence, cheerful bedside manner and many acts of personal kindness, and also for keeping my body and spirit together during a difficult period.

I also wish to thank my beloved children, Thomas and Rebecca, for their patience and tolerance in having to live with this project for far too long. I hope that one day they will think it has been worthwhile. I must also thank Jenny and Nikki for their good humour, despite endless re-drafts which interrupted their lives.

Above all, I wish to thank my dear friend and 'amazing amanuensis' Carol Elliott, who has collaborated at every stage of this work, and who believed in it even when I didn't. Without Carol's invaluable help and encouragement this book would never have been completed. My debt to Carol is inestimable; my regard for her immeasurable.

The Swastika ... became the universal symbol of what is humanly and historically intolerable.

Jean Amery

How can the people of the free countries be made to realise what life was like under the Occupation? ... We could not stir an inch, eat or even breathe without becoming the accomplices of our enemy.... The whole country both resisted and collaborated. Everything we did was equivocal; we never quite knew whether we were doing right or doing wrong; a subtle poison corrupted even our best actions.

Jean-Paul Sartre

In many ways we [in Britain] have led a fortunately sheltered island life, both politically and philosophically, since the mid-seventeenth century.... It is high time that someone hinted of us what we have often said of the Americans: that a long tradition of freedom and fortunate isolation has its price in terms of understanding the circumstances and dilemmas of others.

Bernard Crick

1 Introduction

> Since Hitler's dictatorship is so obviously to be condemned from all points of view, people are tempted to think too little about it. That is why, although we possess an immense mass of literature about the Third Reich so little intelligent use has been made of it.[1]
>
> H. Krausnick & M. Broszat

This book is a study in the ethics of war. It examines a surprisingly neglected aspect of the struggle against Nazism and explores one of the untold stories of the Second World War: the searing moral choices that confronted people in occupied Europe, and the conscience-stabbing dilemmas which arose in counting the human cost of resistance. This study goes beyond previous works by offering a new approach to, and a different perspective on, European resistance and collaboration, by concentrating upon the daunting ethical questions that people had to answer in everyday life with the enemy. The main aim of this work is to fill the gap in the existing literature by providing the first detailed and thorough examination of the ethical dimension of resistance to Nazi tyranny, and to present a comprehensive guide to the moral dilemmas and anguished questions created by German security policy.

This book is also a reflection and meditation on the nature of enemy occupation. The story of resistance to foreign occupation is as old as war itself. It is timeless and topical. The invasion of one's country is invariably a humiliating and degrading experience, but for those living under German occupation, the traumas were intensified to an unparalleled degree by the threat posed by Nazism. Hitler's occupation of Europe was of a radically different nature from previous military conquests, for German policy was based not solely upon a conventional army of occupation but upon an ideological vision of a New European Order: the Thousand Year Reich – with forced labour for millions of people, the ruthless economic exploitation of the occupied territories, and the mass deportation of racial 'inferiors' for slave labour and extermination. Nazi occupation policy added a new dimension to traditional military conquest by forcing people to address agonizing and unprecedented moral choices: how to meet the challenge posed by the Nazi threat to civilized values; how to confront evil in its most radical form without becoming tainted and contaminated by the germ of the German ideology; how to resist Nazism without resorting to Nazi methods.

In spite of the huge number of books which have been written about the Second World War, and an almost insatiable public interest in the central, defining event in twentieth-century history, there is not one study which focuses directly upon the moral issues raised by resistance and collaboration. There are numerous military histories of the Second World War, studies of social conditions on the home front, and a specialist field of studies devoted to the controversial question of the morality of the Allied strategic bombing campaign against German and Japanese cities. Curiously, however, while the ethical issues surrounding obliteration bombing have received extensive analysis and generated fierce public debate, the other major area which gave rise to the most intractable moral problems – the choice between resistance and collaboration – has not been systematically examined, but treated rather casually. It has been mentioned briefly in passing in some historical surveys, but totally ignored in others. Yet of all the questions raised by the occupation years, none is more important than the choice between resistance and collaboration, and there is none which had such profound moral and human costs. There are monographs which touch upon some aspects of this subject, but none which takes the existential issues of resistance and collaboration as its starting-point and central thesis. Given the passions generated by what the French call 'the dark years' this is a rather surprising omission. Despite the expanding literature on resistance in Hitler's Europe, there has been a conspicuous silence about the morality of resistance, and there has been no sustained examination of the vexed ethical issues which resisters had to address when faced with German security measures. It has perhaps been taken for granted that because Nazism was so overwhelmingly evil, therefore resistance was good by definition, and collaboration was bad *tout court*, and that therefore nothing further needed to be said on the subject. The result is a certain evasiveness about some of the more morally questionable aspects of the resistance legacy, and disingenuousness about resistance methods, and the consequences of resistance action. Students emerge from reading the standard academic histories with very little awareness of the mechanisms of control exerted by German security in order to combat resistance, and no firm understanding of the way in which the doctrine of collective responsibility plagued the potential resister with doubt and moral confusion over the human cost of defiance.

COLLECTIVE RESPONSIBILITY

One of the central themes of this book is a study of how resistance movements responded to German security policy, which had at its foundation the doctrine of collective responsibility. This volume provides the first detailed account of collective responsibility, and the moral burden which this practice placed upon resisters. Collective responsibility is the key to the understanding of the true scale of resistance and everyday collaboration. To understand the Nazi occupation of Europe, it is necessary to understand the pervasive influence of collective responsibility. Collective responsibility was a major weapon, often the decisive weapon, in the Nazis' war against subversion in the occupied territories: it included the systematic taking and killing of hostages, reprisal killings, mass deportations, the burning of homes and villages, the imposition of curfews, and collective fines and punishments in order to deter further resistance. Collective responsibility thrived on fear – fear for oneself, but also fear for one's family, friends and neighbours.

On the 26 December 1939 two German soldiers were killed in a bar by criminals in Wawer, a suburb of Warsaw. The Germans rounded up all the men in the area, and in houses where there were several men in a family, the women were forced to choose who should be taken in reprisal. In one house a mother had to choose between her two sons, and another woman had to decide between the life of her husband, brother or father. Every tenth man was shot, including 34 youths under the age of 18 – a total of 106 hostages:

> The significance of the Wawer atrocity was that it was the first time that collective responsibility had been applied and from that moment people realised that 'under German occupation one could die for nothing'.[2]

Any act of resistance could sign one's neighbour's death warrant. Collective responsibility was a vital method by which the Nazis could instil fear, paralyse thought and drown opposition. The Nazi regime devised an elaborate and ingenious series of precautionary measures against disorder. The population of an occupied country was treated as jointly responsible for individual acts of subversion. Hostages were taken and detained in 'hostage pools'. They would guarantee with their lives the behaviour and obedience of the native population. The responsibility for the fate of the hostages was placed in the hands of their compatriots. The populations of the occupied territories were publicly warned that the hostages would be held accountable, answerable and punishable for acts committed by their fellow countrymen, despite the fact that in most cases no relationship or connection had been established between the hostage and the crime. In addition, the German occupation authorities made extensive use of 'human shield' hostages, in order to protect vital military equipment against sabotage. Resisters could only destroy such targets at the expense of sacrificing the lives of their fellow countrymen. The punishment of hostages is based fundamentally on a theory of collective responsibility.

The threat of collective responsibility also hung over non-violent resistance. For example, one important factor in the complicated story of the Pope's silence during the Holocaust was the fear of reprisals against Catholics. The price of taking a moral stand was evident when Holland's Archbishop De Jong sanctioned the issuing of a Pastoral Letter condemning Nazi anti-semitism on 26 July 1942. Five days later the Gestapo arrested all Dutch-Jewish Catholic converts, who had previously been exempted from deportation. They were sent to Auschwitz. Because the Protestant churches had refrained from public protests, the 9000 Protestant Jews were reprieved from deportation. The Pope was horrified by the Nazis' retaliation, and the threat of collective punishment had a considerable bearing on his subsequent behaviour.

Collective responsibility provides an answer to the question which is often whispered but rarely stated openly: why was there so little resistance, and especially so little armed resistance, to the Nazi occupation? When one examines German security policy in detail, the startling thing is not that there was so little resistance, but that there was so much. Much of this constitutes a missing dimension in conventional histories. As we shall see, there was considerable, often widespread, opposition to sabotage and the assassination of German personnel precisely because it led to massive reprisals against the innocent. Many people did not approve of partisan war because it exposed the local community to savage punishment for no clear military benefits. Resistance often inflicted far more damage on the occupied than on the occupier. The policy of unlimited repression was formidable and often highly effective. Resistance leaders came under enormous public pressure to desist from attacks for which local people paid a terrible price in the spilling of innocent blood. From the perspective of those on the receiving end of German collective punishment, the Resistance could appear to be irresponsible and cowardly. Knowing as they must have done that harsh reprisals would inevitably follow the ambush and assassination of German soldiers, resisters beat a hasty retreat, leaving the civilian population unprotected, defenceless and at the mercy of the German security apparatus. The occupation of the homeland by foreigners stirred the potent forces of nationalism. But faced with German reprisals many came to the conclusion that patriotism is not enough. Contrary to popular belief, resisters were initially regarded not as heroes or selfless patriots, but as reckless adventurers who at times needlessly endangered the lives of their fellow countrymen for acts of doubtful value. An important theme which will be explored in this book is the technique of the guilt transfer: the manner in which Nazi security policy succeeded in shifting the burden of guilt and responsibility onto the shoulders of those being persecuted. Collective responsibility raised the problem of the individual responsibility of the resister, who had to face the ethical implications of causing deaths other than those of the enemy. Many of those who opted for reluctant co-operation with the occupation authorities did so because they thought this was a lesser evil than bringing down collective punishments upon the heads of their fellow citizens. Without some grasp of the life and death choices prompted by collective responsibility, we cannot begin to make sense of the occupation years.

JUST WAR AND THE RESISTANCE

This book also examines resistance in relation to the just war tradition. It has often been assumed that resistance was a model of the just war, and therefore this claim has not been scrutinized, but simply taken for granted. Nobody has addressed the question: did the resistance abide by the exacting standards laid down in the just war school, or did it fail to live up to the criteria of a legitimate struggle? Many of the moral principles embodied in the just war tradition became legally enshrined in the Hague and Geneva Conventions. Resistance will be measured against the cardinal principles of the just war and the war conventions.

War brings immense human suffering. Just war theory offers standards for restricting human misery. The protection of civilians has a high priority in all versions of the just war. Direct attacks upon non-combatants are prohibited. Civilians should not be targeted or killed. However, there is a gap in just war theory: the debate within the tradition focuses upon what is permissible to inflict upon *enemy* civilians. It does not address the question which is central to the ethics of resistance: was it legitimate to engage in resistance actions when it was known that the result would be reprisals visited upon *one's own* civilian population? Resisters put their own civilians at risk by exposing them to collective punishments. The voluntary acceptance of one's own death led to the involuntary death of many others. The decision to resist could seal one's neighbour's fate. Some resistance acts were deliberately provocative, aimed at goading the Germans into revenge killings against the civilian population. Could these measures be justified by the plea of military necessity, or were they incompatible with the just war? If resistance undermined non-combatant immunity, it also raised questions about proportionality. The suffering and evil effects of a legitimate struggle must not be disproportionate to the good which is intended. An act which may be right in itself is not permissible if its unintended and indirect evil consequences are of such magnitude as to outweigh the benefits. This just war guideline needs to be interpreted and applied to actual wars. What was an acceptable or an unacceptable number of friendly civilian casualties depended upon the context. Were the deaths of five or one hundred hostages disproportionate to the killing of a German soldier? Were the evil consequences out of proportion to the good that resulted? Did resisters make every effort to keep civilian casualties to a minimum? Was the good achieved by resistance sufficient to offset the moral presumption against actions which jeopardized civilian bystanders? Were there no alternatives to forms of resistance which resulted in so many friendly casualties? These questions will be explored in depth.

The student of resistance faces a further difficulty in trying to understand the complexities of the subject. Because most historians are understandably sympathetic to the resistance cause, they have drawn a veil of silence over some of the questionable means that resisters employed, and there has been a failure to pursue hard and searching questions about the ethics of resistance methods. The moral dimension of resistance has almost been taken for granted. Because it was self-evident that resisters were fighting for a just cause there has been a reluctance to confront embarrassing and potentially damaging questions about resistance methods of warfare. There has been a strong temptation to give resisters the benefit of the doubt by avoiding any discussion of terrorist acts committed by the resistance, and a tendency to turn a blind eye to war crimes carried out by freedom-fighters. By studying resistance, it is possible to chart the ethical ambiguity inherent in fighting even a clearly just war.

There is a need for a more open and intellectually honest examination of resistance methods, and a recognition of the unpleasant reality that some resistance groups violated the laws of war and committed appalling war crimes: acts of terrorism, torture and mutilation; the killing of prisoners-of-war and incapacitated surrendering German troops. Some resistance groups imitated the German doctrine of collective responsibility by terrorizing and then killing the families of informers and collaborators, and by targeting the families of German personnel living in the occupied territories. In practising reverse collective punishments they lowered themselves to the level of the enemy. Some resisters held German prisoners-of-war as hostages, and carried out brutal counter-reprisals. The notion that 'anything goes' in war was a Nazi doctrine that resisters had pledged themselves to oppose at the outset of the struggle. Eventually, however, some resisters abandoned all ethical constraints, and reached the point where for them anything was permissible in the fight against Nazism. Other resisters argued that the resistance could not be allowed to transcend all moral limits, even in the service of a transparently good cause. Beyond a certain point a just cause could become unjust if it employed morally indefensible means such as the mutilation and torture of captured enemy soldiers and collaborators. Such methods incurred the moral opprobrium of those resisters who saw the importance of fighting within the laws of war. They were filled with a sense of shame that the good cause of the resistance was being sullied, and its moral stature diminished by inexcusable methods.

This book propounds a controversial, revisionist thesis. The conventional wisdom about resistance persists: the widespread belief in the myth that resisters were noble, just warriors fighting a clean war. Hence the need for a re-appraisal of the dominant image of resistance, and to call into question some of the most deeply cherished assumptions which underpin our perception of the shadow war. There is a need to acknowledge the enormity of resistance war crimes, and to articulate serious misgivings about resistance methods. The Germans and their collaborationist sympathizers routinely condemned the resistance as terrorists and bandits. Modern neo-Nazi groups may derive satisfaction from the exposure of the repellent methods which some resistance groups resorted to. My argument may be received as grist to their mill. However, my intention, most emphatically, is neither to provide ammunition for such people, nor to damage the credibility and reputation of the resistance. Rather it is to see resistance in all its complexity, and to explore the pangs of guilt and the restless conscience of the scrupulous resister. The restoration of the ethical doubt and moral disquiet of the melancholy warrior provides us with a more complete and accurate picture than the one-dimensional hero of the romanticized myth of resistance. If resistance is to be defended it must meet its critics' strongest challenge: it cannot simply discount such allegations as the fabrication of Nazi sympathizers, by pretending that resistance did not have its darker side. This book challenges the orthodoxy, the received wisdom which depicts resistance as a morally unblemished activity. It is hoped that the book raises troubling and disturbing questions, and will force a re-examination of aspects of the resistance story which had either been ignored or simply taken for granted.

JEWISH RESISTANCE

An important additional reason why I have written this work is my belief in the need to integrate the highly sensitive and deeply controversial questions surrounding Jewish resistance and 'collaboration' into the mainstream of books on European resistance and collaboration. There is sadly still considerable ignorance concerning the life and death issues which confronted Jews, particularly in the period of ghettoization prior to deportation to the death camps. One major aim of this book is to provide the context and framework for such an undertaking, and to be a signpost to the more specialized literature in this area.

There has been a very marked tendency to cordon off a specialist field of 'Holocaust Studies' – usually the preserve of Jewish scholars and students – and to explore the question of Jewish resistance separately, and in isolation from more conventional national studies. The British Jewish author Ronnie Landau rightly cautions against the 'ghettoisation' of the Holocaust, and of the need to:

> lift the Holocaust out of the realm ... of Jewish education, and to set its implications before a wider audience. The lessons of the Holocaust are simply too important, too pressing ... to be imprisoned within the world of the victim.[3]

One unfortunate result of studying resistance through a single-country focus is a tendency to be oblivious to the sensitivities of the Jewish question. The subject of Jewish resistance is relegated to a footnote in many standard general works, and ignored altogether in others: in Henri Michel's *The Shadow War* Jewish resistance merits a mere four pages in a 360-page book; in Jorgen Haestrup's somewhat inappropriately titled *European Resistance Movements 1939–1945: A Complete History*, the Jews of Europe are not even accorded a mention in the footnotes.

The Jewish experience was unique in the grim history of Nazi Europe. While keeping this in mind it is instructive to examine the similarities and parallels in the kind of choices which Jews faced in the ghettos of eastern Europe, to the questions that gentiles faced under German control. Reluctant accommodation to overwhelming force was a Europe-wide response. The same pattern of German terrorism and forced co-operation can be witnessed in varying degrees throughout the occupied territories. The dilemmas of the Jewish Councils were the most extreme manifestation of this phenomenon and can be fruitfully studied in that wider setting. Similarly, if it is questionable to talk of a European resistance movement, one constant factor which did operate throughout Hitler's Europe was German security policy. It varied in intensity according to time and place, but the basic features of state terrorism were on display in all theatres where the occupiers encountered opposition. Therefore it is vital to set the debate about Jewish resistance in its broader European context and to examine the common questions which all resisters had to wrestle with, given the inevitability of punishment based upon collective responsibility.

REMEMBRANCE

> And some there be which have no memorial;
> Who are perished as though they had never been.
>
> Ecclesiasticus (Apocrypha), 44:9

On the walls of the ruins at Oradour is an inscription, 'Souviens-toi' – 'Remember'. Remembrance is a moral obligation that we owe to the millions of victims to the Nazi empire. However, as the Second World War recedes in time and direct personal memory fades, there arises a challenge to develop new ways to present the realities of the Nazi era, while remaining true to the historical record. It is vital to pass on the baton of memory, to capture and stimulate the interest of a younger generation without trivializing or distorting the complex reality of life under Nazi occupation. For the British and American scholar there is the additional challenge that our countries have had no direct experience of enemy occupation, or the harsh choices which this imposed. This makes it all the more difficult to convey what was at stake in the choice between resistance and collaboration. In Britain and the United States there has been a singular lack of interest in, or curiosity about, this aspect of Nazi-dominated Europe. This failure of the imagination is partly attributable to our insular historical experience. Because our countries have not been invaded and garrisoned with enemy troops, we have not had to confront the uncomfortable problems of life under enemy occupation and brutal dictatorship. The noted American scholar Gordon Wright refers to the 'offhand fashion' in which resistance movements have been examined in American textbooks on the Second World War. 'A random check of three widely-used American text books on twentieth-century Europe reveals that the most generous author gives scant page to all resistance movements combined; the second devotes one paragraph to them; the third, not even a footnote. More strikingly still, a recently-published history of the Second World War by an American scholar allots less than one percent of its space to the European resistance groups.' Wright also quotes the view of leading French resistance historian Henri Michel, who accused Americans of perpetuating 'systematic ignorance of the complexities of life with the enemy'.[4]

EMPATHY

> As you view the history of our time, turn and look at the pile of
> bodies, pause for a short moment and imagine that this poor
> residue of flesh and bones is your father, your child, your wife,
> is the one you love. See yourself and those dearest to you, to
> whom you are devoted heart and soul, thrown naked into the
> dirt, tortured, starving, killed.[5]

These words from Eugen Kogon, a Holocaust survivor who was an
inmate of Buchenwald for the duration of the Second World War,
are a powerful endorsement of the empathic approach. Empathy is
a particularly useful teaching device for stimulating and engaging
the interest of a new generation who have no personal experience
of the Nazi era. In waging a war against forgetfulness and oblivion,
the empathic method also provides us with a way of combating
insular thinking. A purely chronological approach can result in our
reactions becoming dulled, whereas to project oneself into the circumstances facing the people studied, is to live through their experiences, and to enter imaginatively into their world, to see it as
they saw it.

The French philosopher Jean-Paul Sartre articulated the ambivalence of sensitive people throughout occupied Europe who felt a
clear moral obligation to resist Nazism, but who also had to face
the fearful question of how they would be likely to respond under
Gestapo interrogation:

> Obsessed as we were by these tortures, a week did not go by
> that we did not ask ourselves: 'Suppose I were tortured, what
> would I do?' And this question alone carried us to the very frontiers
> of ourselves and of the human.[6]

Empathy is not an alternative to conventional historical methods
and evidence, but a vital supplement to it, providing us with an
added dimension and a deeper insight into a period which narrative histories often fail to convey. Judith Miller, while writing about
the Holocaust, makes an important point which can also be applied to the study of resistance in general:

> personal accounts of the Holocaust . . . can accomplish something
> that few history texts can; they stir our emotions; they make us

feel the survivor's pain, the bystander's confusion. In attempting to understand the Holocaust, empathy counts for much.[7]

It requires an imaginative leap, an act of empathic understanding, to comprehend fully the stark choices and evil alternatives which confronted people daily in Hitler's Europe. Try to put yourself in the place of a prospective resister: you are opposed to Nazism, but active resistance carries a heavy blood price. The Nazis made an exact science of inhumanity. One of the favoured methods of the Gestapo was a form of moral blackmail. If a resister did not break under physical torture, his closest male relatives would be threatened with deportation to a concentration camp, and young females – a sister or girlfriend – might be sent to a 'soldiers' house', that is, a German Army brothel. This kind of threat against his fiancée and her family induced a courageous and long-standing resister to reveal the identity and whereabouts of the French resistance leader, Jean Moulin.[8] One female resister committed the mistake of hiding a photograph of her children in her clothing. The Gestapo found it:

> The Germans gave her a choice: Either she would hand over to them all the important people she knew, or else her daughter would be sent to Poland to a house of prostitution for soldiers returning from the Russian front.[9]

The woman's resistance group ordered and carried out her execution before she could reveal their identities under torture. In a similar case, a female member of the French Resistance was arrested and interrogated by the German police, who knew that she could lead them to an escaped resistance organizer whom they were seeking: 'and they know, too, the woman has a daughter: "choose" they tell her, "it's either the man or the child"'.[10] Those who joined the resistance knew that not only would they run the risk of death, but that they imperiled the lives of their families as well. Nuremberg Trial records provide evidence of children being tortured in the presence of their parents, with the aim of making the parents admit everything they knew about resistance. Collective family responsibility was a vitally important consideration which made it extremely difficult for married people, especially those with children, to work for the resistance. Family responsibility was one of the most effective and terrifying weapons of German security, and it imposed the sternest possible moral and psychological test for the potential resister.

WHAT WOULD YOU DO?

Judge not thy neighbour until thou art come into his place.

The Talmud

The ancient rule not to judge your fellow man until you're in his place is good and right.[11]

Yitzak Zuckerman
Commander of the Warsaw Ghetto Rising

Imagine yourself in the shoes of a potential resister or collaborator. Faced with appalling moral choices it is sobering to ask: what would I have done? What would be the consequences of my choice?

(1) You are an engine driver. You are required to drive a 'special transport' of Jews to the border of your country with Germany. Failure to comply carries with it veiled threats of punishment for yourself and your family. Disobedience might result in unemployment, followed by compulsory labour service in Germany.

(2) You are a member of a resistance unit which is about to sabotage a troop train. The Germans have chained women to the front of the steam engine as human shields in order to deter resistance. Would you press the detonator?

(3) You have committed an act of sabotage upon military equipment which has also resulted in the death of 10 German soldiers. As a punishment, the military authorities have threatened to kill 10 hostages each day until the culprits surrender. Should you give yourself up in order to avoid innocent casualties?

(4) You are a Christian pacifist opposed in principle to the taking of life. You have hidden Jews in your house, but your hideout is discovered by a collaborationist policeman who is about to inform the Germans. Should you kill him in order to save the lives of the refugees?

(5) You are the mayor of a small town. An act of resistance has taken place in the vicinity, and the Germans have ordered you to hand over 5 men for a public hanging. If the order is not obeyed, in 12 hours' time the village will be burned, and all the inhabitants killed. Should you sacrifice 5 innocent men to protect the others?

(6) You are a member of a Jewish Council in one of the ghettos of eastern Europe. You have been ordered to provide a list of

10 000 Jews for 'resettlement'. Failure to comply will result in an additional 2000 Jews being added to the list, or the liquidation of the entire ghetto. If you carry out the order, are you guilty of collaboration? How would *you* have coped with a decision of this magnitude?

This book explores the implications of these type of questions, in order to reach a deeper level of understanding of the painful complexities of resistance and collaboration. The pointed question: 'What would I do in their place?' is an integral part of the empathic method. The attempt to reconstruct these awesome moral choices is not a substitute for 'hard' historical research, nor is it an example of 'faction' – the weaving of fact and fiction into a historical 'documentary-drama' in which some of the evidence is made up as we go along for dramatic purposes. Perhaps it requires the skill of a playwright or a novelist to capture the psychological complexity and to plumb the emotional depths of the issues which were involved for individuals torn between alternative courses of action during the German occupation. But this study does not take any artistic licence in order to exaggerate the evidence for dramatic effect. The case studies that I examine in this book focus upon real dilemmas that human beings did have to address, and are based upon verifiable historical events. They have an authenticity that is either diminished or lacking altogether in fictional literature, and in the implausible hypothetical examples that philosophers sometimes employ. Too often moral and political philosophy has been impoverished by what Bernard Williams called 'the morally trivial . . . the cultivation of the banal example'.[12] One exception is the work of R.M. Hare, whose understanding of moral issues was informed by his experience in Japanese prison camps in Thailand and Singapore. Hare criticizes 'those who have lived sheltered lives' and whose moral thinking is derived from fiction. Implausible examples drawn from literature 'lack verisimilitude' and therefore their relevance is 'diminished'. Hare recognizes that, 'the sympathetic imagination plays an important part in moral thought'. Empathy is vital: 'to imagine the real sufferings of another sentient being is to confront the facts – and it makes a difference – that they should really be facts'. In this book I have tried to follow Hare's advice: 'some experience of actual moral perplexities, and of the actual consequences of certain moral choices is a necessity. A few months spent as a coolie building the Burma railway is worth more to one's moral thinking than the reading of a great many novels, or even reports about underdeveloped countries'.[13]

The importance of examining what are, thankfully for us, hypothetical questions, but were an unavoidable reality for many people in Hitler's Europe, is that it is the best way of attempting to enter their world, of stimulating our sympathetic capabilities, and of confronting their plight. It amounts to more than role-play because the effort to use our imagination to comprehend what moral issues were at stake clarifies the precise nature of the choices, the alternatives and consequences of a particular course of action. It is not my job to give neat and tidy answers to these perplexing questions, but rather to spell out the losses and gains, and the human cost involved in alternative decisions. Many of these decisions involved impossible choices, and this in itself tells us a great deal about the calculated psychological terror that underpinned Nazi occupation policy.

The empathic approach can also dispel persistent romantic Hollywood illusions that one often encounters in discussions about life under Nazi occupation. It is not uncommon to find students who have no grasp of the threat posed by collective responsibility, romantically imagine themselves as daring saboteurs blowing up troop trains at night and blithely stating: 'If I had been alive in occupied Europe, I would have joined the resistance.' Indeed, an American Jewish author writes in this vein: 'I'm quite sure I would have become a partisan, a resister, a fighter, at least that's what I hope I would have done.'[14] Although the underlying sentiment is admirable, the empathic method forces us to examine the realities and repercussions of resistance. An American novelist Donald Hamilton articulated the problems in depicting real life in occupied Europe for an American audience:

It always turned out Hollywood when you tried to imagine it. You knew it had not been like that, but you had no idea of how it really had been. When they said, 'underground' and 'Gestapo' it came out, 'Warner Brothers, passed by the State Board of Censors'.[15]

Because it is difficult to imagine such things taking place in Boston, Lincolnshire, or Boston, Massachusetts, in Cambridge, England or Cambridge, USA, perhaps it may be enlightening to ponder the intriguing question: what would have happened if Britain had been invaded and occupied in 1940? Who would have resisted? Who would have collaborated? Because we were not invaded, this enabled us to avoid having to make the hard choices which Europeans were forced to address. This hypothetical question is not frivolous if it helps jolt us out of our insular attitudes, and provides us with an understanding and insight into the dilemmas of others. Its shock value forces us to imagine the circumstances of life under enemy occupation, and the consequences of resistance. Christopher Andrew defends counterfactual history with the telling observation that: 'the main purpose of asking what might have happened is to increase our understanding of what did'.[16]

The most fertile example of speculative imagination can be found in Adrian Gilbert's book, *Britain Invaded*. Based upon a documentary reconstruction of Hitler's plans, Gilbert's work vividly depicts the consequences of a British resistance movement:

> The daring assassination of SS Sturmbannfuhrer . . . Thyrolf, deputy leader of the Liverpool Einsatzgruppen, outside his offices in the Liver Building on 3rd February 1941, brought fierce retribution. Thyrolf had been gunned down by a student from the university; under torture he revealed the where-abouts of the rest of his 'terror gang' – a mixed group of fellow students and dockers from the Port of Liverpool. While they were being rounded up, Heydrich had already telexed . . . that an example must be set. The hostage execution ratio was increased twenty-fold from the standard ten for each German killed, to 200:1. Half were gunned down at the Goodison Park football ground, and the remainder at Anfield. The collective punishment for the people of Liverpool was the withdrawal of fuel, and the halving of basic food rations for three months (a decision which resulted in far more deaths than the executions). Inevitably, incidents like this caused mixed reactions; hatred of the Germans was almost universal in the city – from now on only the most desperate prostitute would have dealings with a German – but this was matched by the fearful reluctance of many to actively support the resistance.
>
> . . . along with the random hostages taken as 'guarantees for good behaviour' the rough total of those arrested and interned during the first two years of the New Order amounted to over 600 000 people. Most of the Jews were shipped over to the mainland. . . . Sadly the British were not impermeable to the antisemitism of the war years, and some Jews were sent to their

deaths as a direct result of action by the indigenous population – perhaps the biggest scar on Britain's post-war conscience.

... just by looking at the map it was fairly clear that England did not lend itself to the classic partisan operations carried out in Yugoslavia and the Soviet Union. Wales and Scotland became the main battlegrounds for this new type of warfare.... Of course the local communities suffered terribly. In certain parts of North Wales and the Scottish Highlands, whole villages were destroyed by enemy reprisals, or abandoned by their inhabitants, who fled into the hills ... the 3000-strong alliance of partisan groups that had declared an 'independent Lakeland' ... stood no chance as the Germans set about systematically destroying the main towns of Keswick and Windermere before sending its sweep and cordon missions into the mountains to isolate and destroy the British.[17]

In an excellent recent study of the German occupation of the Channel Islands, Madeleine Bunting presents a sobering reminder of the lessons to be learned:

The Channel Islands were as close as Hitler got; they were the one bit of British soil he conquered. That is why those blurred black-and-white photos of the Channel Islands' Occupation are so riveting: German soldiers marching past Lloyds Bank, or flirting with Island girls outside Boots the Chemists, or getting directions from a smiling British bobby. That is what life could have been like in Britain with Germans in British streets and in British shops. What happened in the Channel Islands could have happened in the rest of Britain.[18]

The fascination for us lies precisely in what we avoided. Though the questions raised by Gilbert and Bunting are hypothetical, they are not the stuff of fiction. They represent the way we nearly were. Hostages were taken on the Channel Islands. Soon after the German occupation, it became known that some British soldiers were hiding on the Islands. The Germans threatened to shoot 20 hostages if the soldiers were not handed over. In September 1942, English-born Islanders were taken as hostages, after first being identified in registers, specifying place of birth and religion, compiled by the Channel Islands' civil service. 2200 English hostages were interned in German concentration camps until the end of the war, as a guarantee of the good behaviour of the Island populace. Jews and forced labourers were deported with the co-operation and involvement of the local police force and civil administration. There was also a slave labour and death camp on Alderney: an SS camp on British soil. These are chilling reminders of what might quite conceivably have been on the British mainland. In his diary, Jerseyman Bernard Baker pondered and debated the morality of resistance:

> I can of course kill a German, sabotage an aeroplane, destroy a number of lorries but if by so doing I bring heavy punishments to bear on 40 000 people ... and possibly be the cause of sending many able-bodied people to slave in Germany's factories, am I a 'patriot'? or am I a 'traitor'? The question is not so easy to answer as it might appear.[19]

By bringing the problem home to us, empathy can help us reach a deeper understanding of the psychological complexity of life in Hitler's Europe, and provide us with added insights into the cruel dilemmas and ethical ambiguities created by German security policy.

HOSTAGES

While the genre of resistance became a cottage industry after 1945, there was no literature of the hostage camp. Hostages became the forgotten victims of the Nazis. Can we imagine the ordeal of the individual hostage subjected to indefinite detention in a hostage pool? Can we begin to imagine what this kind of incarceration can do to a man: the disorientation and dislocation when every vestige of normal life is suddenly removed? British hostage John McCarthy, in his account of captivity in Beirut, describes the pain of ignorance, the insecurity and uncertainty of what might come next:

> The sense of being under constant threat of execution.
> We were beyond all avenues of appeal. We had no rights or sense of place. We could do nothing to end this situation.[20]

A recurring theme in John McCarthy's imprisonment is the warped sense of time. The hostage was, 'living in a different time scale time was a meaningless progression of wasted hours'.[21] McCarthy's experience provides us with a window of insight into the plight of the hostage in World War Two. Imagine the mental pressure on the hostage, counting away the minutes and hours, brooding on his fate, knowing that his time may be up because of an act of resistance by some unknown compatriot. The psychological deprivation of captivity, with its suspended death sentence, left no senses unimpaired; with nerves stretched and the imagination feverishly working overtime. John McCarthy writes of being, 'forever damaged by the years of fear'.[22] Even for those hostages who survived, something did not survive: their sense of trust in the world. It is important to emphasize the point that the act of holding hostages is as wrong as killing them. The terrorist nature of hostage-taking lies in the threat to innocent life, whether or not the sentence is executed.

The cumulative effect of reading example after example of Nazi hostage and reprisal killings can anaesthetize our sensitivity, numb our sense of proportion and produce compassion fatigue. Statistics don't bleed, and the dry recounting of figures cannot fully capture the human misery, the ruined hopes and shattered lives, the homes and families destroyed. Every hostage and reprisal victim, every casualty of resistance was an individual like John McCarthy: somebody's son, daughter, mother, father, husband, wife, brother, sister, loved one. Each hostage whose future was prematurely ended had hopes, aspirations, wild dreams, just like you or I.

> These hearts were woven of human joys and cares...
> ... These had seen movement and heard music; known
> Slumber and waking; gone proudly friended;
> Felt the quick stir of wonder, sat alone;
> ... All this is ended.[23]

Precisely because the Nazis dehumanized their victims, stripped them of their individuality in killing them by quota, in batches by number, it is important to restore their individual humanity.

METHOD

The subject matter of this work is on the borderline of history, moral philosophy, political theory and literature. Probably for that reason it has fallen into a 'no man's land' between academic disciplines. The educational fixation with neat and tidy academic boundaries has ensured that few have put their heads above the trenches and ventured more than a few paces beyond the demarcation lines before retreating into the shelter and safety of their own recognized territory. This work attempts to remove some of the artificial borders which often act as a barrier to broader understanding. It adopts an eclectic, cross-disciplinary approach to the subject of resistance and collaboration, and draws freely upon a variety of sources and genres and synthesizes the most important findings of specialists in various fields. It attempts to bridge the gap between narrative history and the more abstract concerns of moral and political philosophy. Chronological histories fail to explore the depth of moral issues surrounding resistance and collaboration, and there is a need to link the empirical with the normative. To borrow Michael Walzer's felicitous phrase, this book offers 'moral argument with historical illustrations'.[24]

This book is not a formal exercise in political theory. Nevertheless the occupation years provide a rich source of material for moral and political philosophers to draw upon, and bring into sharp focus many of the key questions concerning human nature and the human predicament – duty, obedience and disobedience, political obligation, loyalty and betrayal, divided loyalties and the problem of how to confront evil. Michael Walzer describes the means/end question as 'the central issue in political ethics'.[25] The perennial problem of means and ends can be studied in urgent and fresh form in the dilemmas of resistance. There is a wealth of evidence concerning the moral confusion and perplexity of people living in Nazi-occupied Europe, stored in the voluminous diaries, chronicles, eyewitness accounts and autobiographies of resisters and victims. I have drawn heavily upon the testimony of Nazi victims, particularly in the chapters on Jewish resistance and collaboration. Wherever possible I have let the victims speak for themselves, so that this volume has become a medium through which their voices might talk to a younger generation of readers who are trying to reach an understanding of the harsh realities of life under Nazi occupation. In places this book has turned into a gathering of witnesses, a compilation of the testimony of victims, survivors and resisters. Much of this rich vein of material has been ignored in conventional histories. This is unfortunate because there are continuities, common links and themes, similar choices which confronted people throughout Hitler's Europe, particularly in their search for an appropriate response to the problems created by collective responsibility. These common threads were woven into a tapestry of misery, but the pattern cannot be detected if we focus only upon the detailed narrative of a single region without taking a step back to see the whole canvas. This work takes a synoptic view of resistance and collaboration.

This book deals with moral responses to Nazism in German-occupied Europe. It does not examine the German resistance movement, which is a separate subject in its own right, and which has generated a vast literature. A few brief observations and points of comparison can be made.

(1) The German resistance was quite unlike resistance movements in occupied Europe. Within Germany resistance to Hitler was an act of treason. In occupied Europe resistance was an act of patriotism, rooted in the soil of the nation.

(2) Although conscientious Germans also faced acute moral decisions and choices, their primary dilemma was the classic problem of political obligation: whether, when and in what manner to disobey their own state. Christians faced with the decision to commit murder by participating in plots to kill Hitler; army officers faced with the repudiation of their solemnly-sworn oath of unconditional obedience to the Fuhrer were confronted by the charge of treason, disloyalty and betrayal of their own country in time of crisis. Hitler was psychologically astute in imposing an oath of loyalty upon the only organized group which could have offered effective opposition to him.

(3) While this book deals extensively with the dilemmas of resisters when confronted by hostage-taking and reprisal measures, we should also remember the guilt, the pangs of conscience of those German soldiers who had grave misgivings at being party to killing innocent civilians. In his *Diaries*, the German Ambassador to Rome, Ulrich Von Hassell, describes an incident in August 1941:

> The whole war in the east is terrible – a return to savagery. A young officer now in Munich received an order to shoot 350 civilians, allegedly partisans, among them women and children, who had been herded together in a big barn. He hesitated at first, but was then warned that the penalty for

disobedience was death. He begged for ten minutes' time to think it over, and finally carried out the order with machine-gun fire. He was so shaken by this episode that, although only slightly wounded, he was determined not to go back to the front.[26]

Von Hassell was executed as one of the leading conspirators to overthrow Hitler in 1944. American soldier J. Glenn Gray recounts the following story:

> In the Netherlands, the Dutch tell of a German soldier who was a member of an execution squad ordered to shoot innocent hostages. Suddenly he stepped out of rank and refused to participate in the execution. On the spot he was charged with treason by the officer in charge and was placed with the hostages, where he was promptly executed by his comrades.[27]

Similar but rare instances occurred in other parts of occupied Europe. Such heroism by ordinary German soldiers should not be forgotten when surveying the volume of German war crimes explored in this book. The plight of the morally scrupulous soldier was summarized by the English constutional lawyer A.V. Dicey:

> He may ... be liable to be shot by a court-martial if he disobeys an order, and hanged by a judge and jury if he obeys it.[28]

2 Myths and Realities of Resistance

Resistance good; collaboration bad.[1]

G. Kren & L. Rappoport

Armed resistance must be understood realistically, not romantically.[2]

R.L. Rubenstein & J.K. Roth

Both terms are vague and defy precise definition; 'collaboration' could mean anything from volunteering for the Waffen SS to buying a picture postcard of Marshal Pétain; likewise 'resistance' could be derailing an enemy troop-train or singing an obscene parody of 'Lili Marlene'! The most that can be said is that collaboration/resistance resembled an old-fashioned hour-glass with collaboration the sand in the upper bulb. In 1940 collaboration predominated and resistance was negligible. As the war progressed, however, and the prospects of German victory receded, the sands of collaboration began to run out while those of resistance multiplied. By the time of the liberation the upper bulb was all but empty, the lower all but full.[3]

David Littlejohn

It is tempting to decorate the occupation with a neat symmetry of heroes and villains. Harry Ree was a British SOE agent who had been parachuted into France in 1943, in order to organize sabotage operations with local resistance groups. After the war Ree gave lectures about his wartime experiences, and he recounts that one of the most difficult barriers to overcome was his audiences' preconceptions:

which were backed up by their enjoyment of a kind of vicarious thrill at hearing about people they insisted on thinking of as whiter-than-white heroes or blacker-than-black villains, or hearing about plots and plays of cinematic unlikeliness.[4]

This tendency is reinforced by the fact that the Nazi occupation of Europe readily lends itself to a kind of '1066 And All That' view of history, in which resisters were 'right and romantic' and collaborators were 'wrong and repulsive'. The parody does contain a plausible half-truth, for there undoubtedly were brave and courageous resisters, and there were also wicked informers and abject collaborators. But as with all caricatures, the main features, although recognizable, are distorted, grossly exaggerated. Corresponding to the demonization of collaborators is a sanctification of resisters – a cult of martyrology, with a debt of honour to preserve the sacred memory of those who voluntarily risked or sacrificed their lives in order to liberate their country. The stark contrast between good resisters and bad collaborators is deeply embedded in World War II mythology.

The origins of this seductive myth are historically important, and can be traced back to the political needs of the immediate post-liberation period. Particularly in France, but also in other countries, there was a kind of 'collective amnesia' about the extent of everyday co-operation with the Germans. It was in everyone's interest to efface the past, and to store away its memory; yet there were countries which couldn't forget the dark years, but couldn't bear to remember them. Painful memories in the nation's consciousness were blocked out and an idealized myth of 'The Resistance' was created and sedulously cultivated.

Popular films and novels helped to perpetuate a highly romanticized view of the resistance. History was rewritten to show that with the exception of a few Nazi sympathizers and traitors, *everybody was in the resistance*. Everyday accommodation and 'bread and butter' collaboration had shrunk from its true proportions into a tiny minority of fascist fellow travellers and fifth columnists, who were unrepresentative of the true nation. Thus the past was remade to suit present requirements. This had its positive side. The mystique of resistance and civic heroism catered to a genuine need for self-esteem and the restoration of national pride. There was, 'a powerful consensus on the need for consensus . . . a tacit agreement not to tear one another apart'.[5]

The myth of massive popular resistance also provided an alibi; it removed the humiliating stain of military defeat and the stigma of collaboration. Resistance enabled the occupied peoples to look the Allies in the face. Everyone could bask in the reflected glory of national resistance. Henry Rousso argues that with a few sentences

in his famous speech in Paris on 25 August 1944, General
'established the founding myth' of the post-liberation era.
spoke of:

> Paris! Paris humiliated! Paris broken! Paris martyred! But Paris
> liberated! Liberated by itself, by its own people with the help of
> the armies of France, with the support and aid of France as a
> whole, of fighting France, of the only France, of the true France,
> of eternal France.[6]

The fact that General Vol Cholditz, with one eye upon post-war
retribution, behaved with discretion in refusing to obey Hitler's order
to destroy Paris, in the manner of Warsaw, was overlooked in the
politics of myth-making. The Gaullist invocation of this self-image
of glorious France, a unified nation of 'the France of all the French,'
which heroically resisted from the first hour of the occupation, and
which achieved the self-emancipation of its capital, obscured the
less than heroic reality of the previous four years: namely that the
overwhelming majority acquiesced in Vichy's collaborationist policies for most of the occupation. Up until 1943 the resistance was
widely regarded as a handful of irresponsible terrorists, a great many
of them Communists who did not represent the French people.
Events looked different when seen through the haze of victory. The
40 million Pétainists of June 1940 became the 40 million Gaullists
of July 1944. Indeed, as late as 26 April 1944, a massive crowd of
Parisians had cheered Pétain on his way to Notre Dame for a requiem
mass for French victims of Allied bombing. Exactly four months
later a similar crowd, perhaps many of them the same people, gave
a hero's welcome to De Gaulle, the man condemned to death by
Pétain's regime as a traitor. This is the winners' version of history.

In his attempt to heal the nation's internal wounds, De Gaulle's
resistance myth was essential because it minimized the extent of
everyday collaboration, and exaggerated the role of resistance. The
more complex and ambiguous truth about the 'black years' was
sacrificed in the interests of political expediency, national reconciliation and post-war reconstruction. The painful confrontation with
the past was deferred; the deep divisions that the occupation exposed and the cruel choices that it imposed, were forgotten, re-
pressed in the national subconscious. The nation reinvented itself
by wiping the national memory clean. In the 1956 documentary
Night and Fog, the film's director, Alain Resnais, was required by

the French film censorship board to remove a scene which showed a French policeman's *képi* (cap) – symbolizing French collaboration in deportations. By drawing a discreet veil over the past, the nakedness of indiscretion and collaboration could be covered up. The most enduring legacy is the myth of resistance: the distortion of painful reality into a medieval morality play, a black-and-white melodrama of clearly defined heroes and villains – selfless resisters overcoming shameless collaborators. The clear-cut and uncomplicated choice between the moral rectitude of resistance and the moral turpitude of collaboration was the projection of the illusory desire of hindsight, with all the uncertainties and moral confusion of everyday life under the occupation removed.

The accretion of myth and legend persists because people would like to believe it to be true; the rewriting of the behaviour of the majority during the occupation into what they felt they should have done, rather than what they actually did. In their hearts at least, everybody resisted. Nevertheless the myth of whole nations opposing the Nazi occupation from the outset was eventually debunked by later generations of historians who provided clear evidence that active resisters were a tiny fraction, less than 2 per cent of the population. There was of course a wider circle of people sympathetic to the aims of the resistance: the two million people in France who bought resistance newspapers, those 'armchair resisters'[7] who risked punishment by listening to the BBC, and the unquantifiable number who simply kept silent, when they could have acted as paid informers. Nevertheless, resistance was a miniscule movement, and the active minority contemptuously dismissed those who wanted to jump on the bandwagon at the last minute, scornfully dubbing them 'Resisters of the 32nd August,': 'Resistance fighters of the Eleventh Hour' and 'Septembrisards': September Resisters, who took up arms after the fighting was over. The carefully stage-managed Paris police strike in August 1944 was a form of last-ditch action against the departing Germans, which gave the police force an alibi to cover their day-to-day collaboration: 'a semi-spurious testimonial as "resistants". They had certainly waited till the very last moment to resist! The result was that there was scarcely a "commissaire de police" in Paris who was replaced at the Liberation'.[8] Many professional army officers who sat out the occupation on half pay rushed to join the FFI at the last minute: the term 'Napthalines' or 'Mothballers' was coined as a term of reproach for those who had stored their uniforms and their patriotism in the cupboard for the four years of occupation.[9] After the liberation 123 000 Parisians applied to the authorities for official recognition of their resistance credentials – between six to eight times the number of genuine resisters.

The fantasy that 'everyone was in the resistance' is an illusion born of the marriage of wishful thinking and hindsight: a perfect illustration of the adage that 'success has a thousand fathers, failure is an orphan'. As Roderick Kedward has observed, genuine resisters took exception to the devaluation of their clandestine activity, and the Gaullist myth 'was challenged by a crescendo of resistance voices as a travesty of history which diminished their minority struggle'.[10] Nevertheless, the reassuring image of a whole people in resistance was used by the country's leaders as a 'quasi-sacred symbol'.[11] and it became difficult to disentangle mythology from reality.

Although the myth of widespread resistance was eventually eroded in the 1960s and 1970s by films like *The Sorrow and the Pity*, what was not challenged was the moral supremacy of the resistance fighting the 'good war' against the evil enemy. This remained on a pedestal. Those who attacked the inaccuracy of the myth of resistance still operated within a framework of values which equated resistance with moral purity and political correctness. Indeed, any discussion of resistance must acknowledge the enormous physical and moral courage that it required to engage in underground warfare in an atmosphere poisoned by suspicion, mistrust, double agents and informers. The Germans regarded resisters as terrorists or bandits, and not as legitimate soldiers who had the right to bear arms. They often fought with inadequate weapons, and if found in possession of a weapon they were liable to immediate execution. Resisters could not save their lives by surrendering because the Germans did not accord them prisoner-of-war status. They were usually tortured if captured alive, and then killed without mercy. In France, 30 000 resisters were shot, and of the 112 000 deported to German concentration camps, only 35 000 returned alive. It must also be borne in mind that, under the conditions of collective family responsibility, the grave risks that resisters ran extended to their families, who would usually be the first target of German punishment if the resisters' identities became known.

'THE BEST OF ALL POSSIBLE WARS'

The official public memory of the Second World War was established after the liberation of the concentration camps in the Spring
of 1945. The Nuremberg Trials provided incontrovertible proof of
the systematic nature and scale of Nazi war crimes, genocide and
crimes against humanity. The liberation of the concentration camps
left a lasting visual image in the public memory of the Second World
War. The haunting photographs and newsreel pictures of the land-
scape of terror – of disease-ridden bodies being bulldozed into mass
graves at Belsen; of bodies abased and stripped of all dignity, stacked
'like cordwood' – these images more than anything else demonstrated that the Allies were fighting 'the good war'. If any war could
be a just war, then this war had to be fought in order to rid the
world of unparalleled evil. As Michael Walzer put it, the Second
World War was 'the paradigm of . . . a justified struggle'.[12] World
War II became widely regarded as a moral crusade in which there
were clearly defined heroes and villains. The enemy were so clearly
evil, and the enormity of their crimes so evident, that this could
not help but make the Allies appear good in comparison. Churchill
and Roosevelt had always said that if the Nazis had triumphed this
would usher in a 'New Dark Age'.

> The British and Americans hailed the liberation of the camps as
> a proper and fitting capstone to their war effort. Liberation pro-
> vided overwhelming evidence that the 'New Dark Age' was no
> mere figure of speech. The deaths in battle of American and
> British soldiers were then invested with a kind of sanctity: after
> the opening of the camps who could say that they died in vain.[13]

The moral clarity of the struggle against Nazism ensured that
events, memories and aspects of the war which did not fit in with
this established version of noble combat were quietly discarded or
forgotten; contradictory images were buried:

> liberation provided an overwhelming moral justification for the
> war, so no embarrassing questions were raised about the Allied
> conduct of the war, in particular British terror bombing. The
> Germans had, in the eyes of the world, lost all rights to blame
> anyone for anything.[14]

This official memory directly affects our perception of resistance and collaboration in occupied Europe. It is almost impossible to view the choice, or complex of choices, between resistance and collaboration, except retrospectively, through the lens of Belsen and Auschwitz. Like looking down the wrong end of a telescope, however, this produces an optical illusion, a distorted image, a false clarity. It foreshortens the complicated nature of the issues surrounding resistance, and turns them into a simple choice between right and wrong.

It ought to go without saying that Nazism was evil – the quintessence of evil – and had to be confronted. But there is a need for a more realistic, cooler appraisal of resistance and 'collaboration'. Precisely because the moral case against Nazism was so overwhelming, there has been a failure to pursue hard and searching questions about the nature, extent, and above all the consequences of resistance activity. The upshot is that a serious examination of the morality of resistance has not been undertaken, but simply assumed. There has been an understandable tendency to treat resistance as *a priori* right, and all forms of 'collaboration' as wrong by definition. Resistance acquired a moral stature, an aura that became difficult to question or dislodge. The trouble with the sanitized myth of resistance is that it whitewashes some of the more morally questionable aspects of resistance activity, and leaves awkward questions unasked. Whereas the established memory of World War II came under challenge by a later generation who asked embarrassing questions about the morality of obliteration bombing and the deliberate targeting of civilians, no comparable debate took place concerning the more dubious aspects of the resistance struggle. Military historians and students of the ethics of war began to apply just war principles in order to assess Allied conduct in the Second World War. Nobody disputed that the Allies had a just cause – a *jus ad bellum*. But the rightness of waging war did not preclude discussion of right conduct within war, and the means employed in achieving victory – the *jus in bello*. The central features of just war theory – the principles of non-combatant immunity and proportionality – were invoked in order to assess the morality of the methods used by RAF Bomber Command, and the United States Army Air Force. The fact that the Nazis started the war and had resorted to barbaric methods did not absolve the Allies from difficult questions concerning their attacks upon civilians, and their violations of the laws of war. The German bombing of Warsaw, Rotterdam,

Coventry, London and Plymouth did not cancel the debate over Hamburg, Rostock, Lübeck and Dresden. Pearl Harbour did not exonerate the US government from criticism over the Tokyo raids or Hiroshima. We judge Allied conduct by its means as well as its legitimate end.

But nothing like this has taken place with regard to resistance. There had been no comparable debate about resistance methods. Historians closed their minds to the true nature of the shadow war. Resistance is still judged largely by its ends – assisting in the overthrow of Nazism in Europe, and the liberation of one's country – and by the courage of resisters. It is assumed that because resisters were brave men and women who risked their lives against an enemy who did not hesitate to use torture, then no further questions need be asked. To do so would be to tarnish the reputation of national heroes. But this is an unworthy form of reasoning which does a disservice to the memory of resisters, because it distorts the difficult and painful choices that they often had to make. To question the British War Cabinet's authorization of civilian bombing in no way detracts from the enormous bravery of Bomber Command crews, with their high attrition rates. But the same logic is not applied to resistance.

Some historians like Alan Milward have questioned the military effectiveness of resistance, and its contribution to the outcome of the war. There has also been a statistical dispute over the number of people involved in resistance activity. But the moral authority of resistance has remained intact. The authors of a standard work on European resistance articulate the widespread sentiment that:

> In one sense or another, most of us are prejudiced in favour of the resistance. None of us is uncommitted.[15]

We still see Nazi-occupied Europe through the eyes of the resistance perspective, or rather through the rose-tinted spectacles of the pervasive myth of resistance. In order to avoid any confusion I will state that I am not uncommitted, I too share the 'prejudice' in favour of resistance. However, we need to fight against the temptation to be biased in favour of our own side if it means distorting the complex issues surrounding resistance and collaboration. We must refuse to be partisan about the partisans, if that built-in bias is to the detriment of accuracy. A fully 'committed', engaged account lacks the detachment necessary to take a step back and to provide a more critical look at the unpalatable aspects of resistance, and to examine the ethical doubts and disquiet of the ambivalent resister with a guilty conscience. We must be prepared to have the courage for an attack upon our convictions, and to unlearn cherished assumptions; to eliminate the adolescent illusion of a black-and-white choice between resistance and collaboration. Even professional historians are not immune from this tendency to give resistance a clean bill of moral health by concentrating upon its aims and not paying sufficient attention to its methods. Thus the distinguished British resistance historian, M.R.D. Foot, states simply that resistance was 'legally wrong [but] morally right'.[16]

> resistance's real strength in battlefield terms was puny. But it had titanic, as it turned out, invincible strength in moral terms.[17]

Furthermore:

> Resisters were prepared to reassert the rule of law against a regime that derided it.... They saw Nazis treating men and women like cattle, and were quite sure this would not do.[18]

This is certainly true of many resistance groups, but quite untrue of others. It is difficult to reconcile these stirring words with the actions of some resisters. The trial of Pierre Laval was virtually a kangaroo court, and the proceedings of many summary executions of collaborators were hardly compatible with the rule of law. The idea that Stalin's or Tito's partisans were trying to reassert due process and the rule of law seems rather questionable, to put it mildly, and the rough justice, and in some cases the plain injustice and atrocities meted out to many collaborators by some resisters (and fiercely condemned by others), seems to fly in the face of such a notion. But Foot is not alone in his estimation of the moral worth of resistance. In a book on *The Spiritual Heritage of Resistance*, the French writer Alban Vistel wrote that:

> resistance was a moral rather than a political phenomenon... for every man of the Resistance commitment implied a break with the mediocrity of the past and rejection of conformism, injustice and degradation; it was a development of a spiritual nature.[19]

According to this view, resistance was a conscious determination to defend basic ethical values of justice and humanity. The danger with this interpretation is that it sustains the seductive myth of the moral grandeur of resistance which we would all like to believe. It constructs an archetypal model of the resistance, an ideal type of the resister which often bears no relation to the practices of actual resisters. As Ralph White points out, 'there was no such thing as a "typical" resister' and consequently 'the evaluation of resistance is a complex problem'.[20] What was true of non-violent Christian re- sisters in Le Chambon, rescuing Jews, might be wholly untrue about anti-semitic members of the Polish Home Army, or among Soviet partisans. The resistance war was many wars in different places, and it is impossible to encapsulate the varieties of resistance struggle within a single phrase. Foot's and Vistel's interpretation of the moral ascendancy of the resistance is simplistic and complacent. The charac- terization of the resister as the embodiment of moral purity, with a clear and untroubled conscience, firmly treading the path of right- eousness, is a superficial generalization not supported by the evi- dence, and it overlooks the less than heroic, morally tainted features of Resistance. It reduces the complexity of life under the Occupa- tion to an edifying epic, a moralizing picture-book story of cow- boys and indians. What is missing is the social and ethical confusion, the ambiguity of moral and political choices. Above all, it ignores the problem of 'dirty hands' and the adoption of questionable methods, and sometimes odious and morally impermissible measures, to further the resistance cause.

We need to distinguish much more clearly between the principle of resistance and the practice of resistance. For if resistance to Nazism was right in principle, its detailed practices were often much more confused and questionable, and a frequent source of debate among resisters themselves. These discussions within resistance movements were not just about tactics and strategy, but concerned the ethics of resistance in the light of German security policy. Some resisters had genuine qualms about the morality of the methods that they employed, and they pondered the central question of political ethics: could a just end become corrupted by unjust means? Many narrative accounts of resistance neglect the fact that ethical considerations were presented at the time, and that resisters de- bated, and were divided over, the moral ambiguities and implica- tions of various resistance methods. I would stress this point because it is not just with the inestimable benefit of hindsight that we can raise questions about the practice of resistance. Rather, moral doubts about the consequences of resistance were raised at the time by resisters themselves. But this was overlooked because it conflicted with the prevailing myth which converted resistance into a sacred object which was beyond criticism. Because it developed into a cult, with its mythical heroes and martyrs, its rituals of remembrance and celebration, any questioning of the received wisdom of resistance was rather like challenging an article of faith. Because of the glorification of *the resistance* one of the most persistent illusions has been the temptation to gloss over, or to edit out the murkier side of the Resistance record. The religious-romantic aura which surrounded resistance ensured a certain silence over its human costs. Discussions of the consequences of resistance were marginalized and minimized, and the victims were denied a voice. Henry Rousso has pointed out the inherent ambiguities in official ceremonies which commemorate VE day in France.

> What dead would be honored in the minute of silence? The martyrs of the Resistance and soldiers killed on the field of battle? Of course, as banners and medals attest. The victims of the concentration camps? Obviously.... And what of all the others?... The hostages who had not participated in the Resistance themselves but who had been executed in reprisal? Those who had been denounced by their neighbours, rounded up by the Vichy police, and tortured by the Milice?[21]

Traditional forms of commemoration for those shot as hostages, or in reprisals, were inappropriate and might raise unpleasant questions about the necessity of resistance. They became the lost, forgotten victims of the German occupation. The manufacture of a mythical past aided the wiping out of unpleasant memories. Memory is selective, and those fragments that did not fit were suppressed or buried. Hollywood-style films often depicted the epic quality of resistance, and helped to sustain an enduring image of its heroic side. The cult of 'the resistance' turned resisters into sacred icons of the anti-Nazi struggle. The French historian, Jean-Pierre Azema, describes the popular perception of the archetypal resistance hero:

> The collective memory of ... the Resistance tends to be a confused picture of secret agents, avengers and outlaws with something of the Western hero or the knight [with spotless reputation]

about them, machine gun in hand, blowing up hundreds of factories and trains. A number of amazing, even fantastic episodes certainly took place but they were the exception rather than the rule.[22]

What was missing from these glorified romances of armed resistance was a reckoning of the human cost, the blood price that had to be paid. The forgotten epilogue to such tales of derring-do was the list of names of hostage and reprisal victims: for example, the 15-year-old boy, and the 76 other innocent reprisal victims killed after an act of railway sabotage at Ascq in 1944. This particular stretch of track on the main line from Antwerp to Paris had been sabotaged three times at the same inhabited spot. Even the most unimaginative resisters must have realized that their actions endangered the local population. It has been suggested that they could have considered moving their operations to the forests south of Lille where the Germans had no easy pretext for reprisals.[23] The countless victims were lost in the swirling mists of nostalgia for an imagined past, an idealized lost land, the pantheon of true patriots. In bestowing upon resisters the glamour of the outlaw, in transforming them into epic heroes – Robin Hood or William Tell figures – the grim complexities of the shadow war and hidden victims of the actual past could be denied.

One of the aims of this book is to challenge the received wisdom of the resistance experience: to demythologize it without attempting to belittle it; to see it for what it was, and not as some romantic holy crusade. Although numerous historians have scaled down the legend of universal resistance, and have demonstrated that very few people were active members of resistance groups, the pervasive image of resisters as just warriors waging a just war, by methods which were within the laws of war, remains intact. This is the myth of the resister as freedom fighter, actively supported by the rest of the population, and embodying their ideals and aspirations. This myth dies hard, and some accounts of resistance border on the hagiographical, conferring a wholly unreal, saintly status, upon resisters and resistance activity. An illustration of this comes from David George, who applies a just war model to armed resistance by partisans living under Nazi occupation. He writes that:

the moral right of wartime Resistance was the right of self-defence against the tyrannical aggression of Nazi rule ... a right not limited to its military agents. Exercising these rights did not violate the Just War principle that prohibits attacks on innocent non-combatants; the violence was discriminate. It is also arguable that the means employed were proportionate to the ends they adopted, both in the sense that an economy of force was employed and in the means being compatible with the end pursued. Means and ends of resistance were inter-connected, both being grounded in law and limits.[24]

The trouble with this statement is that it is based upon wishful thinking and uncritical adulation. It constructs an ideal standard of how resistance perhaps *ought* to have behaved, in accordance with the principles of just war theory, but it bears very little relation to the realities of resistance. These comforting certainties ring hollow when we examine resistance methods. The aims of resistance were just: to liberate one's country from Nazi oppression. However, some of the means of resistance were not grounded in any limits which derived from the laws of war or the just war tradition.

RESISTANCE METHODS

those who want to wage wars and revolutions must be prepared to kill people, to kill their compatriots – even their friends and relatives.[25]

Milovan Djilas

I met a Chetnik accompanied by one of our men. 'Where are you taking that man?' I asked the soldier. 'That's my own brother', replied the soldier. 'I'm going to finish him off in the ravine. He had no mind for our sufferings. He betrayed us.'. . . 'Do you know our policy regarding the captured Chetniks?' 'I do, but I tell you, he's my brother. I have the right to judge him.'[26]

Milovan Djilas

The decision to resist the Germans by violence was sustained by the firm conviction that resisters were fighting a just war. It was easy for resistance to occupy the moral high ground against unprovoked attack and Nazi occupation policies. It was harder to maintain that moral superiority when faced with difficult choices about how to resist Nazi rule. This proved to be a contentious issue which raised questions about the strategic worth, and the ethics of resistance to tyranny. Some of the methods that resistance employed were without military necessity or moral justification, and led to a lowering of the ethical sensibility of the resistance. As we shall see in later chapters, the assassination of German soldiers had little effect on the outcome of the war, and led to frightful suffering caused by German retribution. Resisters could not be absolved from their share of responsibility for the consequences. In particular, Communist Party policy was to use brutal measures against German troops, who would thereby be provoked to atrocious retaliation. Some resistance groups engaged in the torture and mutilation of German soldiers prior to execution, and to other methods which are explicitly prohibited by the just war tradition and the laws of war – attacks upon German hospital trains and unarmed Red Cross convoys; the poisoning of wells, and attacks upon the families of German personnel. Some resisters tortured collaborators. The torture of informers could provide important information, but it debased the resistance and it brutalized the torturers. Was it an acceptable method of waging war by people who held themselves to be civilized, and who were fighting against the barbarism of the Nazis? Was this the use of illegitimate means in the pursuit of a legitimate end? Some resisters had genuine doubts about the morality of the activities that they engaged in, realizing that a just end could become corrupted by unjust means. Some methods, such as the intimidation and killing of the families of collaborators, the taking of family hostages, the mutilation and torture of German soldiers, and the killing of prisoners-of-war, were a blot on the resistance record. They sullied the honourable cause for which resisters fought and died. Most histories of European resistance ignore the dark side of the shadow war, partly because exposure of such morally repugnant means might tarnish the reputation of the resistance. The adoption of such controversial methods tends to undermine the otherwise unassailable moral position of the resistance. The moral outrages of the resistance were disregarded because the Allied cause was crowned with success, and because the justification of the war was sufficiently strong. Hardly anyone objected to resistance tactics because the war against Nazism was a moral crusade in which the Allies could do no wrong. Victory vindicated the use of means which in other circumstances would have been seen as questionable. In 1945 nobody was in the mood for accusations of atrocities committed by resisters. Victors' justice meant that violations of the laws of war only became war crimes if committed by the Germans.

The grim record of partisan warfare during the Second World War offers evidence of a massive decline in standards, and a slide away from adherence to the principles of just war theory. Guerrilla war developed and degenerated into a savage form of combat with morally destructive consequences for the combatants and for the civilian population. The insecurity of German troops was answered by terror. Critics of partisan war have questioned its necessity, given the disproportionate reprisals, and the ghastly record of brutality that it engendered. It was in truth a vile and squalid war fought by methods of barbarism.

The glamorization of resistance in the post-war era obscured the often widespread opposition to violent resistance among the civilian population. The post-war myth conferred retrospective respectability and legitimacy upon resistance, and drew attention away from the fact that the resistance represented an unpopular minority for considerable periods of the occupation. It is difficult to gauge public opinion in an occupied country, but it is clear that large numbers of people questioned whether it was justifiable to sacrifice so many innocent hostages and reprisal victims for the sake of putative benefits. In many countries, public opinion was clearly and firmly against provoking the Germans, and resistance leaders came under enormous pressure to refrain from unnecessary attacks. Often resisters were deeply unpopular because their actions led to savage but avoidable reprisals.

In October 1943 when 5 Norwegians were summarily shot after a German troop train had been sabotaged, thousands joined in a public demonstration against the saboteurs. The gravity of this problem was apparent at every stage.[27]

Irate Norwegians were not the only critics of what they regarded as fruitless human sacrifices. A microfilmed report by one of the leaders of the Danish resistance was smuggled to London in January 1942. It stated that 'Anyone who tried to commit sabotage today would probably be condemned by a majority of Danes'.[28] Secret reports to SOE in London warned that the Danes were not 'ripe' for sabotage, and:

As late as May Day 1943, Socialist speakers contemptuously referred to Underground combat teams as 'little groups of fanatical provocateurs'. . . . The public mood at the time was accurately defined by Aage Peterson, who himself belonged to a sabotage team. . . . People are utterly scandalized. Nobody dares to shelter us. Nobody will accept an illegal newspaper. They are scared of us.[20]

Similar stories from other parts of Europe confirm a pattern of unpopularity. During the 1944 Warsaw Uprising, the Polish Home Army encountered a widespread defeatist attitude among the population of the capital. As the street fighting dragged on there was:

a growing conviction that all the efforts and sacrifices were futile [and] civilian behaviour towards insurgents was eventually affected. Now a sobering question was asked of the insurgents. 'What have you done for us?' . . . Towards the end there were instances when civilians refused to give lodgings to non-wounded insurgents. . . . The attitude . . . was progressively hostile . . . the questions were asked, 'Why does the Uprising continue? Why this bloodbath?'[30]

In the considered judgement of Norman Davies, the foremost British historian of Polish history:

There can be little doubt that the decision to launch the Warsaw Rising represents for the Poles the most tragic mistake in their recent history.[31]

Despite being undertaken for 'the most honourable motives' by men who fought selflessly for their country, it had 'the most baleful consequences for the very cause which it was intended to serve'.[32] Because the Rising had little chance of success, was politically unrealistic and tactically inept, Bor-Komorowski and the Home Army resistance were guilty of 'gross irresponsibility'[33] in failing to take into consideration the consequences of collective responsibility: 225 000 civilians killed, and Hitler's order for the city of Warsaw to be 'razed without trace'. In the suburb of Wola German security forces carried out the wholesale execution of 8000 people. Similarly, at Ochota, 40 000 people were murdered and hospitals were set on fire with their patients and staff inside. 550 000 civilians were despatched to Pruszkow concentration camp, and 150 000 sent to the Reich as forced labour. It was one thing for Polish nationalists to adopt the heroic mode of resistance and to proclaim the obligation 'to fight, whatever the cost' for the idea of Poland. It was quite another thing to count that cost in Polish lives, and to accept the responsibility for the losses that ensued.

Commander Stephen King-Hall relates how on one visit to France he had been told of an incident in the vicinity in which some partisans had ambushed a German convoy, killing two Germans:

> As a result the Germans went to the nearest village and shot a number of men as reprisals. My informant asked me what good this attack ... had done and assured me that the countryside had been anxious to see the partisans subdued. I heard similar stories in Belgium.[34]

Most Europeans wanted to be freed from the yoke of German occupation, but they wanted to be liberated by Allied armies, not by the fire and sword of resistance. We can only speculate about the response of the mass of the population in the USSR and Yugoslavia. After the war, the official histories were written by Communist historians on the winning side, and the view of the peasantry was not heard. But if the death of five hostages in Scandinavia could produce mass protests against armed resistance, it is not unreasonable to suppose that reprisals on the scale of Kragujevac, Kraljevo and Kiev, which resulted in thousands of deaths, produced an intense detestation of guerrilla warfare. In one German anti-guerrilla reprisal measure alone, in May–June 1943, 158 villages in the Osveia and Rossony districts of Western Russia were burned and totally destroyed. All able-bodied men were deported to Germany as slave labour, and all the women, children and old people were murdered.

> When the partisans returned there were corpses everywhere. . . . Many thousands had been murdered.[35]

Military historian John Keegan describes Milovan Djilas' memoirs, *Wartime*, as 'the key text of the Yugoslav war and one of the most brilliant literary achievements of the Second World War itself'.[36] As Tito's chief lieutenant, and one of the leading figures in the partisan movement, Djilas' testimony provides compelling evidence of the way in which brutalization became routine in guerrilla warfare.

Many resistance memoirs are a mixture of self-glorification, inac-
curacies and exaggerated tales of heroism. Djilas, however, provides us with an unflinching account of what resistance entailed in
practice, and he does not shy away from the more questionable
aspects of underground war. Drawn into a spiral of atrocity and
retaliation, Communist resisters were not over-scrupulous about
avoiding civilian casualties, and did not err on the side of restraint.
Djilas admits that Communist methods antagonized the Yugoslav
peasantry because 'they killed too many people'. The Chetniks gained
support because they were more cautious about incurring reprisals.

> It became increasingly clear to me that our imprudent, hasty
> executions . . . were helping to strengthen the Chetniks. Even more
> horrible and inconceivable was the killing of kinsmen and hurl-
> ing their bodies into ravines – less for convenience than to avoid
> the funeral processions and the inconsolable and fearless mourners.
> In Herzegovina it was still more horrible and ugly. Communist
> sons confirmed their devotion by killing their own fathers [who
> had refused to join the partisans]; and there was dancing and
> singing around the bodies. . . . By retrieving the bodies from the
> ravines and giving them solemn burial, the Chetniks made im-
> pressive gains, while pinning on the Communists the horrible nick-
> name of 'pitmen'.[37]

One of Djilas' kinsmen, a fellow Communist, 'even ventured to
tell me that in the command they were executing people "for nothing".'[38] Djilas informed the Supreme Staff that 'unjustified executions were being carried out'.[39] Some resisters like Djilas underwent
a radical change. As the old certainties deserted them, they questioned their most deeply-held assumptions and beliefs. Djilas concluded that such methods 'turned undecided, vacillating peasants
into bitter adversaries'.[40]

Thus the means and methods that resistance groups employed
to achieve a just end need to be examined much more critically,
and much more self-critically, in the honest manner of veterans of
the underground struggle like Djilas. For although the *principle* of
resistance was morally right, the *practice* could often be wrong,
dubious or foolhardy; and many resisters were deeply ambivalent
about the ethics of waging a one-sided war in which the losses to
their own civilian population might be totally out of proportion to
the gains. There was widespread opposition to armed resistance,

sabotage and assassination precisely because it led to massive reprisals against the innocent, and resulted in unnecessary civilian
casualties. On 14 July 1944 – Bastille Day – over a month after the
D-day landings in Normandy, the Resistance in Marseilles, which
was still under German control, laid a wreath on the city's war
memorial dedicated: 'To those who fell before us, comrades of the
Resistance.' Attached to the wreath was a box of the type used to
carry mines, with a notice saying, 'Achtung – Minen'. On hearing
of this, the German commander closed the cemetery to civilians
and ordered his troops to fire at the box. Nothing happened, and a
German soldier was sent to inspect the box. On opening it, he
found that it was full of stones. As a reprisal for this gesture of
symbolic resistance, 30 hostages were killed.[41] That this was a tragedy,
nobody can deny. That it was a military necessity, few will believe.

Similarly, when partisans knew that the war was effectively over,
continued attacks against retreating German troops only resulted
in needless loss of life. The timing of resistance is important in
assessing its morality. Two partisan attacks in the last week of the
war, three days after Hitler's death, led to a massacre of the civilian population in the Carnia region of north east Italy. On 2 May
1945, partisans engaged in sniper fire, causing 80 casualties among
German troops, who had signed a ceasefire before retreating towards
Austria.

In reprisal, a horrible massacre of civilians was carried out in
the village of Avanzis; the partisans had fled into the mountains.
51 defenceless civilians were killed in cold blood, including women
and children, and 25 left wounded.[42]

Another ambush in the village of Ovaro resulted in over 25 deaths:

The villagers . . . were furious . . . the villagers wrote on the walls
of Ovaro that the killings were the result of an irresponsible
partisan attack [at the mass funeral] . . . there were shouts of
'Death to Communist partisans'.[43]

Greek Communists kept up a similar barrage of attacks on retreating Germans. They too were ineffective, and could have been
avoided: unnecessary civilian deaths could have been prevented.
Those who would condemn the bombing of Dresden as wanton
destruction are compelled by the same logic to regard these attacks

as pointlessly provocative, militarily senseless and morally inexcusable.

The disparity between the modest achievements of routine resistance and the high level of human suffering and material destruction sustained in reprisals necessitates a reassessment of the dominant image of the shadow war. After the war the resistance fighter was canonized and turned into a national saint: a figure of towering stature who was beyond the reach of criticism. This myth of the noble freedom-fighter dies hard. It is the last bastion to fall in our minds. But we must demolish this icon and replace it with a more accurate figure which reflects the moral complexity of resistance. Some of the practices of resisters were painfully at odds with their principles, and we must no longer venerate resisters as objects of idolatry. When assessing resistance, the human cost must always be counted, and it is difficult to avoid the general conclusion that armed resistance often achieved only moderate results at disproportionate costs.

3 The Moral Grey Zone: Collaboration

This is, perhaps, the most fundamental lesson of our study: ordinary people, simply doing their jobs, and without any particular hostility on their part, can become agents in a terrible destructive process. Moreover, even when the destructive effects of their work become patently clear, and they are asked to carry out actions incompatible with fundamental standards of morality, relatively few people have the resources needed to resist authority. A variety of inhibitions against disobeying authority come into play and successfully keep the person in his place.[1]

Stanley Milgram

In order to avoid unnecessarily antagonizing the indigenous population, the Germans preferred to work with the co-operation of prominent local politicians and administrators, rather than with the active minority of vociferous but unpopular fascist collaborators who might plunge their country into civil war and chaos. Ideological identification was less useful to the Nazis' scheme of economic exploitation than creating a semblance of normality which obscured the extent of their control. A period of docility enabled the population to adjust more easily to the new state of affairs, and for the Germans to introduce changes gradually. Because the screw was turned slowly, people became habituated to obedience. Thus, after the initial traumas of defeat and occupation, everything returned to normal but everything was subtly different; everything was the same but nothing was the same, as an eerie period of 'abnormal normality' set in.

Under these conditions, ordinary people continuing to do their normal jobs provided a far greater contribution to the Nazi occupation than the activities of the relatively small number of ideological collaborators. In the long term this form of accommodation proved to be more insidious and corrosive, and did far more harm than the more blatant and overt forms of ideological and military collaboration. Richard Cobb noted the psychological insights of German propaganda immediately after the occupation of France in understanding and exploiting the 'conservatism' of ordinary people, and of the need for the occupying forces to use tact and self-restraint in order to encourage the resumption of a life as normal as possible:

> to reassure their perhaps unwilling, certainly surprised and be-wildered hosts ... through a sense of continuity, however arti-ficial and deliberately misleading that sense may have been. The main thing was to convince middle-of-the-road opinion – the tim-orous, the peaceable, the unadventurous, those always concerned above all to keep out of trouble – that for all essentials, life was much the same as it had been, and that all the old, reassuring landmarks were still in place.[2]

A quiescent population was far more manageable and economically efficient than one that required to be kept in place by brute force.

> Most people want to be reassured, and will indeed cling to re-assurance all the more desperately in the face of apparent dis-aster. The first requirement of any 'occupant' is to supply that reassurance. . . . Hence the posters of the correct German soldiers lifting up little French children.[3]

Armies of occupation are not renowned for their finesse, and the Germans conducted a none-too-subtle campaign to win the hearts and minds of the vanquished. After absorbing the initial shock of military defeat and occupation people still had to survive, and a 'life must go on', 'business as usual' attitude, became widespread. Once people settled back into their normal routines this provided the Germans with desperately needed personnel, an invaluable pool of labour from which to draw. The day-to-day administration of the state, and guaranteed industrial and agricultural production, was indispensable to the Germans. In between the extremes of a tiny minority of active resisters, and a small, but larger, minority of active collaborators, the vast majority of people engaged in pass-ive co-operation, or 'bread and butter collaboration'[4] simply in order to preserve their existence. People had to make a living. Food had to be produced, and the distribution of food through the ration card system guaranteed the 'bread and butter' collaboration of many people, whether they liked it or not. Essential services like coal mines had to run in order to provide gas, electricity and heating. Factories which declined to work for the Germans were deprived of raw materials. This resulted in their workers becoming unemployed, and led to the threat of deportation to Germany as forced labourers. If they refused, their unemployment and other benefits would be withdrawn, and their families would suffer.

In the mundane, everyday sense of reluctant accommodation and a grudging adjustment to adverse circumstances, most people collaborated most of the time. However, if co-operation was the rule and resistance the exception, given the ideological nature of Nazi occupation policy, the question soon arose as to where to draw the line between legitimate and illegitimate dealings with the German authorities. Given the everyday compromises of life under the occupation, the borderline was not always clear. Were shopkeepers who put German language signs in their windows to solicit extra business guilty of collaboration? Where did self-interest end and collaboration begin? 'Collaboration is an endlessly elastic concept that is not easy to define. Was anyone who worked, directly or indirectly, for the Germans a collaborator?'[5] Were the 35 000 industrial workers who remained at the Renault works – one of the largest industrial plants in Europe – collaborating because they turned out military equipment for the German Army? And what of the lucrative commercial collaboration of leading industrialists like Renault? At what point in making compromises was one compromised? When did accommodation to unfavourable circumstances shade over into active collaboration and doing the Germans' dirty work for them? When did compromise turn into complicity, collusion and consent?

In order to explore the moral implications of this issue more fully, it is illuminating to look at various occupations under the occupation. Although everybody was faced with moral choices during the years of German rule, most people tried to avoid them in their private, family lives. In their public lives, however, these choices and decisions became inescapable.

OCCUPATIONS UNDER THE OCCUPATION

No occupying power ... can administer territory by force alone. The most brutal and determined conqueror needs local guides and informants ... the study of military occupation may tell us as much about the occupied as about the conquerors.[6]

M. Marrus and J. Paxton

Many professionals stayed at their posts out of a sense of public duty, and in order to shield the general population from the worst effects of Nazi domination – taking orders while attempting to lessen their impact. However, they were soon faced with a gradual increase in Nazi demands, and found it difficult to reconcile German orders with their patriotic duty, or their humanitarian feelings. The initial compromise was unavoidable, and the eventual consequences unforeseeable. Professional groups such as doctors, civil servants, railwaymen and policemen became embroiled in the implementation of policies which went far beyond administrative continuity and stability. They became intermediate links in a chain of evil that ended at Auschwitz. Ironically, the normally commendable virtues of skill, competence and taking a professional pride in one's job – using problem-solving rationality to find the most efficient and economical means of working – could prove deadly under the abnormal conditions of Nazi rule. The longer the occupation dragged on, we find broader and broader circles of complicity. At what point did one become an accessory to Nazi crimes?

Doctors

Doctors frequently rendered invaluable service to resistance groups, but the nature of their work confronted them with acute dilemmas. Because too many French doctors gave false exemption certificates, German doctors had to be present at medical examinations to determine the fitness of workers for compulsory labour in Germany. Under German military occupation rules, doctors and hospital staff were required to report the identity of any wounded person to the authorities. Obedience to this rule could result in the arrest of resistance suspects. Disobedience could jeopardize the families of medical personnel. After Heydrich's assassination in Prague, German security discovered that one of the killers had been wounded, and all 7000 doctors in Czechoslovakia had to swear a written oath stating that they had not treated a man fitting the description of the suspect. Any doctors offering aid to the assassins risked the lives of their entire family.

Doctors were also required to reveal the identity of Jewish patients, and any male who had been circumcized. Medical co-operation with the 'Jewish Question' resulted in a severe crisis of conscience for many Dutch physicians. In Holland in May 1943, the German authorities issued an ultimatum to categories of Jews who had previously been exempted from deportation – converts to Christianity, and Jews in mixed marriages. They could either choose 'voluntary' sterilization or deportation. The Germans also insisted that Jewish and Dutch doctors, rather than Germans, perform the operations. Sterilization conflicted with Jewish law, and was opposed in principle by the Roman Catholic church. Some Jewish doctors suggested the wholesale resignation of the medical profession, but the Germans would have treated this 'strike action' as sabotage, and the doctors and their families would be threatened by deportation or death. If they conformed to the Nazi decree, and the racial doctrine underlying it, the doctors would compromise the most basic medical tenets, and their religious principles. If they refused to perform the operations, it would be at the expense of the lives of those to be deported. One doctor said that 'for his family's sake he was reluctantly compelled to co-operate, but that in future he would look upon himself as a criminal'.[7] At what point did compromising with Nazism mean compromising oneself? When did the behaviour of the doctors in acting under duress become active collaboration?

Civil Servants

Civil servants engaged in a policy of administrative accommodation with the Germans, which slid imperceptibly into collaboration. For example, every Czech civil servant had to swear an oath of allegiance to Germany. Simply remaining at one's post meant compromising one's professional standards and patriotism. It was difficult to determine where the borderline of unavoidable co-operation ended and active collaboration began. Public services had to be provided. Even remaining at one's post provided the Germans with continuity, stability and invaluable expertise. Throughout the hierarchy, from Secretaries-General to middle-grade officials and the humblest worker in the typing pool, civil servants were involved in an elaborate system of administrative control: processing identity cards, ensuring that everyone was photographed and finger-printed, and preparing a racial questionnaire which helped to define, isolate and target Jews. Civil servants were required to compile a census of the population which enabled the Germans to determine who was eligible for compulsory labour service in Germany. The Dutch churches urged civil servants to resign rather than administer this conscript labour scheme. In October 1940, Dutch public servants (who included schoolteachers and university staff) were obliged to certify their 'Aryan' status in questionnaires which classified the racial origin of public employees. 'This . . . was to be the acid test for all Dutch civil servants'.[8] Most complied, and by attesting their Aryan origins, made it easier to bring about the disqualification and dismissal of Jewish colleagues.

> Without the compliance of Holland's civil employees, the Germans never could have been so successful in their deportation of Jews in Holland. A Dutch official in charge of designing identity cards created a pattern so intricate that it was more difficult to forge than the German identity card. The designer's feelings about Jews was irrelevant. He was a man who was proud of his job.[9]

André Tullard, a leading civil servant in the French police, compiled a massive alphabetical index of Jews based on a census that the Germans had requested the French police to carry out. In October 1940 Jews were required to register at police stations, providing information concerning their home address, nationality (whether a French Jew or a refugee), and their profession. By completing the paperwork and devising his elaborate filing system, Tullard, who took a professional pride in doing a good job, made it infinitely easier for the Germans to locate and isolate Jews for eventual round-ups. Although he did not realize it at the time, Tullard's dossiers became death lists, and a key instrument in France's contribution to the Holocaust.

In the purge trials after liberation, a recurring theme throughout Europe was the judgement that the normal performance of one's job was not culpable, but that excessive zeal constituted active collaboration, and 'aiding and abetting the enemy'. The principle was straightforward; its application was fraught with difficulty in weighing up the mass of circumstantial factors which made up working life with the enemy. The moral purpose was to purify the country, and to punish collaborators. However, it proved impossible to establish exact gradations of collaboration, especially as many public servants claimed that they engaged in simultaneous resistance and collaboration. If there were over-zealous officials, there were also anonymous public servants who smuggled out ration cards from the Central Food Office in Rotterdam, or who forged ration and identity cards, which provided a lifeline for fugitive Jews and resisters. In over 150 Dutch towns and villages the public registers essential for the compilation of deportation orders disappeared, as civil servants co-operated with the underground in throwing a spanner in the works. Some people collaborated by day and resisted by night. Civil servants were especially well placed to provide inside information and assistance to the underground. A leading member of the Dutch Resistance testified to their value:

> There were the Burgomasters, or Mayors, who, longing to resign from the posts which had become so distasteful under the Nazi regime, were persuaded by us, for the sake of their fellow countrymen, to remain where they were. 'If you resign', we told them over and over again, 'Nazis will be put in your place – and things will be blacker than ever for all of us. Stick it out . . . keep up the passive resistance as much as possible; make things as difficult as possible for the Nazis'.[10]

Nevertheless this policy created a crisis of conscience because one of the tasks of the Burgomaster was to serve as head of the local police when the Germans required Dutch participation in Jew hunts.

Railway Workers

Railway workers played a prominent part in deportations, and were implicated at every stage. They provided a well-oiled bureaucracy for the smooth-running of trains: from the sidings worker cleaning out wagons and affixing destination labels, to the signalman and the engine driver who took the train to the border of Germany. It is important to stress that it was Dutch, Belgian, French train drivers, and not Germans, who took responsibility for the trains within their own borders. Timetable officials drew up schedules, not only for German troop trains, but also for 'special transports': Jew transports, with their human cattle wagons, which were specifically timetabled to travel at night in order to avoid arousing public sympathy. When Jews were rounded up in French towns, they were transferred to the deportation centres in the reassuringly familiar green and white buses run by the 'Compagnie des Transports', thus implicating its drivers and management.[11]

Collaboration cannot be examined in isolation from resistance. The extent of railway collaboration also tells us something about the realities of resistance as opposed to the myths which surround it. Thus, French railway workers had a reputation for militancy, and contained a disproportionate number of socialist and communist resisters in their ranks. The Head of French Section SOE claimed 'Throughout the history of the Resistance the railwaymen were almost one hundred per cent the keenest and most resolute resisters'.[12] Yet between March 1942 and August 1944, 76 000 Jews were transported from France in 85 special trains, including transports which consisted solely of children. As Roderick Kedward astutely observes:

> When historians of the Jewish persecution ask why [these trains] were allowed to leave France without a single major act of derailment or sabotage to interrupt their passage, the damaging answer is that although many people felt the Jewish deportations were morally indefensible, there were not enough people who felt their own lives and freedoms threatened by the deportations to produce an effective ... response.[13]

Kedward adds that when STO, the Compulsory Labour Service, conscripted Frenchmen to Germany, the response of the railway workers was different and involved widespread sabotage. Given the opportunities and information available to railwaymen, the question arises 'why the Resistance's apparent ability to disrupt any train at will did not seem to have prevented trains departing for the death camps'.[14] What does their inaction tell us about resisters' priorities and the relative unimportance attached to the plight of foreigners and Jews?

A similar story emerges from Holland. In May 1940 the five trade unions representing administrators and workers endorsed a Dutch railway management declaration of loyalty to the Germans, and agreed to administrative co-operation if the Germans left the railway network in Dutch hands. 112 000 Jews were deported in 98 freight trains, yet the 30 000 railway workers attempted no sabotage or disruption of these transports.[15] Individual railwaymen were troubled by the ethical implications of serving the Nazis: 'In isolated incidents, engineers apparently reported sick to avoid running trains with Jewish deportees, but replacements could always be found'.[16] Despite the reluctance of some workers, hardly any resistance was offered: 'No train, no single train, failed to run on schedule'.[17] Indeed, throughout Europe the only confirmed case of railway sabotage against 'Jew transports' occurred in April 1943, when Belgian railway workers unbolted cattle wagons containing their human cargo, and 150 Jews escaped from Transport No. 22.

The sheer scale and efficiency of railway collaboration raises uncomfortable questions about the extent of working class collaboration in general, prompting one commentator to make the provocative point, 'The widespread view that European labour's resistance to the occupying power was instinctive and class-based is one of those pious myths that fail to withstand serious scrutiny.'[18]

Police Forces

The police were always at the sharp end of Nazi occupation policy. Having sworn to uphold the law of the land, they found their land under enemy control. As the executive arm of the conquered state, and the enforcement agency of their country's law and order policy, the police force was in the most exposed and difficult position of any professional group in having to superintend and execute Nazi occupation legislation, which frequently conflicted with the traditional laws that had been in force prior to the invasion. Policemen were required to organize and participate in manhunts, combing an area for political fugitives and resisters, and to round-up Jews for deportation. The whole ethos of their profession militated against disobedience, yet the enforcement of these measures posed the most acute moral questions for decent policemen. Nationalist, humanitarian or religious beliefs could conflict with the ingrained professional habits of a lifetime, causing a profound crisis of conscience. In May 1943 the Catholic hierarchy in Holland 'forbade the collaboration of Catholic policemen in the hunting down of Jews, even at the cost of losing their jobs'.[19] John Sweets illustrates the moral confusion and complexity of life under enemy occupation by relating the story of a policeman who engaged in simultaneous collaboration and resistance.

> The head of the 'gendarmerie' for the region around Clermont-Ferrand became, posthumously, a hero ... because he died in deportation. But at the time of his arrest by the Germans he was marked for execution by the 'Front-National'. Allegedly, he had distracted the Germans' attention from non-communist groups by revealing to them the locations of 'Francs Tireurs et Partisans' (FTP) units. This same official had acted to protect individual

Jews from persecution. His story should sound a note of caution for those students of ethics or morality who would see the history of wartime France in clear shades of black and white – the good resisters versus the bad collaborators. To sort out the interwoven threads of heroism, treason, good and evil, is exceedingly difficult. In wartime France, everything was complicated.[20]

Numerous policemen retired rather than be a party to inhuman orders. However, this carried with it the risk of punishment, and the latent threat of collective family responsibility. One Dutch policeman used his inside information and the cover provided by his uniform to run an escape line. His wife stated, 'It's no trouble to us. We've got no children for them to take reprisals on; so what have we got to lose?'[21] The local population benefitted in many ways by having a sympathetic indigenous police force, rather than a specially selected Nazi import. The local force was better placed than any other group to provide vital information and warnings to the Resistance about impending raids. It could also engage in passive resistance: delaying tactics, an unco-operative and obstructionist attitude, and the removal of files containing incriminating evidence against fellow countrymen. Nevertheless, as Nazi Germany had created the perfect model of a Police State, there was constant SS and Gestapo supervision of local forces, and a credibility gap would emerge if the native police were persistently ineffectual. The local police had to demonstrate successful co-operation in executing German demands. This, coupled with the constant threat of reprisals, often placed policemen in an impossible position. Gerhard Hirschfeld wisely cautions that:

> The personal risks faced by the individual policeman should not be forgotten. His responsibility for the livelihood and even the lives of others frequently brought with it much greater personal dangers than those faced by other employees in the public service. From July 1942, officers who had been guilty of an 'offence' against the occupying power, or had refused to undertake a task assigned to them, had to answer for their conduct before a special German SS and police court. This fact alone throws a revealing light onto the extremely precarious situation of the Dutch police. It would be completely unjustifiable to make a sweeping condemnation of the entire police system.[22]

Rauter, the SS Chief in Holland in charge of anti-Jewish affairs, decreed:

> I will act against any policeman who disobeys an order from the German police to arrest Jews. We will not only dismiss such policemen from the service, irrespective of whether they are state police or municipal police, but there must also be disciplinary proceedings against them.[23]

Rauter ordered the arrest of the parents and families of policemen who resigned or went underground. In Denmark, the Gestapo drew up lists of the most unreliable policemen, and in a co-ordinated operation, SS and German Army units occupied every police station in the country on 19 September 1944. Nearly 10 000 officers were arrested, and over 2000 were deported to German concentration camps. Those suspected of underground activity were severely beaten and tortured. Thousands were placed in internment camps.

Although there were numerous humane acts by policemen, how does one weigh individual resistance against institutional police collaboration, which conferred a kind of legitimacy upon Nazi measures? Throughout occupied Europe, the Germans were desperately short of manpower, and were stretched thin across vast areas. They were particularly handicapped by limited numbers in ordinary security and law and order tasks, and were heavily dependent upon the local police. There were only 3000 German security police for the whole of France, and in Saint-Etienne, for example, the Gestapo had only five men to cover a city of 200 000 people. Therefore, the participation of the French police force of over 100 000, including 10 000 in Paris, was essential for the success of German repression. The French police was one of the most centralized forces in Europe: it administered the census of the population; it did all the paperwork, and through Tullard's elaborate filing system, made a major contribution to the Final Solution. A similar story can be told for Holland, where the Germans had only 1000 civilian officials and were reliant upon the co-operation of the Dutch civil service and police. Westerbork and other transit camps for Auschwitz were run primarily by Dutch SS volunteers, not by the Germans.[24] The post-war testimony of Wilhelm Lages, Head of the German Security Police in Amsterdam confirmed:

The main support of the German forces in the police sector and beyond was the Dutch police. Without it, not 10% of the German occupation tasks would have been fulfilled. . . . Also it would have been practically impossible to seize even 10% of Dutch Jewry without them.[25]

Clearly the number of resistance and Jewish victims would have been considerably fewer if the Germans had to identify and arrest them all. Equally clearly, collective and family responsibility and other reprisal measures were no idle threat, and played a not inconsiderable part in guaranteeing police co-operation. Indeed, there is a link between the small number of German personnel in the occupied territories and the resort to drastic action. The limits on German power, and the sense of vulnerability of its occupation force, made it rely ultimately upon security measures, and above all, the threat of ruthless reprisals to intimidate the population into compliance.

AVERTING THE WORST: THE DILEMMAS OF COLLABORATION

> It is the logic of our times,
> No subject for immortal verse,
> That we who lived by honest dreams,
> Defend the bad against the worst.[26]
>
> C. Day Lewis

In a dreadful moment in history it was argued that one only carried out unjust laws in order to weaken their severity, that the power one agreed to exercise would have done even more damage if it had been placed in hands which were less pure. What a deceitful rationalization . . . which opened the door to unlimited criminality! Everyone eased his conscience, and each level of injustice found a willing executor. In such circumstances, it seems to me, innocence was murdered, with the pretext that it be strangled more gently.[27]

Benjamin Constant, 1815

In a well-known example from the literature of moral philosophy, Bernard Williams presents the dilemma of Jim, a visiting botanist who walks into a South American village where Pedro, an army captain, is about to shoot 20 Indians, randomly selected from the villagers, as a punishment for a non-violent protest against the regime. As a special 'guest's privilege' Pedro will release 19 of the victims if Jim will select and kill one of them himself. There is no means of negotiation with Pedro, and no prospect of saving all 20 people, because the village is surrounded by heavily-armed troops. If Jim refuses to accept the wager, he personally will have killed no one, and his hands will be clean of direct involvement in shedding human blood. However, his inaction will result in 20 deaths. If he kills one of the villagers, 19 other lives will be saved . . . but at the expense of the murder of an innocent person by Jim. What should Jim do?[28]

Some commentators have described Jim's dilemma as 'far-fetched'.[29] It is certainly questionable in its small print. One wants to know what this political innocent is doing abroad in a country with such a record of human rights' violations and roving death-squads. Also the 'guest's privilege' is artificially contrived and trivializes the genuine dilemmas which have confronted people in real life, and because it ignores the complex circumstantial factors which cloud the decision. Nevertheless this philosophers' parlour game has urgent equivalents under the Nazi occupation. Jim's dilemma may be interpreted as a stark parable of reluctant collaboration as a necessary evil to avert even greater evils. It also illuminates the appalling complexity of the dilemmas of the occupation, and leads us to question the delusive simplicity of unqualified condemnation of collaboration as a traitorous activity. Like Jim, the peoples of occupied Europe wished that the situation had never arisen. Like Jim, they had to make choices that nobody should be forced to contemplate. Like Jim they became accomplices to evil and accessories to crime, compromising their own principles in order to avert greater crimes and worse evils.

In the post-liberation purge trials the classic defence of limited collaboration was always a variation on the theme of 'the lesser of evils', 'averting the worst', the 'double game' and the 'shield philosophy'. The standard justification of government officials and civil servants was that they could not abandon their country to its fate, nor could they shirk their responsibility for representing the national interest. For example, the Germans detained two million French prisoners of war, and treated them as bargain hostages in order to exert pressure upon the French authorities, blackmailing them into compliance with German demands. French policy was dictated by the fate of the prisoners. Collaboration with the enemy meant that officials would act as a shield or a buffer to protect their own people. An examination of this argument will illustrate the moral complexity and ambiguity of resistance and collaboration, and it will take us into what Primo Levi called 'The Grey Zone' in which so many people were condemned to live under enemy occupation. In this moral grey area one tone delicately shaded into another: subtly moving from compulsion to reluctant co-operation to active assistance to connivance to collusion and complicity.

In the early years of the war, and especially in 1940, resistance was quite without practical importance. Because there was no means of challenging Nazi domination, working with the enemy seemed unavoidable in order to guarantee basic goods and services. Some form of co-operation was an inescapable yet humiliating necessity dictated by superior force. The only questions were: what form that co-operation should take, and what were the limits of collaboration? Government officials confronted a real dilemma. If co-operation with the enemy was a painful necessity, an expedient to prevent the execution of more extreme measures, they soon found themselves being drawn deeper and deeper into carrying out the crimes of the Nazi occupation regime. The limits of collaboration kept expanding. Nowhere was this more evident than in the dealings of the Vichy government in France: the only country under occupation to adopt an official policy of state collaboration. Commitment to collaboration often for the most honourable motives led down a path which was not immediately apparent, and Vichy officials became prisoners of their initial decision. Reasonable collaboration resulted in unreasonable German demands. Moral contamination became unavoidable as the Germans required Vichy to do more and more of their dirty work for them, entrapping its officials by deliberately creating conflicts of conscience.

Marshal Pétain and Pierre Laval believed that they had to reach an understanding with the Nazis in order to moderate the excesses and limit the damage of the occupation; to salvage what they could from the wreckage of military defeat: to compromise in order to save lives. The justification adduced by Pétain and Laval at their trials was couched in terms of the 'Shield Philosophy'. Pétain:

> I used. . . . power as a shield to protect the French people. . . .
> Will you try to understand the difficulty of governing in such

conditions? Every day with the enemy's knife at my throat, I had to struggle against his demands.[30]

The policy of temporizing, inertia, and creating what Laval called 'an atmosphere of artificial confidence among the German representatives'[31] had saved France from the perils of total occupation and national extinction. Pétain again:

I prepared the ground for liberation, by keeping France alive, though in pain. What good would it have been to liberate ruins and cemeteries?[32]

Critics have questioned this defence of the Shield Philosophy, arguing that at best it is an over-simplification, and at worst a self-serving excuse. The argument also lost much of its force when the Germans occupied Southern France in November 1942. Nevertheless, taken on its own terms, limited collaboration had shielded the country from the rule of the Paris-based ultra-collaborationist French Nazis, or the direct rule of the Gauleiter. The examples of Czechoslovakia under Heydrich and Poland under Hans Frank served to emphasize the point. The threat of 'Polonization' was the central argument for Vichy's existence, saving the country from the same fate as Poland by playing the 'double game': partial compliance with German demands in order to mitigate the harm and to subvert Nazi excesses. The joke about Laval's strategy was that when the Germans asked for a chicken he gave them an egg.

At some indeterminate point, however, reluctant accommodation based upon good intentions, shades into collusion, and the conquerors played upon this to exact a higher price from the timorous French. The Germans viewed collaboration in a very different light, captured in the contemporary joke 'Give me your watch and I'll tell you the time.'[33] They skilfully exploited French fears, drawing the Vichy regime into greater and greater complicity. The policy of defending the bad against the worst – agreeing to the commission of limited harm to avert greater harm – faced the Vichy authorities with appallingly difficult questions. After the invasion of the USSR, there was an upsurge of Communist resistance in France. The first assassination of a German occurred in Paris on 21 August 1941. Hitler demanded pitiless reprisals, and the German High Command selected 100 hostages for execution, in two batches of 50. As an object lesson, to impress the population with the consequences of defiance, it was announced that the bodies would be publicly displayed at the Place de la Concorde. However, in order to exploit French susceptibilities and blackmail Vichy into co-operation, the German Foreign Office devised a devishly cunning plan to implicate French officials. The first batch of 50 hostages would be reprieved if the French agreed to set up an 'Extraordinary Tribunal' to eradicate Communist resistance. Also, the number of hostages would be reduced to 10 if they were selected and executed by the French themselves. The Germans imposed a five-day deadline for the French to reach a decision. After urgent and tortuous discussions between the French judiciary and civil service, the Vichy regime agreed to enact retrospective legislation, backdated to the time of the assassination. French judges tried, unsuccessfully, to mitigate the sentences. Maurice Gabolde, Minister of Justice, described the choice which confronted him:

> If the French government could obtain through its own courts 10 death sentences, followed by execution, of notorious communists, there would be no execution of substitutes. It was a tragic dilemma. From the point of view of the interests of the French authorities, it would have been better to let the occupying authorities carry out their reprisals: but how many families would have been in mourning, and what a drama of conscience.

Many of those involved in this drama were 'quite shaken' by the alternative presented, but the Vichy courts of appeal set up 'special sections' to deal with 'terrorist crimes':

> The law came into effect immediately, and its retroactivity made it possible to judge condemned persons for deeds committed previous to its publication, which was the only way of avoiding numerous executions of persons condemned in replacement.[34]

As Minister for Justice, Gabolde was fully aware of the cruel irony of his position: sanctioning flagrant injustice in order to save lives:

> At the same time we had continued our efforts to have the number of condemnations to death reduced. Out of 10 which were demanded we saved first three, and finally five.
> The 'special section' condemned only three. The drama of conscience among the judges must have been terrible.[35]

The complex problem facing the judiciary was compounded by the fact that De Gaulle's Free French Resistance Movement in London had urged judges to remain in office and take the oath of allegiance to Pétain, as Head of State, in order to mitigate the evils of the occupation. To be effective at all, they had to co-operate with the enemy. After the liberation, resistance ministers admitted that the judges had saved thousands of lives by avoiding the strict application of the letter of the law, and by passing lesser sentences upon captured resisters than the death penalty. Hanging over them was the threat that if they resigned, neo-Nazi French ultra-collaborationists would take their place, and would impose much harsher penalties. Even if their action could be justified in utilitarian terms in saving lives, the judges' decisions compromised their professional ethics and rudimentary principles of justice, and left them morally tainted. As Peter Novick noted, the judges' 'dilemma became excruciating when it extended to a choice between sentencing some innocents to death, in the name of French justice, or seeing a larger number executed by the Germans'.[36]

Having embarked upon this path, Vichy officials soon found themselves having to go that extra mile down the collaborationist road. Once the principle of collaboration had been established, and the precedent of participation in killing innocent people had been accepted, albeit reluctantly, the path became broader and easier to traverse. Pierre Pucheu, as Minister of the Interior, and Jean-Pierre Ingrand, as the Ministry's liaison officer to the Germans, became responsible for the selection of hostages to be shot by the Germans. In October 1941, after the shooting of a German officer at Nantes, Pucheu was presented with a list of 100 hostages drawn up by the Germans. He persuaded them to reduce the number to 50, but the list still contained 40 veterans from the First World War. Pucheu protested at the proposed punishment of patriots for a crime committed by Communists. The Germans supplied an alternative list, containing 44 Communists and 6 other hostages. Pucheu said nothing. The Germans interpreted this as silent assent. In effect, Pucheu had tacitly condoned the doctrine of collective guilt and responsibility. He tried to justify his action to a friend:

I did what anyone, as Minister of the Interior, would have done . . . I could not allow 40 good Frenchmen to be shot.

'But how could you, Pucheu? How could you choose the hostages to be shot?'

I didn't choose them. I simply let the Germans give me a different list.

'You had no right to do that, my friend. Whether ex-Servicemen or Communists, they were all good Frenchmen. You had no business to choose; the massacre should have been left entirely to the Germans.'[37]

Although on one level Pucheu's behaviour could be seen as an attempt to shield the French from the Germans – after all, 50 lives had been saved which would have been lost without his intervention – on another level it was an attempt to save one group of Frenchmen at the expense of sacrificing another group of Frenchmen. At this level of collaboration it is almost impossible to disentangle genuine humanitarian motives from Vichy's pursuit of its domestic political agenda to rid the country of Communism. The shield became a screen behind which Vichy settled old scores with the enemy of the Popular Front era. This also proved congenial to the Germans, and there was a convergence of interest between the German and French authorities over the elimination of a common enemy. What began as the mitigation of Nazism ended as its imitation.

Police Collaboration

... if you are always afraid of dirtying yourself, you never get anywhere.[38]

Pierre Laval

The moral complexity of institutional collaboration is further illustrated by the role of the French police under the leadership of its Secretary General, René Bousquet. In May 1942 Bousquet refused to acquiesce in Heydrich's plan to reorganize the French police under direct SS control. Bousquet also declined to recruit large numbers of extremists from ultra right-wing parties. Resistance veteran Jacques Delarue argues that by his obduracy and insistence on the independence of the French police, 'Bousquet had spared France from a very grim future. In Poland . . . and Czechoslovakia, the German police controlled the entire local services.'[39] As with the French judiciary, the Resistance instructed policemen not to resign, but to remain at their posts.

Bousquet agreed to the principle of co-operation between the

French and German police, on condition that the Germans did not interfere in the administration and conduct of the French force. However, ultra-collaborationists conducted a hostile press campaign and organized rallies condemning the weakness and vacillation of Vichy and 'openly accused Bousquet of protecting Jews'.[40] Karl Oberg, Head of the SS and German Police in France, threatened to hand over police powers to the pro-Nazi ultras, because Vichy was regarded as too dilatory in its pursuit of suspects. As part of the Oberg–Bousquet Agreement of 29 July 1942, Bousquet persuaded the Germans to renounce their proposed reorganization, in return for a more active policy in repressing resistance. Bousquet obtained a guarantee that French policemen would no longer be placed in the invidious position of having to select and arrest French hostages for German executions. Bousquet's aim was to revoke the Hostage Code of September 1941, and to ensure that only those found guilty of specific offences against the occupation forces should be punished by the Germans. It is significant that Jacques Delarue paid tribute to Bousquet's efforts to avert reprisals: 'It is understandable that the general secretary of the police could at this moment rightly feel proud.'[41]

Bousquet's legitimate objective of protecting innocent French lives could not have been achieved without co-operation and compromise with the German authorities. The logic of the lesser of evils still entailed the taint of corruption. Bousquet chose dirty hands rather than washing his hands of the problem. This left an indelible stain. But it is important to ask what choice did officials like Bousquet have except the policy of containment and minimizing casualties? That Oberg violated the agreement 13 days later by ordering the execution of 88 hostages for the death of eight German soldiers only served to illustrate the weak bargaining position and inherent powerlessness of the occupied when faced with a ruthless army of occupation. If the road to hell is paved with good intentions, it is littered with the reputations of those who would appease tyranny in order to moderate it.

If leading figures like Laval and Bousquet became reluctant accessories to Nazi crimes, there were always more extreme ideological collaborators waiting in the wings for their opportunity to become willing executioners of the Nazis' plans. Charles Maurras, the ageing leader of the reactionary 'Action Française', in numerous public pronouncements, defended and justified the German practice of shooting hostages to deter resistance, and even urged that the families of exiled Gaullists be held hostage. In his collaborationist newspaper, 'L'Oeuvre', Marcel Deat exceeded any German propaganda requirements by calling for British subjects living in unoccupied France to be taken hostage after RAF raids on the Renault raids in March 1942. He recommended to Pétain that 'for every innocent Frenchman murdered by the RAF, one hostage to be shot'.[42]

The threat from the far right was not a figment of the imagination. Laval and Bousquet had limited room for manoeuvre, and were constrained by the fear that non-cooperation with German demands might precipitate an even worse outcome. Joseph Darnand, the Head of the Milice, was congratulated by the SS for his exemplary behaviour in hunting down Jews. Because of Bousquet's obstructionism he was replaced as police chief in January 1944 by Darnand. In conformity with the German doctrine of collective family responsibility, Darnand drew up lists of known resisters and arrested their families, using them as a supply pool for future hostage executions.

Vichy and the Jews

Vichy's anti-semitic policy, and its aid to the Germans in deporting Jews has been the subject of many detailed studies, notably Marrus and Paxton's 'Vichy France and the Jews'. Lack of space forbids a thorough analysis, but it is important to be clear about the nature and purpose of French collaboration with the Germans over the 'Jewish Question'. Many of Vichy's own anti-semitic laws and policies were taken in advance of any Nazi requests for co-operation, and often exceeded German measures. Vichy adopted its own independent, indigenous response to the 'Jewish Question' and 'mounted a competitive or rival anti-semitism rather than a tandem one'.[43]

As Vichy saw it, the Jewish problem consisted of the recently arrived stateless foreign Jews – 200 000 in total – who had fled to France as a safe haven from Nazi persecution in the 1930s. With the scarcity and privations of wartime, they were regarded as an unwanted refugee population. Vichy policy was directed at expelling this alien minority. However shabby, inhumane and xenophobic, Vichy's measures 'were not intended to kill'.[44]

The most infamous action was the 'Grand Rafle' of 19 July 1942, when 5000 French police rounded up 13 000 Jews in Paris for deportation. A total of 76 000 Jews were expelled from France. Although there is no dispute that the Vichy government, its civil service and police apparatus consented to, and directly participated in, the deportation of Jews from France, the question of perception and intention remains vital. The unfolding chronology of events is central to the understanding of the Holocaust, and scholars repeatedly confront the question: who knew what, when? Did the French consciously aid and abet the Germans in carrying out mass murder? Marrus and Paxton note that 'like everyone else, Vichy's leaders were slow to fathom the scope of the Final Solution'.[45] Because atrocity propaganda from the First World War had been shown to be false, there was considerable scepticism about mass killings in eastern Europe. Because the Germans desperately lacked manpower, and given the secrecy in which the Holocaust was shrouded, the official reason for deportations – that Jews were being sent to labour reserves in the east – seemed plausible in 1942. The French collaborated with deportation, not extermination. As Holocaust scholar John P. Fox observes, 'one may certainly accuse the Vichy authorities of callousness and inhumanity, but not of mass murder'.[46]

In June 1942 the Germans ordered the deportation of all Jews from France, but Laval attempted to save French Jews by relinquishing foreign Jews. An SS report to Berlin dated 25 September 1942 stated:

> an attempt was made to arrest Jews of French nationality. The political situation and . . . Laval's views on the matter do not permit action . . . such an action would have severe consequences. . . . The Reichsfuhrer SS concurred in this opinion and ordered that no Jews of French nationality are to be arrested for the time being. Large scale Jewish deportations are therefore impossible.[47]

When the nature of genocide became clearer by 1943, Fox notes that this 'intensified Vichy police and government efforts to prevent French Jews from being deported'. Bousquet informed the Germans that 'no French police personnel would assist them with any transports that included French Jews. . . . French obstructionism served merely to confirm their other doubts about how far they could count on French cooperation.'[48] Numerous German security reports referred to the unreliability of the French police in combating resistance, and in being less than zealous in implementing manhunts for Jews.[49] Laval's biographer notes that Laval 'fought very hard for the French Jews'.[50] In the most balanced and thought-provoking analysis of Vichy's complex role, John P. Fox points out that there is 'no basis' for the accusation of conscious and deliberate Vichy complicity in 1942 in the Nazi programme of genocide. Fox is the only scholar to have drawn attention to the striking similarities between Vichy's choices and the decisions of the Jewish councils in eastern Europe. He argues that when a clearer picture emerged in 1943 'the actions of Vichy France indeed paralleled the practical and moral dilemmas of the eastern Judenrate'.[51] Vichy France sought to protect its own citizens, French Jews, by handing over foreign Jews. In drawing a clear comparison with the invidious choices that the Jewish Councils confronted – by sacrificing some Jews in order to save others – Fox asks whether this requires us to 'moderate' the harsh judgement of Vichy and to grant it 'a greater degree of "understanding" because of the human dilemmas involved'.[52]

French involvement in the deportation of Jews is deeply troubling, but it cannot without serious distortion be equated with the willing participation of Ukrainian, Latvian and Lithuanian police in the Final Solution. Bousquet and Laval were not inhuman monsters like Mengele or Heydrich, but flawed, imperfect characters with all the weaknesses and vacillations of ordinary human flesh. They faced disturbing, almost impossible choices, and became tainted and compromised by contact with their country's conquerors. Whether their form of collaboration mitigated Nazism or facilitated it will depend upon whether we regard Jim as the murderer of one Indian or the saviour of 19.

CONCLUSION

The evaluation of the shield theory is a deeply controversial and unresolved issue. There is no consensus on the overall assessment of Vichy. Among historians, opinion is divided over the wisdom, morality and effectiveness of the strategy of reluctant accommodation. Robert Paxton concludes his study of Vichy France by asserting that 'the shield theory hardly bears close examination'.[53] John P. Fox, however, argues that there was a shield, and that it worked:

> That the position would have been far worse had Vichy not acted in the way it did, or had 'allowed' the Germans free rein to pursue whatever policies they wished, there can be no doubt.[54]

These conflicting conclusions are reflected in the ambivalence of Stanley Hoffmann's response. On the one hand he asserts that 'there is enough evidence behind the thesis of Vichy, the shield that protected the French body politic while London and the Resistance forged a sword to allow the French public to face its wartime record without too much shame'.[55] Yet Hoffman could also write that:

even if Vichy had saved France from . . . the fate of occupied Poland, even if Laval did his best to delay the arrest of French Jews, the moral price was horrendous. . . . Vichy France made moral choices which no government should be willing to make.[56]

The most considered and measured judgement was pronounced by Gordon Wright:

The men of Vichy faced some of the thorniest moral issues and personal dilemmas of our time. . . . Laval repeatedly confronted this dilemma of the lesser evil: when he thought the choice lay between shooting 10 hostages or seeing the Germans shoot a hundred, when he turned over the foreign-born Jews on the theory that he could thus save French Jews, when he believed that nobody else could keep the super-collaborators out.

It is difficult to dissent from Wright's conclusion:

If the men of Vichy failed to resolve any of these dilemmas . . . perhaps their failure should inspire as much pity as contempt.[57]

The shield theory is not wholly specious. There is more in it than its critics allow, but less than its apologists admit. One cannot dismiss it out of hand. Equally, one must recognize that the shield philosophy provided a convenient excuse, and in some cases a perfect alibi, for those whose motives were less than pure. The problem in any given case is to determine whether an accused collaborator was genuinely playing a double game, or whether that defence rested on a triple bluff. The trial of Paul Touvier in March 1994 illustrated the difficulty in arriving at a fair judgment. Touvier had been the Intelligence Chief of the pro-Nazi anti-semitic Milice in Lyon. He was charged with authorizing the execution of seven Jewish hostages, and that he was therefore guilty of 'crimes against humanity' – a crime which carried no statute of limitations. Touvier's lawyers tried to minimize his role by playing the classic defence that he was acting under constraint, but had tried to avert the worst. On 28 June 1944 members of the French Resistance assassinated the Vichy Information/Propaganda Minister, Philippe Henriot. Touvier claimed that the SS Commander in Lyon ordered 100 hostages to be shot as a punishment. He asserted that his immediate superior in the Milice had negotiated with the Germans, and had succeeded in reducing the number to 30. Touvier alleges he was ordered to carry out the killings, but that he in turn managed to get the figure reduced to seven, although he personally had to select them from a batch of 30 men rounded up by the Milice. The killing of the seven Jews was carried out at the cemetery of Rillieux-la-Pape, near Lyon, by a Milice firing squad.

Touvier argued that he should not be seen as an accomplice and a murderer, but rather as the saviour of the reprieved hostages. Touvier's lawyer compared his behaviour to Oscar Schindler in saving 1200 Jewish lives. Before the trial he stated 'Touvier is Schindler'.[58] This Schindler defence is a rather questionable comparison, to put it mildly, given that Touvier had volunteered for an organization whose oath bound its members to destroy 'Jewish leprosy'.

The trial exposed the extent to which Vichy had been drenched in duplicity. The trial of Paul Touvier was in microcosm the trial of Vichy France – its police, its law courts, and even the right-wing, anti-semitic network within the Catholic Church which had hidden Touvier after the war. It was 'Vichy's day in court fifty years after the fall of the regime.'[59]

The passage of time should not tempt us to rehabilitate collaborators, nor to accept their claims at face value. But coming to terms with the past in a dispassionate way should force us to acknowledge the genuine complexity of the choices which faced decent men who practised 'reasonable' collaboration, yet who were overwhelmed by events. The Tribunal at the Nuremberg Trials ruled that the plea of superior orders under duress was a legitimate defence if it could be demonstrated that the harm caused by obeying the order was not disproportionately greater than the harm that would result from not obeying the order. Many co-operated with the Germans not out of conviction but out of fear of the consequences of disobedience. The latent threat of collective responsibility cast its shadow over the cruel choice of either working for the Germans or facing punitive measures for oneself or one's family or country. One cannot discount putative duress when assessing the moral and psychological complexities of collaboration. We should never lose sight of the fact that it was German security policy that placed the peoples of occupied Europe in an unenviable, often morally intolerable position. Nevertheless, they could not evade the stark moral choices which faced them, for if they did not act many lives would be lost in any event. It is important to recognize the good intentions of those collaborators who, operating from a position of weakness under pressure from the conqueror, tried to reduce the severity of Nazi rule while facing an uncertain future, or the prospect of indefinite German domination. It is also imperative to differentiate them from those fanatical ideological collaborators who willed a German victory by Nazi methods, and had been bought body and soul by the Germans. Jim is not Pedro, and even if Jim facilitates Pedro's work, he does not elect to become a willing executioner, but rather the protector of the innocent.

4 Moral Choices in Occupied Europe

It was one of those rare times when everyone was faced with a moral choice, even though the choice most people made was 'life as usual'.[1]

Ted Morgan

The Occupation, by putting people against a wall and forcing them to make the kind of choices that people should perhaps never be asked to make, pushed them into ambiguities.... This was a time of heightened sensitivities.... Situations that had never seemed in need of questioning now began to be questioned, and new situations arose for which no response had been formulated.[2]

Frederick Harris

Throughout Hitler's Europe people were forced to choose, and to find answers to tragically difficult and unprecedented questions. Jews were often faced with a stark choice between bodily death or spiritual annihilation. The Christian resister confronted the necessity to lie, to deceive, to murder. Officials were faced with the need to violate all professional standards. The occupation years raised profound ethical problems concerning individual responsibility, professional ethics and conflicting duties. Life and death questions. Questions of adherence to pacifist religious principles or saving lives. Questions of patriotism, honour and treason. Questions of political obligation and disobedience: obeying the law or following the dictates of one's conscience. Questions of utilitarian ethics: choices between a greater or lesser evil. Questions central to the just war tradition which has shaped western attitudes towards violence: when, and under what conditions were killing and violence justified? Questions for every resister to ponder: even if one had a just cause, did one have a right to use any method to defeat Nazism, or were there limits to what was permissible? Disturbing questions concerning the human cost of resistance actions, which jeopardized the lives of one's fellow countrymen, and whether the price in human suffering was disproportionate to the ends being pursued.

These questions could, and indeed did, divide societies. Households were riven. The occupation years left lasting scars on the body politic: families and friends bitterly divided, communities torn apart by internal strife, and in some countries civil war; the convulsions of the post-liberation purge of collaborators; haunting and unforgettable images of shaven-headed women with swastikas daubed on their foreheads, taunted contemptuously by jeering crowds for engaging in 'horizontal collaboration'.

The trial in Bordeaux in January 1953 of 21 members of the *Das Reich* division of the SS exposed the deep divisions within French society. The Oradour Trial was especially traumatic and painful because 14 of the defendants were not Germans but French nationals from Alsace. They claimed that they had been conscripted unwillingly to serve in the German armed forces, and had been compelled to act against their will out of fear of reprisals against their families if they disobeyed orders. Although they had participated in the massacre of 642 French civilians, their subsequent punishment of forced labour provoked an outcry in Alsace. Fearing secessionism in the area, the French government proposed an amnesty, and in February 1953 the Alsatians were freed. The granting of the amnesty was condemned in the National Assembly by Deputies representing Oradour-Limousin; numerous protest strikes and demonstrations broke out, plus pilgrimages and vigils in Oradour itself. The history of the German occupation was viewed in differing ways in Strasbourg and Limoges.

> The Oradour affair demonstrated that the fault lines created by the Occupation were not simply ideological. They were also geographical, a reflection of the different situations existing in different parts of occupied France.[3]

Although an extreme case, the Oradour trial illustrated the inherent tension between the demands of justice and the requirements of national reconciliation. The granting of amnesties was a deeply divisive issue throughout Europe. It was difficult to separate peacetime politics from the just punishment of war criminals, and the shadows cast by the occupation lasted long after the end of hostilities.

A poignant illustration of the depth of feeling that the occupation years inspired can be found in the memoirs of Henri Frenay, the founder of one of the earliest resistance groups, 'Combat'. Frenay had been a general staff officer in the defeated French Army. After the armistice many patriotic French servicemen faced a crisis of conscience – wanting to continue the struggle against their 'hereditary enemy', but recognizing the legality of the Vichy regime, and its legitimacy in the eyes of the majority of French people, and also disciplined to obey the legitimate authorities – the subordination of the military to political control. Frenay's mother shared the common feeling of the overwhelming majority in seeing Marshal Pétain as the saviour of the nation in the darkest hour in its history. She suspected her son's loyalty, and after some tense questioning he reluctantly informed her that he was not going to sign the oath of allegiance to the new Head of State:

> Barely able to control herself, she turned pale, then interrupted me curtly in a quiet but terrifying tone. . . . You're trying to hurt our country . . . and if you think I'm going to keep quiet about it . . . well, you're wrong! I love you dearly, as you know – my children are my whole life – but I believe that patriotic duty comes before maternal love. I'm going to denounce you to the police! I must stop you from doing evil.

Although stunned by this outburst, Frenay replied:

> Such an act on your part would cause an irreparable breach between us. I respect your conscience; please try to respect mine. But if you insist on doing what you've just threatened to do, don't bother to call for me on your deathbed, for I shall not come.[4]

The choices confronting the peoples of occupied Europe varied from profession to profession, and from year to year. People saw things differently in 1940–1941 when the German army had swept everything before its path and had seemed invincible, from the way in which the situation was perceived in 1943–1944, with the changing fortunes of war, and with the German armies on the retreat and heading for defeat. What appeared to be the calculated, expedient collaboration dictated by considerations of *real politik* in 1940 looked increasingly like *surreal politik* by 1944. The choices also varied in intensity from country to country – ranging from the 'velvet glove' policy in the Nazis' showpiece, its model protectorate of Denmark, to the comparatively lenient treatment of western Europe, to the mailed fist in eastern Europe. In the words of Hitler's biographer Joachim Fest:

For all that the [eastern] campaign was strategically linked with the war as a whole, in its nature and in its morality it signified something else entirely. It was, so to speak, the Third World War.[5]

The war in the west was fought largely within the laws of war, the attitude of the German authorities to the civilian populations being strict, but 'correct'. In the east, however, Germany waged a war of extermination, an ideological crusade, outside the laws of war and the Geneva Convention, at the express command of Hitler. The differences between the two types of war and occupation conditions need to be constantly borne in mind when assessing opposition to Nazism, because not all forms of resistance can be measured and evaluated by one absolute yardstick of right and wrong. There were important differences of circumstance facing resisters in different countries – some imposed by the Germans, some dictated by geography and different historical and cultural traditions. What was feasible in the mountains of Yugoslavia or in Russia's Pripet Marshes, was out of the question in the Channel Islands or in Holland. What might be unnecessarily provocative and avoidable for ordinary Belgians was vital and inescapable for Jews in the Warsaw Ghetto or in the private hell of the concentration camps.

A question which might have been a cause for soul-searching in the Channel Islands would not have been an issue at all in Poland or Serbia – indeed it might have been regarded as a form of moral self-indulgence. Given the correctness and propriety of German behaviour, Channel Islanders debated what was the appropriate response to the civility shown by German soldiers? Should one reply in kind to a friendly soldier who has offered his hand in a courteous greeting, or should one ignore the outstretched hand? Should his warmth be answered by the cold shoulder? Were manners and politeness suspended for the duration?

One of the greatest dilemmas of the Occupation . . . namely, how much social interaction with the enemy was compatible with patriotism? Every islander, from young children to the Bailiff, had to decide what kind of behaviour they were going to adopt towards the enemy.The simplest human exchanges became the subject of anguished moral searching.[6]

How did one respond to the German soldier billeted in one's house? Did one, in Kantian terms, treat him as an end in himself? Or did one see him as the personification of 'the enemy'? Vercors' famous short story, 'The Silence of the Sea' centres around the refusal of a Frenchman and his niece to speak to the young German soldier billeted with them, despite the fact that he is not a Nazi, reveres French culture, and has excellent personal qualities. Silence is their only weapon. Their stubborn silence and determination to let life go on as normal, and to change nothing, even down to the smallest detail of their daily routine, as if the soldier didn't exist, is a symbol of the mute defiance of the powerless. The story becomes a parable of the virtues of stoicism and self-respect under conditions dictated by the adversary.

Sartre reports an accident involving a German colonel whose car had overturned in one of the main streets in Paris. Ten Frenchmen hurried to help free him from the wreckage. Although they may have hated him as an enemy: 'Was that man an occupier lying crushed under an automobile? ... the concept of an enemy is only completely firm and clear if the enemy is separated from us by a barrier of fire.'[7]

NOT BY BREAD ALONE

In their moral deliberations, Orthodox Jews in the eastern ghettos and camps debated whether to fast on holy days in order to keep their commandments, or to eat the little amount of food they had in order to keep up their strength. 13-year old Elli Friedmann described her experience at Auschwitz:

> My assignment to the night shift coincided with Yom Kippur. Before we leave for work in the evening we are served our breakfast and at 12 midnight, the lunch ... on the night of Yom Kippur I could not have my breakfast before leaving for work because it is served too late ... after the beginning of the fast. The midnight meal, naturally, I had to forego. And the supper in the morning.

Although ravenous, Elli writes:

> I started my second night of work without food, by now having fasted thirty-six hours.[8]

For other Jews who questioned their faith, to eat could be not just a way of staying alive but an act of symbolic defiance against God's indifference, and a rejection of a 'dead' former way of life. Elie Wiesel in Auschwitz:

> Yom Kippur. The Day of Atonement. Should we fast? The question was hotly debated. To fast would mean a surer, swifter death. We fasted here the whole year round. The whole year was Yom Kippur. But others said that we should fast simply because it was dangerous to do so. We should show God that even here, in this enclosed hell, we were capable of singing his praises.
>
> I did not fast, mainly to please my father, who had forbidden me to do so. But further, there was no longer any reason why I should fast. I no longer accepted God's silence. As I swallowed my bowl of soup, I saw in the gesture an act of rebellion and protest against Him.
>
> And I nibbled my crust of bread.
>
> In the depths of my heart, I felt a great void.[9]

A similar dilemma faced a group of Hasidic Jews in Buchenwald, when a Ukrainian kapo offered to sell them some sacred religious objects (a pair of Tefillin) that he had stolen, in return for food.

> The Ukrainian's price – four rations of bread – created a moral problem for the Hasidim. To do without this much bread was to risk death; to sell the bread was therefore to risk committing the sin of suicide. What did they do? They sold the bread, bought the Tefillin and then, to quote a survivor, 'prayed with an ecstasy which it would be impossible ever to experience again.[10]

A group of Hasidic Jews who ran the brush factory at the Plaszow labour camp declined to work on Yom Kippur, and prayed instead. The practice of their religious beliefs under these conditions raised wider questions, because it jeopardized the lives of others through German reprisals. Other workers pleaded with them to return to work. The SS learned of the incident and shot the 'malefactors' and randomly executed some of the other workers.[11] At what point was their adherence to religious principles outweighed by the obligation not to endanger others? Should they have refrained from their ritual observance in order not to imperil the lives of their fellow workers?

Jewish parents with new-born sons faced a difficult choice. The practice of circumcision is an integral part of the Judaic faith. But it provided the Germans with an easy test for determining whether any males were Jewish. One Jewish woman testifies:

> At the end of November 1941, I was taken to the Jewish hospital, where I gave birth to a baby boy. Under the circumstances, circumcision could have been a question of life or death. If the baby was then left with a Christian family he might be recognized as a Jew. We nevertheless decided that he should be circumcised.[12]

For Jewish couples in Nazi-occupied Europe, the natural decision to have children was in effect to pass sentence upon them: to condemn them to death.

CHRISTIANS AND THE ETHICAL PROBLEMS OF RESISTANCE

> Although it is certainly not true that success justifies an evil deed and shady means, it is impossible to regard success as something that is ethically quite neutral. . . . In the last resort success makes history. . . . Simply to ignore the ethical significance of success is a short circuit created by dogmatists who think unhistorically and irresponsibly; and it is good for us sometimes to be compelled to grapple seriously with the ethical problem of success. As long as goodness is successful we can afford the luxury of regarding it (ie success) as having no ethical significance; it is when success is achieved by evil means that the problem arises. In short, it is much easier to see a thing through from the point of view of abstract principle than from that of concrete responsibility.[13]
> Dietrich Bonhoeffer

> Only those who cry out for the Jews may sing Gregorian chant.[14]
> Dietrich Bonhoeffer

There is a tendency on the part of secular scholars to underestimate the power and importance of beliefs that they do not share. Given the enormous influence of Christianity in shaping European civilization, and the large numbers of Christians scattered throughout Hitler's Europe, it would be a mistake to neglect the important role that Christians played in resistance groups. Many of the most significant dilemmas can be seen in the tensions between obedience to the Commandments and compassion for the persecuted. In St Paul's Epistle to the Romans, Christians are enjoined to obey the 'powers that be' because the State is a divinely ordained institution. Many Christians, particularly in the Lutheran tradition, have taken this to mean an almost unqualified obligation to obey the State. Certainly St Paul's epistle was a major factor within Germany, acting as a powerful restraint upon political disobedience to the Nazi regime. One historian has even gone so far as to assert: 'The thirteenth chapter of the Epistle to the Romans contains what are perhaps the most important words ever written for the history of political thought'.[15]

The initial problem for Christians was the conundrum of how to confront evil in the form of Nazi state power whilst 'rendering unto Caesar'; how to be their brother's keeper while their brother was being systematically mistreated. In practice it could come down to a stark choice between obeying the Commandments to tell the truth, not to deceive and not to kill, and the need to save innocent lives. In a decree dated 13 December 1940, the German authorities compelled priests in Norway to reveal incriminating information given to them under the seal of the confessional if German security police demanded it. The penalty for non-cooperation was imprisonment, despite the fact that Norwegian law upheld the silence of the confessional. There was a massive protest by the clergy, and the seven bishops of the Norwegian Church lodged an official protest against this attack on the pledge of silence. Nevertheless the decree remained 'in the interests of the state'. Similar measures were adopted in other parts of occupied Europe, notably in Catholic Poland. Roman Catholic resisters sought absolution for killing Germans and collaborators, and for participation in group acts which involved the spilling of blood. Priests who ministered to resisters found the political obligation to obey 'the powers that be' clashed with ecclesiastical law, nationalist sentiment and humanitarian feeling.

On 15 October 1941 the German authorities passed a law in Poland specifying the death penalty for any Jews who were found outside their ghetto without permission, and for anyone who knowingly provided a hiding place for Jews. 'Any Christian who learned that a Jew was breaking the law had an obligation to report the crime or be subject to the same punishment.'[16]

What Bonhoeffer called the 'safe road of duty' would have required the obedience of immoral laws, and inhuman decrees. To obey the law and tell the truth under Nazi rule might result in the certain deaths of hundreds of people. The alternative to this 'safe conscience' was a clear one which accepted the responsibility for one's actions. But even this clear conscience was threatened by the problem of 'dirty hands'. Many people, either for reasons of temperament, religious convictions or compassion, were unwilling to engage in violent resistance. Although they were not prepared to take lives, in many cases Christians and pacifists were attracted to working in organized escape lines in order to save the lives of persecuted refugees. They drew a moral distinction between humanitarian aid and physically harming the enemy. However, although this form of illegal and clandestine work was easier to reconcile with their consciences, the circumstances of Nazi occupation tested their non-violent beliefs to the limit. If helping victims was the natural thing to do, it could lead to unimagined consequences.

The story of Marion Pritchard, a 22-year-old Dutch woman who saved the lives of over 150 Jews during the war, illustrates the dilemmas of peace-loving people living in dark times who felt that they had to do something.

In 1942 I was asked by friends in the resistance to find a place for a man . . . and his three small children aged 4 years, 2 years and 2 weeks. [Because the countryside was safer than large towns, they moved into a farmhouse belonging to a friend.] [We] built a hiding place in the basement in case of raids, which we had at times. One night four Germans and a Dutch Nazi policeman came to search the house. Everyone was in the hiding place, and they didn't find it. But a short time later the Dutch Nazi returned alone. He had learned that Jews were often in hiding places, and that if you returned just after a raid, you might catch them in the house. That's exactly what happened. Erica [the baby] started to cry, so I let the children come up. When the Dutch policeman came back, I had to kill him with a revolver a friend had given me, but I had never expected to use. I know I had no choice, but I still wish there had been some other way. An undertaker in town helped me dispose of the body by putting it in a coffin with another body. I hope the dead man's family would have approved.[17]

Of the 25 000 Jews hidden in Holland over 8000 were captured, often through the assistance of informers. Try to imagine yourself in Marion Pritchard's shoes – especially if you are sympathetic to non-violence and to pacifist ideals – what would you have done? In taking in Jews, in hiding children, you have assumed a responsibility for the lives of others which might override personal convictions about the intrinsic evil of killing.

Christians who decided to participate in resistance activities, often for the most humane reasons, found themselves drifting towards a moral whirlpool where traditional rules and guidelines no longer operated. Resisters were ineluctably drawn into a series of unforeseen actions as a logical consequence of their commitment to oppose Nazism. Sometimes resisters had to kill a comrade who was too seriously injured to be moved, rather than let him fall into enemy hands to face torture, and the inadvertent betrayal of his fellow partisans. Resisters had to confront the means-end question in its most acute form, pushing the conundrum to its limit, to the point where there are no longer any limits, and everything is permitted.

In a short article written immediately after the war – and one of the few studies to explore the ethical issues of resistance – the Scottish Presbyterian minister Alexander Miller describes the moral maelstrom into which Christian resisters had been drawn and which threatened to submerge and drown their moral universe:

Not to resist Nazism was to acquiesce in it. There was no living alternative at all. Yet to resist Nazism was to be plunged into the same chaos. For to resist one must stay alive and one could stay alive only by forgery and deceit. Ration books must be forged or stolen. Propaganda and organization must be carried on clandestinely and by trickery. . . . Even within the Christian groups the traitor or the potential traitor must be liquidated without hesitation if not without compunction, since not only might the lives of the group members themselves depend upon it, but the good cause itself. . . . But drive this to its logical limit, and where does it take us? Presumably if a man may be liquidated as a danger to the good cause, the same man may be tortured to make him yield information vital to the good cause. If he resists torture himself, would it not be more effective to torture his children before his eyes?[18]

Miller incisively depicts the cumulative moral deterioration which could occur. For most resisters, the duty to oppose Nazism was necessary and obvious. But as with all versions of the means-end problem, the struggle against the evils and injustices of Nazism could only be waged effectively at times if resisters were prepared to adopt similar methods to those of their opponent. Resisters found themselves crossing moral lines and barriers, at first slowly and with hesitation, then with greater rapidity: trickery, lying and deception could lead on to the assassination of Germans, the murder of fellow countrymen; the torture of informers and the torture of relatives of informers. Resistance could coarsen the greatest idealist. Unless they abdicated any personal involvement or responsibility, washed their hands of the problem and adopted a cautious, wait-and-see attitude, resisters could not help but get their hands dirty.

In 1945 Miller questioned a group of French and Dutch Christians who had engaged in forgery, lying, torture and murder while in the Resistance.

> I put the obvious question . . . Forgery, 'liquidation', torture – if these may be used, then, 'Is everything permitted?' The reply was clear and quite crucial: 'yes: everything is permitted – and everything is forbidden'. In other words, if killing and lying are used it can only be under the deepest sense of personal guilt that no better alternative can be found. That is a sure safeguard against carrying on torture, for example, just for the fun of the thing, as Nazism or nihilism would permit.[19]

The Polish Catholic resister Wladyslaw Bartoszewski relates how the Polish Underground made stringent efforts to find out the names of Polish informants and security police officials who had specialized in denouncing or blackmailing Jews in hiding.

> We obtained our information directly from Christian Poles who worked for the security police with the knowledge of, and under orders from, the underground organisations. In this way we managed to unmask several dozen confidence men whose cases were turned over to the special court.
> . . . the sentences passed on traitors by the special courts were carried out by the young, self-sacrificing men acting for the underground Polish government at great personal risk.[20]

The Underground was scrupulous in its efforts to ensure that only the guilty were punished, and was deeply conscious of the need to avoid tragic errors. In addition:

> Those who carried out death sentences had to bring all of the documents and papers they found on the condemned person to their superiors. During the fall of 1943 I came into the possession of a notebook that had been found on Borys Pilnik who had been executed... near Warsaw in the summer of 1943. Pilnik was the leader of a whole group of blackmailers who hunted down Jews living in the 'Aryan' sector, including people who were married to non-Jews. They would then force these unfortunate people to pay for their silence. This criminal's notebook was a veritable record of his heinous deeds. In it he had carefully noted the names, and in some cases the addresses of the people who had been blackmailed so far, and he had pedantically entered records of the amounts of extorted money. In addition, it contained names and addresses of people who were potential victims for blackmail or denunciation, some of which were followed by a question mark. For example, it read: 'The daughter of the Rabbi?' followed by the address, or, 'Mixed marriage? – needs to be investigated', or the initials and address of an unknown person with the addition: 'Valuables'. When we were able to find the victims, we informed them immediately and told them that their tormentor was no longer alive.[21]

A less harrowing example can be found in the Protestant Huguenot community of Le Chambon in Southern France, where thousands of Jewish refugees were concealed and eventually smuggled to Switzerland, under the leadership of the pacifist pastor, André Trocmé, and his wife Magda. They believed in the overriding necessity of saving as many innocent lives as possible, and that to refuse to help refugees would be an act of harmdoing (a sin of omission). Nevertheless, for these devout Christians, such actions still gave rise to real doubts and quandaries. Clandestine action entailed breaking the Commandments, and this caused them guilt and anguish, however compassionate the cause. One lie led to another untruth – a chain reaction of deception – until all of their most deeply-held beliefs had been compromised.

in Le Chambon in the beginning of the 1940s, concealment meant lying – lying both by omission and by commission. It meant not conveying to the authorities any of the legally required information about new foreigners . . . and it meant making false identity and ration cards for the refugees so that they could survive in Vichy France.

But for Magda and the other Chambonnais, the making of counterfeit cards was not simply a matter of practicality. It raised profound moral problems . . . duplicity for any purpose was simply wrong . . . none of those leaders became reconciled to making counterfeit cards, though they made many of them in the course of the Occupation. Even now, Magda finds her integrity diminished when she thinks of those cards. She is still sad over what she calls 'our lost candour'.[22]

In addition to questions of personal integrity, there were wider considerations. Non-violent opposition to the authorities could also result in the imposition of collective punishments – mass deportations; the burning of villages; massacres. Le Chambon was fortunate in being under the benevolent control of Major Julius Schmahling, military governor of the Haute-Loire in 1943–44, a decent man who turned a blind eye to the rescue plans, and prevented the SS legions from moving into the village. Most places were not so fortunate. Hiding Jews and other 'outlaws' carried the death penalty. But it also jeopardized the lives of one's family and possibly one's neighbourhood or village. For example, in Poland, a family of eight people were shot because they had hidden one Jewish child. In a similar incident, five Poles in a family, which included a 13-year-old and a one-year-old baby were killed after it was discovered that they had hidden four Jews. The practice of collective family responsibility guaranteed that an act of compassion towards a Jew put the lives of one's own family at risk. Was the rescuers' primary responsibility towards family or total strangers? As one Jewish survivor has written:

> Harbouring a Jew was like living with a time bomb . . . who has the right to ask another to risk his life in order to save his own?[23]

Jewish resister Yisrael Gutman asks:

Are we capable of imagining the agony of fear of an individual, a family which selflessly and voluntarily brings into their own home someone threatened with death? There is no moral imperative which demands that a normal mortal should risk his life and that of his family to save his neighbour.[24]

Capital punishment was supplemented by the infamous 'Nacht Und Nebel' (Night and Fog) decree in December 1941. Whole families were deemed to be collectively responsible for any acts of resistance to the New German Order, and members could be spirited away secretly into the 'night and fog', finding themselves in a concentration camp at dawn. This deterrent measure, designed to strike fear into any potential enemy of the Reich, caused the most profound conflicts of loyalties between obligation to one's family and community, and obligation to persecuted individuals, encapsulated in the question that the Mayor of Le Chambon asked the Trocmés when the first fugitive sought shelter:

Do you dare to endanger this whole village for the sake of one foreigner? Will you save one woman and destroy us all?[25]

This was no rhetorical question. In February 1944 the Germans were informed by Ukrainian collaborators in the ethnically mixed area of Galicia in eastern Poland that about 100 Jews were being hidden in the Polish villages of Huta Pienacka and Huta Werchobuska. With the help of Ukrainian policemen the Germans surrounded both villages and burned them to the ground. The soldiers:

Assembled all the farmers together with their families and locked them in the barns. They even locked the cattle in the stables. Then they set fire to the entire village . . . [They] stood guard to make sure that no living thing, human or animal, would escape from the burning buildings. The village burned all day.[26]

The formidable practical problems involved in rescue activities should not be forgotten. How could one keep young children quiet, not only during a raid, but under everyday circumstances, with the constant uncertainty that one's neighbours might be informers – especially when the children were too young to understand that they were not allowed to make any noise or to play outside? Without a ration card, how could the basic necessities of food, clothing and soap be provided? With tradesmen and other callers, how could refugees be effectively concealed? If a Jew became ill and needed medicine, could the local doctor and chemist be trusted? 'How does one call a doctor for someone who does not exist?'[27] What if the refugee died? How was one to dispose of the body? Under these conditions, and with a network of paid informers, and vicious neighbours who derived no material benefit from denunciation, the effort to practise Christian charity – to love one's neighbour, and to be one's brother's keeper – was fraught with danger.

Holocaust survivor Leon Wells recounts the story of two Christian families in Lvov. The beloved youngest son in a family said to his mother:

'Look, our electricity meter is running. Who has lights during the day?' We were in the basement. The mother looked at him and decided the next day that she had to send him away. Eight years old! A kid! ... They sent him 400 kilometres away so he couldn't betray us accidentally.

In the second family:

The son liked to have a drink. So the mother couldn't tell her son that they hid Jews, because if he had a drink he might talk out. And the wife, being mad at him, could tell on him. So they didn't tell the son that the father was hiding Jews. Not because they were afraid, not because of any anti-semitism, but because it was a simply human thing: if he drinks and if he has a problem with the wife. . . .

Once committed to the rescue of Jews, dishonesty went beyond the deception of German officials and extended to one's own family, friends and neighbours. Leon Wells concludes by raising the problem of collective family responsibility:

People don't realize what it meant to hide somebody, to sacrifice. I ask audiences continuously, 'How many of you would have risked your lives to save a stranger? . . . How many would risk your lives for a complete stranger? [and] . . . the life of the whole family.[28]

A morally questionable form of rescue occurred when Christians were prepared to engage in illegality, deception, the falsification of records, but only if this resulted in the conversion of Jewish children to Christianity. One Greek priest in Slovakia:

> Agreed to verify that certain Jewish families had converted to Christianity before 1938 (thus exempting them temporarily from deportation), even if they had not, provided parents were willing to have any children in the family actually baptized into the Greek Orthodox faith.[29]

In effect this amounted to spiritual blackmail. The parents could only secure the false certificates necessary to save their children's lives at the price of conversion to Christianity, and the renunciation of their own faith. Ironically, these Jews could only avoid the racial anti-semitism of the Nazis through this revival of medieval religious anti-semitism. Bodily death could only be averted through spiritual death. In Lawrence Langer's words:

> 'It is a kind of annihilation, a totally paradoxical killing of the self by the self in order to keep the self alive'.[30]

PARADOXES OF RESISTANCE

> I dreamt that I had come
> To dwell in Topsy-Turveydom!
> Where vice is virtue – virtue, vice:
> Where nice is nasty – nasty, nice:
>
> Where right is wrong and wrong is right –
> Where white is black and black is white.[31]
>
> W.S. Gilbert

The paradox of resistance is that normally honest, law-abiding and patriotic citizens had to turn their values inside out. Normal ethical rules could not apply in the abnormal context of Nazism. Lying became a virtue, law-breaking and refusal to obey the authorities became a patriotic duty. This transformation meant that many decent people either condoned, acquiesced in, turned a blind eye to, or actively engaged in deception, theft, robbery, forgery, sabotage, murder and terrorism. Thus we find devout Christians violating the Commandments, and facing the necessity of lying, stealing and committing murder; orthodox rabbis granting permission for abortions in the ghettos, despite Halachic law which forbids the practice; doctors breaking the Hippocratic Oath; civil servants and administrators deliberately losing files useful to the Germans; Post Office workers intercepting, opening and destroying mail containing informers' letters of denunciation to the German authorities; patriotic policemen breaking the law by forging identity papers, and a range of other groups prepared to break their code of professional ethics and confidentiality for humanitarian purposes.

An extreme, and probably unique example of the degree to which ordinary moral considerations had been suspended is given in the memoirs of the French resister and SOE agent, Philippe de Vomecourt:

> After a conversation on a train about British pilots eating carrots to improve their night vision, I discovered from an oculist in Paris that heroin had the opposite effect. I asked London for a supply of heroin. 'What for?' they asked. 'Never mind what it's for', I replied. 'I'll tell you when the operation is successful.'
>
> The kilo of heroin which they sent to me must have taken a lot of argument and persuasion on their part to procure. It was sent by the American diplomatic bag from London and delivered to the Military Attaché of a then neutral embassy.
>
> Now I had to find a way of feeding heroin to the German pilots. Who were the only people in regular contact with the Germans, and able to administer the heroin to them secretly? The whores.
>
> There was a large concentration of German night-fighters around Tours, so I went to the people running the whorehouses there and explained what I wanted to do. They agreed to gather together a number of women who were keen to work for the Resistance.
>
> A few of the Germans who patronised the brothels were already drug addicts. To them, the whores sold the heroin; they promised they would not sell it to any but Germans. Other German pilots, who were often the worse for drink by the time they found themselves in a room with a whore, were tempted to try the heroin – 'just a little sniff to see what happens'. The result, of course, was a temporary feeling of well-being, which encouraged the young men to try a little more, and so they were led into addiction.

When a pilot refused to take the heroin, the women put some of the 'snuff' into cigarettes, and they were 'hooked' in that way.

It was an effective form of Resistance. A substantial number of night-fighters stationed in the Tours area found their vision deteriorating. With each monthly medical examination, they saw less and less.

Unfortunately, the Luftwaffe's doctors became suspicious of the high incidence of deteriorating vision in its pilots, and German security forces eventually found the source of the problem.[32]

Two of these patriotic prostitutes were tracked down and shot.

RESISTANCE IN THE CONCENTRATION CAMPS

There is reason to believe that a person who fully adhered to all the ethical and moral standards of conduct of civilian life on entering the camp in the morning, would be dead by nightfall.[33]

William G. Niederland

In the space of a few weeks ... the deprivations to which they were subjected led them to a condition of pure survival ... in which the room for choices (especially moral choices) was reduced to zero.[34]

Primo Levi

In the exceptional circumstances of the camps, normal codes of morality could not be adhered to in the desperate struggle for survival. It is questionable whether one could or should judge these wartime dilemmas by peacetime standards. The Underground condoned or tolerated acts which would have been ordinarily rejected as too awful even to contemplate. Rudolf Vrba described an incident in Auschwitz when 15 men were marched to Block Eleven, the punishment block. Among the men were some members of the Underground. The resistance movement faced a hard choice about the need to protect the rest of the organization:

The situation became ... grave in the extreme. If these men cracked under torture, it would mean more than their deaths, more than fierce reprisals against the rest of us. It would mean that the underground movement would be liquidated.

The leaders of the underground were fully aware of the danger and took swift evasive action. They smuggled poison into Block Eleven and within a few hours the men . . . were dead. Rather than risk revealing the names of their comrades, they had committed suicide.[35]

In Lawrence Langer's words, the world of the camps 'requires us to suspend our sense of the normal'.[36]

Auschwitz inmate Josef Garliński points out that 'The fight against informers . . . was one of the movement's chief tasks'. The killing of dangerous informers and spies was essential if the resistance movement was to grow; but no-one was sentenced to death without the fullest investigation (under the conditions) of the details of their alleged treachery. There were to be no kangaroo courts, precisely because 'The underground soldiers had the ambition to be better than their oppressors.'[37] However the form of death had to be disguised in order to avoid SS reprisals. In desperation, the underground resorted to what can only be described as a low-level form of bacteriological warfare. One resistance member who worked in the hospital block befriended the chief Gestapo informer, Stefan Olpinski, in order to carry out the death sentence imposed by the underground court, and 'managed to persuade him to accept a sweater containing typhus-infected lice'. Garliński adds that their activity was not confined only to spies:

In the hospital laboratory, Witold Kosztowny bred typhus lice, which were thrown onto the coats of the most hated SS men . . . typhus did get into the SS barracks and caused serious losses there.

He concludes:

The fight against the informers, and the attempts to infect S.S. men with typhus are a graphic illustration of what Auschwitz was like and what methods were used there to win the battle for life and to combat the inhuman lawlessness of the S.S. men. It is impossible for people living in safety today to judge . . . years later, these desperate struggles.

A former Auschwitz prisoner, Adeleide Hautval, expressed this very clearly:

I don't think anybody in the world today has the right to judgement or decision as to what he himself would have done in those completely improbable conditions with which one stood face-to-face in places like Auschwitz.[38]

The problem raised here is partly methodological, but it is also one of sensitivity, and the limits of judgement.

Prisoner doctors became unwilling accomplices in the brutalities of Nazism. The SS and Nazi doctors drew them into a web of complicity with killing; involving healers in the machinery of murder, tainting them by active participation in the selection process of who should live and who should die. They faced the same paradox which confronted leaders of the Jewish Councils in the ghettos – that it was necessary to participate in the selection process of killing some people in order to save others.

Consider the conflict of conscience of Jewish doctors in Holland, who had to sit on Selection Boards in order to decide who was healthy and who was unhealthy: who was fit for deportation, who was not. Doctors could only use delaying tactics to slow down deportations if they agreed to participate in the process and to operate the principle of selection itself. The alternative was to let Nazi doctors do the job, in which case 'every examinee would be given a one-way ticket to Mauthausen'. When Nazi doctors were employed, they passed everyone, including 'acute asthmatics, serious heart cases and the like'.[39] It is important to emphasize the point that at this stage, Dutch Jewish doctors cannot have been aware of the Nazis' ultimate aims of genocide. The doctors attempted to protect the physically weak from the ravages of deportation to the slave labour camp at Mauthausen, with its notorious stone quarry, where only the fittest could survive for any length of time. The situation was reversed in the concentration camps themselves, where prisoner doctors had to separate the fit from the unfit, knowing that the latter were thereby condemned to death.

The agonizing choice that confronted prisoner doctors was how far to co-operate in the selection on the train ramps and in the camps, sifting the healthy and those able to work from the unhealthy:

Thus, prisoner doctors were pressed by their Nazi medical rulers into a moral dilemma which, however resolved, had to result in a sense of guilt: one could save lives only by contributing to Auschwitz selection policies; one could avoid that involvement only by refusing to exercise one's capacity to save lives.[40]

In his memoir, *Medical Block Buchenwald*, Walter Poller describes the terrible dilemma which faced medical personnel with limited power and opportunity. It was impossible to save everyone, and thus it became necessary to choose almost arbitrarily those that they could help.

> As a rule in the great majority of cases they were obliged to watch helplessly as thousands of wretched men grew languid and died or were murdered. They could only intervene in a few exceptional cases, and then only at the risk of their own lives . . . they were confronted with the dreadful decision of choosing from a thousand men one single prisoner whom they could keep alive.
>
> Imagine a doctor who comes to a barracks where there are a hundred people perilously ill with typhus, and yet possesses only enough medicine to win five of these lives from otherwise certain death. He must decide on which five to give the medicine.
>
> The greater his sense of responsibility, the more difficult will he find the task of making his decision. . . . We political prisoners found ourselves in a similar situation.[41]

As well as helping the Resistance to kill informers, prisoner doctors performed abortions (at a time when abortions were more widely regarded as intrinsically wrong) and killed new-born babies because the concentration camp authorities had decreed that new-born babies and their mothers were to die. Women prisoner doctors were forced to behave in a manner totally alien to their nature and to their training as paediatricians. Olga Lengyel gives a harrowing account of the dilemmas that doctors faced:

> As soon as a baby was delivered at the infirmary, mother and child were both sent to the gas chamber. That was the unrelenting decision of our masters. Only when the infant was not likely to survive or when it was stillborn was the mother ever spared. . . . We . . . whose responsibility it was to bring these infants into the world – the world of Birkenau-Auschwitz – felt the burden of this monstrous conclusion which defied all human and moral law. . . . How many sleepless nights we spent turning this tragic dilemma over in our minds. And in the morning the mothers and their babies both went to their deaths.[42]

The doctors devised a plan which would at least save the mothers. All the children would have to pass for stillborn.

Unfortunately, the fate of the baby always had to be the same. . . . we pinched and closed the little tyke's nostrils, and when it opened its mouth to breathe, we gave it a dose of a lethal product.[43]

This was no isolated or exceptional story. Ella Lingens-Reiner, a German doctor who was incarcerated in Auschwitz as a political prisoner, also reluctantly agreed to perform late abortions on Hungarian Jewish women in 1944:

I asked one of my colleagues – a deeply religious Polish woman. . . . how she could bring herself thus to operate on healthy women. She said that those women themselves begged to be relieved of their unborn children, and that the only way to save the mothers from death in the gas chamber was to sacrifice the children. Indeed, this treatment was lenient compared with the earlier procedure, when nearly all pregnant Jewish women were gassed. If one of them happened to give birth in the camp, the child was immediately drowned. . . .
   Yet, it was even more frightful to see nursing mothers kill their three or four-month-old babies, by choking them or giving them twenty sleeping tablets, so as not to be sent to the gas chamber with the child. Many of these women had elder children hidden outside in the care of non-Jews, and wanted to keep alive for their sake.[44]

Sara Nomberg Przytyk, a Polish Jew, also assisted women doctors in Auschwitz after being informed of the secret killing which necessarily surrounded the birth of Jewish children. A Jewish doctor called Mancy told her:

'Our procedure now is to kill the baby after birth in such a way that the mother doesn't know about it.' 'What? You kill it?'
   'It's very simple', Mancy continued. 'We give the baby an injection. After that, the baby dies. The mother is told that the baby was born dead. After dark, the baby is thrown on a pile of corpses, and in that manner, we save the mother. I want so much for the babies to be born dead, but out of spite they are born healthy.[45]

On the first occasion when Sara helped, the Jewish woman doctor:

> told me to bring her a bucket of cold water. . . . Finally, the baby
> was born. Mancy put her hand over his mouth so he could not
> cry, and then she put his head in the bucket of cold water. She
> was drowning him like a blind kitten. I felt faint.[46]

Judith Sternberg Newman was a nurse who had been deported
to Auschwitz. She was unaware of Nazi policy towards Jewish mothers
and their babies. She relates how her happiness at the birth of a
baby boy in her block suddenly turned to a new understanding of
the concentration camp universe:

> Three hours later, I saw a small package wrapped in cheese cloth
> lying on a wooden bench. Suddenly it moved. A Jewish girl em-
> ployed as a clerk came over, carrying a pan of cold water. She
> whispered to me, 'Hush! Quiet! Go away!' But I remained, for I
> could not understand what she had in mind. . . . She took the
> infant and submerged its little body in the cold water. My heart
> beat wildly in agitation. I wanted to shout 'Murderess!' but I
> had to keep quiet and could not tell anyone. The baby swallowed
> and gurgled, its little voice chittering like a small bird, until its
> breath became shorter and shorter. The woman held its head in
> the water. After about eight minutes the breathing stopped. The
> woman. . . . said to me, 'We had to save the mother, otherwise
> she would have gone to the gas chamber.' This girl had learned
> well from the SS and had become a murderess herself.[47]

Adina Blady Szwajger, a Polish-Jewish paediatrician in the Warsaw Children's Hospital relates how in September 1942, the Germans organized mass deportations from the Warsaw ghetto to
Treblinka. Many children were so sick from hunger-related diseases
that the train journey would have been too much for them. So she
practised a form of mercy killing in order that the children should
have a quiet and peaceful death, rather than expose them to the
horrors of the railway journey:

> I . . . got two large containers of morphine . . . I took the mor-
> phine upstairs. Dr Margolis was there and I told her what I wanted
> to do. So we took a spoon and went to the infants' room. And
> just as, during those two years of real work in the hospital, I had

bent down over the little beds, so now I poured this last medicine into those tiny mouths.... downstairs there was screaming because ... the Germans were already there, taking the sick from the wards to the cattle trucks. After that we went in to the older children and told them that this medicine was going to make their pain disappear. They believed us and drank the required amount from the glass.[48]

Abraham Lewin, a teacher in the Warsaw Ghetto, was preoccupied with the fate of his family during the great deportations in the summer of 1942. On 24 August he wrote in his Warsaw Diary:

The matter of my mother is causing me great anguish. What can be done for her? I have given my permission to put her to sleep ... rather than give her over to the executioners. But J [Lewin's brother-in-law], who was a doctor refuses to carry it out. Even the devil could not have conceived of such a situation.[49]

It seems impossible to assimilate the experiences described here to normal moral discourse; and after the concentration camps it has become necessary to rethink our whole understanding of the world. The ghettos and concentration camps were a truly topsy-turvy world, deliberately designed to disorientate and confuse the victim: a world where doctors became killers; where the traditional male chivalry of 'life-boat ethics' in which women and children were rescued first, was turned upside down. Women and children were the first to go into the gas chambers: a world where madness was a sane response, and where 'sanity' was itself a form of madness. In André Malraux's words, 'it was a world in which the impossible was always possible.'[50]

One of the most frightening aspects of Nazi control was the manner in which compassionate people had to adapt rapidly to crude Fascist notions of Social Darwinism: the weak and the helpless were, according to the Nazi biological vision, 'life unworthy of life'; superfluous – 'useless mouths' – and to be sacrificed in order that the strong and healthy might survive. Jewish doctors occasionally had to kill dangerous lunatics whose behaviour threatened to get the whole medical ward 'selected'. As Terence Des Pres points out, the resistance movement in Auschwitz was compelled 'to make its own "selection" in strategic mimicry of the Nazi procedure'. One survivor reflected:

it was the cruellest task that any Underground has ever faced . . . the Nazi system was so thorough that anti-Nazis, too, had to use death as a tool.[51]

Sara Nomberg Przytyk describes a selection process in which a beautiful young woman had been chosen for the gas chamber, and cannot comprehend the injustice of her selection:

> She is really young and pretty. Why did they write her number down? I trembled at that terrible logic, as though there were some justification in killing the sick, the elderly, and the unattractive. I looked at the old faces, the bowed heads, and I felt sorry for them.[52]

Przytyk stops at the point where she finds herself thinking according to the 'terrible logic' of Nazi values.

The ultimate moral degradation can be found in the reflections of prisoner doctors like Olga Lengyel, whose psychological pain and residual guilt at her own corruption by the brutalizing environment of Auschwitz is captured in a haunting passage:

> And so, the Germans succeeded in making murderers of even us. . . . The only meagre consolation is that by these murders we saved the mothers. Without our intervention they would have endured worse sufferings, for they would have been thrown into the crematory ovens while still alive.
>
> Yet I try in vain to make my conscience acquit me. I still see the infants issuing from their mothers. I can feel their warm little bodies as I held them. I marvel to what depths these Germans made us descend![53]

I have let these eye-witnesses and participants speak for themselves, and at length, because no short summary can adequately convey the nature of their experiences. Indeed, conventional language and vocabulary seems grotesquely inadequate as a means of conveying the impossible decisions that these women faced. Concepts of human dignity and ethical choice, based upon traditional moral theories, seem incapable of conveying what was at stake. It would be impertinent to attempt to pass moral 'judgement' upon those caught up in these situations where language and the boundaries of moral choice have been strained beyond their recognizable limits.

'CHOICELESS CHOICES'

Lawrence Langer has described the crisis into which the Nazis had plunged these victims as a 'choiceless choice'.[54] Langer is the pioneer moral cartographer in this dark continent, pushing back the boundaries of moral theory in order to explore the black hole in the moral universe which has appeared in the centre of Europe. Traditional moral language is based upon categories of good and evil, right and wrong, blame, guilt and responsibility: a vocabulary of purpose. 'The moral systems that we are familiar with are built on the premise of individual choice and responsibility for the consequences of choice'.[55] It can encompass choices between a greater and a lesser evil. But the notions of choice, control and responsibility crumble before the realities faced by concentration camp victims. It is easy when discussing resistance to romanticize the subject, and to adopt a 'grammar of heroism'; 'language has no difficulty celebrating humanitarian impulses'.[56] Yet many of the alternatives facing resisters elude our traditional moral conventions and categories, based upon normal behaviour in ordinary circumstances. With the erosion of moral certainty and the disintegration of our traditional moral universe, we are left groping for an adequate vocabulary to describe and account for the universe of the concentration camps. It seems impossible to assimilate the experiences described above to normal moral discourse; neither deontological theories nor utilitarian or consequentialist theories of ethics seem capable of explaining or providing a resolution of the dilemmas involved. After the concentration camps, it has become necessary to rethink our whole understanding of the world. In the search for a suitable language, we may have to revise our grammar or invent a new lexicon in order to describe the indescribable choices discussed in this chapter.

There are other examples of 'choiceless choices' – individual dilemmas in wartime Europe which were so exceptional that no general moral lessons could be drawn from them, and where traditional moral rules offered no guidance. Take the case of a group of 90 men, women and children hiding from the German authorities in a cave in the mountains of Yugoslavia. A German security patrol approached within ten yards of the cave without spotting its entrance. At that moment, a new-born baby began to cry, and although the mother tried to calm the child, it continued to cry out. The people were afraid that they would be discovered, and someone whispered that the baby should be killed because it was putting everyone at risk. The mother held out the infant, but nobody had the willpower to carry out the act, and so the mother strangled her own child.[57]

There was also the agonizing dilemma of a pious orthodox Jew who was offered a bargain with the devil by a camp guard at Auschwitz. He could ransom his own son from certain death, but only at the expense of condemning someone else. Unable to decide what to do, this simple, righteous man consulted a rabbi in order to ascertain whether Jewish (halacha) law could give him guidance. The rabbi was unable to find a precedent, and could neither rule for nor against such a course of action. Although sorely tempted, the father concluded that while the 'natural' thing to do was to save one's own child's life, the rabbi's hesitation indicated that the Torah would not allow such a decision, and so the son perished.[58]

Sometimes personal survival could only be secured by placing others at risk. Wherever deportation quotas had to be filled, one could only save oneself at another's expense. In her diary, the young Dutch Jew Etty Hillesum wrote: 'Everyone who seeks to save himself must surely realise that if he does not go another must take his place.'[59] An identical dilemma weighed on the conscience of Yitzak Zuckerman in the Warsaw Ghetto: 'Each of us bears his guilt and knows exactly that he remains alive instead of someone else.'[60] Thus collective responsibility, and shouldering the burden of a common fate, acted as a restraint upon the human impulse to escape, robbing this form of resistance of any grandeur and heroism it might otherwise have had.

A thirty-year old Jewish woman from Krakow who was imprisoned in Auschwitz related how four German soldiers came to her house soon after the beginning of the occupation. One of the soldiers put his gun in her hand and ordered her to shoot her entire family – her baby, husband, father and mother. Horrified, Felicia shrieked and gave the gun back to the soldier.

> The soldier repeated his order, this time adding his condition: 'If you don't do it, I will kill them. But not so simply. They will die in slow agony . . . .
>
>   I shrieked like a madwoman, 'No, I will never do that!' The soldier . . . stepped over to the highchair, where the baby sat. 'Is that your baby?' he asked. 'If you don't do as I say, I will kill your baby.' One of the soldiers then gave me a gun. 'Shoot' said

the first soldier. As I stood transfixed, immobile, he swung the little boy upside down and called to one of his men to hold on to the baby's feet. And then, each holding a foot, they tore my child in two . . . my child, my own little baby boy . . . right before my eyes. The Germans threatened, 'this is what we will do to your family if you don't shoot them. Tear them to pieces. Bit by bit. Do you hear? Now, shoot!' I screamed and screamed and began to shoot. I shot everyone, everyone.[61]

THE CASE OF OSWALD RUFEISEN

One of the strangest stories of the Second World War concerns the remarkable life of a young Polish Jew called Oswald Rufeisen. Although Jewish, he managed to pass himself off as a half-German, half-Polish gentile. Because he could speak German fluently he came to serve as a translator and personal secretary to a regional German police officer. By performing duties which included reading out death sentences in Polish to prisoners, he earned the trust of the German commander. He used his privileged position to pass important secrets to Jews, and to Polish resistance groups about forthcoming raids. Nevertheless, in his capacity as translator, Rufeisen had to participate in *Aktionen* – raids which would result in reprisals against villages suspected of harbouring partisans.

In the summer of 1942 a German soldier was shot and killed by resisters in the village of Simakowo. The Wehrmacht demanded punishment, and the village was surrounded. More than two hundred men were rounded-up and taken to a field outside the village. As translator, Rufeisen had to tell the head of the village that unless those who helped the partisans were identified, every tenth man would be shot. This would result in the death of 25 men. In addition, the village would be burned to the ground. The village chief denied that anyone was a witness or accomplice to the crime. Rufeisen wanted to avert a mass execution, but time was running short. He exploited the humane feelings of the German in charge of the expedition by arguing that it would be wrong to kill 25 innocent people for the death of one soldier; instead the guilty party should be found. He had to do something quickly. He stressed the consequences of doing nothing to the head of the village, and asked him to select two people of whom the village would want to be rid. One was a mentally retarded young man who didn't understand what was happening. The other was a forester who had previously acted as an informer for the Germans. He had denounced a boy who had illegally possessed a gun. The boy was executed by the Germans. The forester pleaded with Rufeisen to tell the Germans that he was innocent of the crime, and that he would reveal the partisans' hide-out in the forest. By saying this in front of the entire village he had condemned himself to death at the hands of the partisans in any case:

> by following the wishes of the head of the village I would be saving not only many of the local men, but also partisans in the forest. It was a tragic game.... Here I was not yet twenty and I had to decide in a split of a second a matter of such magnitude.[62]

Rufeisen deliberately mistranslated the information, and the retarded youth and the forester were shot. Looking back, Rufeisen questions whether he had the right to decide who should be sacrificed. Nevertheless, he had acted:

> simply out of a desire to save human lives.... I could have said that these people should not concern me and just translate as I was supposed to do. But mine was a struggle to save people.... The risk was that among the German soldiers who were there some might have been from Silesia. Some of them might have known the Polish language.... This was a terrible risk.... Maybe at the time this was the only way out? But now I ask myself if I had the right to designate as guilty and sacrifice for the others even the retarded youth. Still, under the circumstances, I had to decide right away. I could not have hesitated.
> Today my conscience is not clean. The truth is that the forester did not deserve mercy. He was a collaborator.... But even this does not give me the right to decide about his death. Particularly since I knew he had eleven children.... As you know his house was burned....
> No one can enter into the situation as it was then at the time.[63]

CONCLUSION

Surely there has never been a generation in the course of human history with so little ground under its feet as our own. Every conceivable alternative seems equally intolerable. . . .

The great masquerade of evil has wrought havoc with all our ethical preconceptions.[64]

Dietrich Bonhoeffer

The German occupation inflicted unforeseen circumstances and unfamiliar moral choices upon Europe's population. It presented a challenge to all normal thinking and demanded a recasting of thought. No-one was prepared for the moral inferno into which all values were hurled. It ravaged inherited norms and moral assumptions, and turned acquired standards and preconceptions upside down. Right and wrong, permitted and forbidden, guilt and innocence, truth and lies: the accumulated set of values that western civilization had created and nurtured were placed in turmoil. Des Pres talks of 'the visible wreckage of moral and physical being'.[65] The Nazi occupation generated a historical and above all a moral crisis without parallel, in which all acknowledged ethical guidelines were thrown into upheaval. Religious and humanist beliefs were shaken to the foundations.

Ordinary people faced extraordinary choices and awesome dilemmas, without any guidance from the Bible, or from the storehouse of wisdom contained in the history of western thought. Traditional theories of ethics had not had to address the kinds of questions posed by the radical evil of Nazism. Conventional thinking, all textbook ethics seemed grotesquely inadequate, if not irrelevant, to people abandoned by man and God. People were severed from their moral moorings and cast existentially adrift. Because there was no analogue in human experience, each choice had to be improvised, each decision had to be fashioned anew amid the rubble of the entire set of values by which mankind had lived. Buchenwald survivor Eugen Kogon wrote of the 'smashing of the old familiar world with its values' and how 'utter failure met any attempt to apply once valid social standards to a concentration camp environment'. In order to survive the mind had a develop a 'protective crust'. 'Not only the hands, the soul had to grow calluses'.[66] Resistance to Nazism entailed more than human sacrifice and the loss of one's life. Resistance required the erosion of ethical inhibitions and the blunting of moral sensibilities. Resistance entailed a loss of innocence and spelt the death of idealism.

5 German Security Policy and the Moral Dilemmas of Resistance

GERMAN SECURITY POLICY

> The practice of executing scores of innocent hostages in reprisal for isolated attacks on Germany in countries temporarily under the Nazi heel revolts a world already inured to suffering and brutality. Civilized peoples long ago adopted the basic principle that no man should be punished for the deed of another. Unable to apprehend the persons involved in these attacks the Nazis characteristically slaughter fifty or a hundred innocent persons.[1]
>
> Franklin D. Roosevelt

> The leading principle in all actions.... is the unconditional security of the German soldier. The necessary rapid pacification of the country can be attained only if every threat on the part of the hostile civil population is ruthlessly taken care of. All pity and softness are evidence of weakness and constitute a danger.[2]
>
> High Command of the Wehrmacht, Order 16 July 1941

> It is better to be feared than loved.[3]
>
> Machiavelli

The aim of German security policy was to create a sense of insecurity among the local population through the ruthless application of the classic terrorist precept, 'Kill one, frighten ten thousand.' Throughout occupied Europe opposition was to be crushed unmercifully by a policy of *Schrecklicheit*: calculated terror and political intimidation, aimed at depriving the civilian population of the will to resist, and reducing it to a state of quiescence. With his usual clarity Hitler formulated the Third Reich's answer to the problem of resistance:

> We must be ruthless....
>   terror is the most effective political instrument.[4]

Force ... is not enough to ensure total domination; admittedly it is still the decisive factor but no less important a factor is that intangible psychological faculty which a lion tamer must have if he is to dominate his animals.[5]

Hostage taking and reprisal killings were the normal and well-publicized official response to acts of resistance, and a primary means of subduing the civilian population – pacification through indiscriminate, random terror. No one was targeted in particular, and therefore no one was safe – potentially anyone and everyone was threatened; after an act of resistance any foreign national was deemed to be a legitimate target. As M.R.D. Foot observed, 'They were not particular whom they shot, so long as they shot somebody.'[6] In effect, the Germans treated the entire population of an occupied country as hostages.

Hostage Taking

The taking of hostages plainly falls under the rubric of terrorism.[7]
Noam Chomsky

Hostage-taking has a long history in the annals of human warfare, extending back to ancient times. In previous centuries of conflict between aristocratic armies or rival royal dynasties, only 'important' persons were deemed worthy of hostage status: only their lives had sufficient value to count as a likely restraint upon enemy misconduct. Countries or tribes which had signed a peace treaty frequently exchanged important hostages as a form of mutual security for compliance. This acted as a safeguard against ill-treatment. Their lives were offered as a pledge of good faith in order to guarantee the observance of treaties. The practice became obsolete in the eighteenth century.

With the democratization of society from the French Revolution onwards came the transformation in status of ordinary people: the leap from kings' servants to democratic citizens. This in turn heralded the modern age, with the democratization of warfare in the form of mass conscription. If, however, everybody was now important, this brought with it the threat that anybody was a potential hostage. This became increasingly evident in the 19th and 20th centuries with the more widespread resort to hostage-taking during the American Civil War, the Franco-Prussian War, the Russian Civil War (1918–21) and the Spanish Civil War.

It is important to mention this long historical tradition of hostage-taking, for the Nazi regime did not invent the practice, although it did add further refinements to an age-old institution. What the Third Reich did was to extend the practice drastically, and to apply the logic of hostage-taking in a far more coherent and systematic manner than had previously been employed. It is also worth pointing out that there was nothing specifically or distinctively 'Nazi' about the practice. During the Second World War, hostage-taking was not initiated by the leadership of the Nazi Party or regime, nor was its implementation prompted by the Gestapo, the SS or the SD, but rather by the German Army, which reverted to the custom and practice of the Prussian Army from the time of the Franco-Prussian War, of taking civilian hostages to guarantee the safety of its troops, supplies and military equipment from guerrilla attacks. This was consolidated during the German occupation of Belgium in the First World War.

Hostage-taking was the centrepiece of German anti-resistance measures during the Second World War. Whereas in previous conflicts hostage-taking played only a minor role, under the Nazi occupation it was elevated into a major weapon of warfare. In World War II the practice became more widespread than at any other time in history, and the killing of hostages occurred on an unprecedented scale. It amounted to a reign of terror. Moreover, hostage and reprisal killings were usually taken as a first, not a last, resort, and were regarded as the normal method of combating disobedience. The German Army, with the approval of the Nazi regime, made extensive use of the policy of killing innocent members of the civilian population as a deterrent against sabotage and assassination. The essence of the hostage system lay in the fact that people were detained and executed without trial for offences which had been committed by other people: their fellow countrymen. The principle of collective responsibility lay at the heart of the institution.

Excesses occur in all wars, but the practice of taking and killing hostages throughout Europe was planned, organized and instituted by the German Army and authorized by the German government from the outset of the war. Hostage killing was not some sporadic, improvised initiative taken by hard-pressed local officers in 'the heat of battle', but rather an officially sanctioned policy of state terrorism emanating from the High Command of the armed forces, and approved and ratified by Hitler. German Army service regulations stipulated that only a high-ranking officer – a divisional commander or above – could order the taking and shooting of hostages. This was confirmed at the Nuremberg Trials, where evidence was produced from Army Regulations, Section 9: the Hostage Law of the German Wehrmacht.

> Hostages may be taken only by order of a regimental commander, an independent battalion commander or a commander of equal rank.... Furthermore, only senior officers holding at least the position of a division commander can decide on the fate of the hostages.[8]

Broad policy directives came from the nerve centre of the German army in Berlin, and allowing for the differences of conditions between western and eastern Europe, there existed a basic uniformity of policy: an agreed framework of methods for dealing with resistance.

Hostage-taking was a precautionary measure. The German fear of subversion and underground warfare was such that a *Hostage Code* was introduced, which set out fixed penalties for different types of resistance activity. Hostages were to answer with their lives for the security of the occupying forces. The authorities devised a sliding scale, or hostage tally, for every German soldier killed or wounded. During the Polish Campaign in the autumn of 1939, the German Army operated according to an official quota: for every German soldier killed by Polish resisters, 10 Poles would be executed. As the war intensified in ferocity the quotas increased in severity. The precise implementation of the hostage policy reflected Nazi racial classification. In calculating reprisal punishments, the Nazis applied a racialist scale of values. According to their human equation, a German life was worth five Danish lives, ten French lives and a hundred Polish lives. Walter Kuntze, the acting Commander-in-Chief of the 12th Army in Serbia, articulated a widespread sentiment in the German Army in an order dated 19 March 1942:

> It is better to liquidate 50 suspects than lose one German soldier.[9]

He implemented this doctrine by ordering that in areas which had been mined by partisans Serb hostages in the immediate vicinity should be used to clear the minefields. Similarly, in the occupied areas of the Soviet Union, the infamous SS Dirlewanger regiment, composed of some of the worst criminals from German jails, employed the technique of forcing women and children to march across minefields which protected partisan hideouts. In 1942, during 'Operation Cottbus', over 4000 people died 'spotting' mines.

The disproportionate and inhumane nature of German reprisals was rooted in racialist assumptions concerning the human worth of different subject peoples. The Nordic and Aryan peoples of northern and western Europe were inherently superior to the racially inferior Slavs and Jews of eastern Europe. Thus, whereas a Serb or a Pole caught engaging in non-violent resistance such as hiding Jews, or producing an underground newspaper, was likely to be shot on the spot alongside his family, a Norwegian or Dutchman would normally be sent to a labour camp for the same offence. A Frenchman or a Dane might be punished for what he did. A Pole or a Jew was additionally punished for what he was.

As a rule, life became cheaper the further east one went. Thus, depending upon the Nazis' general political and racial objectives, their hostage policy was governed by 'pre-determined quotas'[10] which varied from country to country, but which increased in severity wherever organized resistance grew. In each country there existed an arithmetic table to be learned by rote by divisional commanders. For every German soldier killed or wounded, Nazi mathematics dictated a simple equation, as follows:

	Killed	Wounded
Denmark	5:1	2:1
Holland and France	10:1	5:1
Poland: 1939	10:1	5:1
1940	50:1	25:1
1941	100:1	50:1

In the USSR, Yugoslavia and Greece the 'going-rate' settled at 100:1, although 300:1 was not infrequent, and the campaigns against partisans in the Balkans and on the eastern front degenerated into a generalized terror in which the grim calculus of accurate bookkeeping was lost. A sliding scale was also applied in the event of resistance assassinations of German collaborators in occupied countries. Nazi mathematics calculated that for the less serious death of a pro-German Pole or Greek, a ratio of 10:1 would suffice.

In September 1941 General Keitel, Chief of the High Command of the Armed Forces, issued instructions for handling unrest in the

Occupied Territories. Although originally designed for the Eastern Campaign, the Hostage Decree came into general use wherever violent resistance occurred throughout Europe.

> It must be kept in mind that a human life is often considered to be of no value in the countries concerned, and a deterrent effect can only be obtained through unusual severity. In these cases . . . the death penalty for 50 to 100 Communists must be considered an appropriate atonement for the life of a German soldier. The manner of the execution must intensify the deterrent effect.[11]

When high-ranking Germans were killed as opposed to ordinary conscript soldiers, the ratio increased further. In retaliation for the death of General Krech in Athens, 300 Greeks were executed on 15 August 1944. They were officially classified as 200 Greek citizens and 100 Communists. The German authorities usually attributed resistance activity to 'Communists', irrespective of who was actually responsible. In order to comply with the spirit of Keitel's directive, it was not sufficient that hostage and reprisal killings were publicized. Frequently they took place in public before an assembled population for demonstrative effect. Public executions were clearly a more dramatic and effective method of instilling fear and terror than merely reading an official notice after the event.

In eastern Europe and in the Balkans, the public hanging of influential personalities replaced shooting, in order to achieve the desired deterrent effect. The victims would be left hanging in a prominent place – in the town or village square – for three to seven days. In the USSR, firing squads were ordered to aim at, or below, the waist, the result of which was that many victims were buried alive, dying in agony from stomach wounds and suffocation. In addition to 'increasing the deterrent effect' there were also practical reasons for this grim practice, as an Army Order spelled out:

> In cases where children are included among the hostages [aiming at normal height] such persons may escape execution altogether . . . and would have to be despatched by hand of officer in charge of the burial party.[12]

As a supplement to the Hostage Code, Hitler initiated the Night and Fog (Nacht und Nabel) decree in December 1941. The execution of innocent prisoners was not sufficient, and a greater deterrent was required. Resistance suspects, or sometimes members of their family, mysteriously vanished without trace, spirited away into the night and fog, only to find themselves in a concentration camp at dawn. Most NN prisoners were taken to Natzweiler, Ravensbrück or Mauthausen. One survivor wrote: 'They could have shot us all in a day and be done with it' but German security forces 'wanted . . . a sort of revenge drama, almost a cat-and-mouse torment instead of instant death . . . Resistance, you see, was our sin. . . . Natzweiler was geared not so much to kill us, but to destroy our ability or desire to resist. It was an ongoing antiresistance laboratory.'[13] The Night and Fog order produced acute insecurity in the relatives of those who simply disappeared without warning to some unknown destination. The next of kin would never know their whereabouts or fate. The ingenuity of German security turned state terrorism into an art form. It was a powerful psychological restraint to discourage patriotic activity.

HOSTAGE SELECTION

> To me, terrorism assumed its most distressing form in the taking of hostages. . . . The plight of families from which members had been taken as hostages never failed to move me.
>
> Bill Jordan, SOE Agent[14]

No single, definitive rule governed the choice of hostages throughout occupied Europe. The selection method and treatment of hostages varied from place to place, and depended upon the initiative and discretion of local army commanders, and the general policy of the German High Command towards the particular country under occupation. The victims came from all walks of life. In many districts 'hostage pools' were established in existing prisons, containing about 150 prominent members of the local population – where mayors, doctors, priests, teachers, lawyers – would be detained as a deterrent against subversive activity. In larger cities, between 400–500 people would be held in hostage depots, like Romainville Fort in the suburbs of Paris.

Soon after the invasion of Poland, hostages in some areas had the responsibility of preventing acts of sabotage in their communities and of apprehending anyone guilty of subversive activity. Lists of guard hostages were published under a German decree of February 1940:

In the event of subversive action, if the culprit is not found those persons whose names are posted on this list must answer before the law. The penalty for an act of sabotage is imprisonment or death.

It is in the interest of the population, and especially the interest of the 'hostages', to keep watch over the public security and to prevent any subversive activity.[15]

In some areas, ex-servicemen or released prisoners of war were re-imprisoned and/or threatened with deportation to Germany. In France, the Supreme Commander specified that all persons already in prison would automatically be regarded as hostages, and that university students should be added to the list.

Keitel issued an additional High Command Order on 28 September 1941 which instructed military commanders to have a pool of hostages available at all times in order that they might be executed if and when German troops were attacked. Prisoners were known by the sinister or macabre title of 'todes kandidaten' – candidates for death. The Order stipulated the following provision:

It is opportune for the military commanders to have always at their disposal a number of hostages of different political persuasions, ie:

1. Nationalists
2. Democratic middle class
3. Communists

It is important that among these are leading personalities or members of their families. Their names are to be published. In case of attack, hostages of the group corresponding to that to which the culprit belongs are to be shot.[16]

Men could not be certain when they left home in the morning that they would return at night. In some places, people were chosen at random: an area of a town or village would be sealed off, and every man unfortunate enough to be in the vicinity would be rounded up from the streets or their homes, and taken into custody to fill the hostage pool. In other places hostages were not detained, but had to report to the authorities at specified times, but were otherwise 'at liberty', and were only detained prior to the arrival of a prominent German official, as a security for the good behaviour of the town.

The hostages' lives were the Germans' security. Therefore the actual killing of hostages was the clearest sign of the breakdown of German security measures. The deterrent had failed to deter. Subsequent German policy was to increase the deterrent by threatening to kill a higher number of hostages, in order to ensure future compliance. There was some initial confusion within the German Army over the question of whether the hostage order applied to and included women, but this issue was clarified by an official pronouncement in Yugoslavia:

> It was contrary to the viewpoint of the German soldier and civil servant to take women as hostages.[17]

Officially only men were to be treated as hostages, although wives and female relatives of partisans were subject to reprisal punishment under the principle of collective family responsibility. Occasionally, however, women were taken hostage. In areas of eastern Europe where large sections of the male population had been either deported to work in Germany as slave labour, or had fled to join the partisans, the Germans felt they had little option but to use women as hostages. Also, in areas under SS and not German Army control, there was less concern for traditionalist Wehrmacht chivalry and scruples over holding women as hostages. In short, whereas hostages were usually chosen from the male population, German reprisals frequently degenerated into wholesale slaughter, and included women, children and babies.

Field-Marshal Kesselring, Supreme German Commander in Italy, issued a typical warning to the Italian people against supporting the resistance movement:

> Every village where it is proved there are partisans or in which assaults against German or Italian soldiers have been committed or where attempts to sabotage warlike stores have occurred WILL BE BURNED TO THE GROUND. In addition all male inhabitants of such a village over eighteen years of age WILL BE SHOT. The women and children will be interned in labour camps.[18]

Public warnings were issued throughout Europe. A proclamation in the small town of Covolo in Italy typifies German Security policy:

> For every member of the German Armed Forces, whether military or civilian who becomes injured FIFTY men, taken from the

place where the act was committed, will be shot.

For every soldier or civilian killed, ONE HUNDRED MEN also taken from the place where the incident occurred will be shot.

Should several soldiers or civilians be killed or wounded ALL THE MEN OF THE PLACE WILL BE SHOT, THE PLACE SET ON FIRE, THE WOMEN INTERNED, AND CATTLE CONFISCATED FORTHWITH.[19]

It is beyond the scope of this book to chronicle a detailed history of German hostage and reprisals' policy, but some notorious incidents may be taken as representative of what happened in every country under military occupation. They illustrate the extensive, systematic and meticulous nature of German security measures.

(1) *France*: The shell-like remains of the village of Oradour-sur-Glane near Limoges, in Central France, have been left as a shrine: a permanent war memorial for all the towns and villages which fell under the shadow of the Swastika. In one of the most infamous and well-publicized massacres of the Second World War, 642 villagers out of a population of 652 people were murdered – allegedly as a reprisal for resistance activity in the area. On 10 June 1944, four days after the Normandy landings, 445 women and children were locked in the church, which was then set on fire; the men were shot.

Alongside the village of Lidice, Oradour has become a symbol of German atrocities. The revelation of the incident caused international outrage. British wartime secret agent E.H. Cookridge has written that:

> The massacre of Oradour will forever remain the most horrible and shameful page of the history of German war crimes.[20]

Appalling though the events at Lidice and Oradour were, to see them as the worst war crimes committed by the German forces is the result of a limited imagination and perspective, and a failure to comprehend the nature of the war on the eastern front. Without wanting to enter into some macabre calculation of relative suffering, I would endorse the view of Max Hastings:

> It is important to remember that if Oradour was an exceptionally dreadful occurrence during the war in the West, it was a trifling example of what the German Army had been doing on a national scale during the war in the East, since 1941.[21]

Hastings quotes an SS veteran of the Russian campaign, who had taken part in the destruction of Oradour, and who was astonished at the international publicity that Oradour had received: 'in our circumstances . . . it was nothing'.[22]

The official German record of hostages executed in France was 29 660.

(2) *Holland*: In reprisal for an attack upon an army vehicle near the village of Putten in 1944, in which one German soldier was killed and another wounded, 150 houses were burned down, and all 622 male inhabitants were deported to Germany. 590 died in labour camps.

After the attempted assassination of Hans Rauter, the Chief of Police and the SS in Holland, 263 Dutch civilian hostages were executed.

Over 2000 Dutch hostages were killed during the occupation.

(3) *Greece*: It was estimated at the Nuremberg Trials that of a total of 6500 Greek villages, approximately 1600 villages with a population between 500–1000 people were burned and destroyed in areas of partisan activity. On 5 October 1943, as a punishment for the death of a regimental commander, and for an act of telephone sabotage, the village of Akmotopos was destroyed, and its entire population executed. During a Wehrmacht raid in August 1943, 317 villagers from Komeno were massacred, including 74 children under the age of ten, and twenty entire families.[23]

At Nuremberg, prosecuting lawyers summed up German atrocities in Greece by stating:

> In Greece there are a thousand Lidices – their names unknown and their inhabitants forgotten by a world too busy and too cynical to remember.[24]

A total of 91 000 Greeks died as hostage or reprisal victims during the German terror campaign, and an additional 68 000 Greeks were executed for resistance-related activity.

(4) *USSR*: It is difficult for a normal imagination to comprehend the sheer scale and savagery of German atrocities in occupied Russia. One writer has summed up the overall result by observing:

> There was one Oradour in France, and one Lidice in Czechoslovakia, there were hundreds in the Soviet Union.[25]

More than 1700 towns, 70 000 villages, and 100 000 farms were destroyed during the German occupation, leaving 25 million Russians homeless. By any standards this was an occupation of unprecedented brutality. We do not have accurate figures for the total number of hostage and reprisal killings in the USSR, but some notorious incidents stand out. In Kiev after a bomb had exploded in German Headquarters in 1942, 1256 people, including children, and women with babies, were executed in reprisal. Earlier in Kiev, in October 1941, retreating Soviet partisans had planted delayed-action mines in the centre of the city, causing a great loss of life in buildings occupied by German military personnel. As a fitting retribution for the destruction of a hotel lodging German troops, the entire Jewish population of the city – 33 780 people – were executed at the ravine known as Babi Yar outside the city.

Probably the greatest single massacre happened after the Germans captured the Ukrainian industrial city of Kharkov in the autumn of 1941. The army declared that it was only able to feed 150 000 of the remaining quarter of a million inhabitants. The remaining 100 000 had to dig a huge grave, where they were machine-gunned, and their bodies bulldozed into the pit.

(5) *Poland*: A similar story could be told about Poland: over 300 villages were destroyed. In the district of Lublin, the entire population of the village of Jozefow was wiped out in retaliation for the death of a German family. As one Polish emissary observed:

We have thousands of Lidices in Poland.[26]

The Governor-General, Hans Frank, boasted in February 1940, after only five months of occupation:

In Prague ... large red posters were put up announcing that seven Czechs had been shot that day ... if I wanted to have a poster put up for every seven Poles who were shot, the forests of Poland would not suffice for producing paper for such posters.[27]

(6) *Yugoslavia*: After the ambush of a German police car in the village of Skela, 50 Communists were hanged in Belgrade. As a punishment for failing to report the presence of the guerrillas,

15 villagers were shot and all 350 houses in the village were burned to the ground.[28] Throughout Serbia placards were posted in villages, notifying the population of the serious consequences of resistance activity. These placards epitomized the methods of German state terrorism:

> By a mean and malicious surprise attack, German soldiers have lost their lives. German patience is at an end. As atonement, 100 Serbs of all classes of the population have been shot to death. In the future, 100 Serbs are to be shot, without consideration, for every German soldier who comes to harm as a result of a surprise attack by Serbs.[29]

In keeping with this policy, 2100 hostages (mainly Jews and Communists) were executed in reprisal for an ambush in October 1941, which resulted in the loss of 21 German soldiers.[30] In Valjevo, 10 German soldiers were killed and 24 wounded. The commander of the hostage pool wrote to a friend:

> in the last eight days I had 2000 Jews and 200 gypsies shot in accordance with the ratio of 100:1 for bestially murdered German soldiers, and a further 2200, likewise almost all Jews, will be shot in the next eight days. This is not a pretty business. At any rate, it has to be, if only to make clear what it means even to attack a German soldier....[31]

The infamous massacres at Kraljevo and Kragujevac will be discussed in the next chapter.

COLLECTIVE RESPONSIBILITY AND THE MORAL DILEMMAS OF RESISTANCE

> Hostages are inhabitants of a country who guarantee with their lives the impeccable attitude of the population. The responsibility for their fate is thus placed in the hands of their compatriots. Therefore, the population must be publicly threatened that the hostages will he held responsible for hostile acts of individuals.[32]
>
> Commander-in-Chief of the Army in France,
> September 12, 1940

Reprisals followed resistance as night follows day. In the light of German security policy, and especially given the disproportionate scale of German reprisal measures, serious questions need to be addressed concerning the appropriateness and legitimacy of certain types of resistance. Despite the enormous personal courage and self-sacrifice of most resisters, was it right for them to engage in acts of resistance which would in effect be passing a death sentence upon many innocent hostages? Given the German practice of publishing lists of the names of detained hostages, was it right to persist in resistance activities when it was certain that the scale of punishments would be increased? Lawrence Langer relates the story of Joseph K, who:

> recalls placards posted in his town listing the names of ten residents who would be summarily executed if there was an attack on a German. Heroic endeavour, whether as resistance or sabotage, thus could become not only potential suicide, but as Joseph K insists, a version of murder.[33]

Resistance attacks were also liable to end in punitive action against Jews, who were frequently selected in disproportionate numbers as hostages, or in other reprisal punishments. The assassination of two Germans in Paris on 13 February 1943 resulted in the deportation of 2000 additional Jews to the death camps.

Under the circumstances, were assassinations or repeated minor sabotage absolutely necessary and unavoidable, or even merely useful? In the case of Soviet and Yugoslav partisans, was it justifiable knowingly to commit acts of resistance which were deliberately intended to goad the Germans into stunning reprisals? Yet set against these questions, we need also to acknowledge the alternative dilemma: not to engage in resistance because of the human cost of these security measures was in effect to abandon the struggle, to submit to German terrorism. The failure to resist could have been construed as acquiescence in national degradation and the continued occupation of one's country. Did reflection on the morality of struggle weaken the ability and resolve to resist?

The whole rationale underlying the seizure of hostages and reprisal killings was to place the burden of moral responsibility upon the potential resister. Everyone was held to be jointly responsible for the actions of resisters: the many would suffer the consequences of the defiance of the few. Collective responsibility was specifically

designed to make the innocent pay for the guilty, and for the resister to think long and hard before embarking upon a course of
action which would have such calamitous consequences for his fellow
countrymen. Not only did the punishment not fit the crime, but
there was no connection between the offence and those punished.
Hostages themselves could exert no direct control over the behaviour
of resisters, and were not personally responsible for resistance actions, even though they carried the collective responsibility of the
community. It is a fundamental rule of justice that a person's life
may not be arbitrarily taken. Hostage killing was a vicarious punishment of the innocent as a deterrent against further resistance.
The idea that an innocent person may be killed for the crimes of
another went against every principle of natural law and elementary justice. Hostages were killed without any semblance of a judicial hearing. Without question the doctrine of collective responsibility
was illegal, inhumane and arbitrary. Nevertheless, should resisters
have modified their behaviour in response to collective punishment?

Before joining the Resistance, individuals had first of all to resolve in their own minds the private dilemma of conscience: to
fight or not to fight, to kill or not to kill. But in addition, resisters
had to contend with the certain death of large numbers of innocent people shot as hostages or in reprisal killings, whose deaths
were a direct result of their acts of overt resistance. This placed an
enormous moral burden upon resisters when deciding upon the
importance of a given act of resistance. Doubt-ridden resisters had
to do some hard moral thinking before they embarked upon a precarious venture with often incalculable consequences.

There is a vital moral difference between:

(a) risking one's own life and coming to terms with the probability
of torture and a violent death;
(b) placing at risk the lives of 10, 50, 100 or more of one's fellow
citizens who have not been consulted on the subject.

Everyone has the right to sacrifice himself. Does he have the right
to sacrifice others? Thus, resisters who had to face the question of
whether it is right to take up arms against tyranny and whose moral
scruples sanctioned the taking of life, which they accepted as their
personal responsibility, were saddled with the consequences of the
doctrine of *collective responsibility*. Even if it was legitimate in itself
to resist Nazism, could it be justified in the light of German reprisals?

'SIPPENHAFT': COLLECTIVE FAMILY RESPONSIBILITY

> Can you imagine anything more dreadful than taking severe
> measures against the mother of a young man who has helped
> him to go and fight with the allies of his country? Can you imagine
> anything more despicable? losing sons in a war is a terrible trag-
> edy. Taking severe measures against the mother of a boy who
> wants to fight for his country's allies, I am suggesting to you, is
> despicable. The one is a tragedy; the other is the height of bru-
> tality. Do you not agree?
>
> Sir David Maxwell-Fyfe[34]

Maxwell-Fyfe's question to Field Marshal Keitel at Nuremberg
exposed the practice of collective family responsibility. Some Free
French resisters had been captured on the eastern front. Keitel
issued an order: 'detailed investigations are to be made ... with
regard to relatives of Frenchmen fighting for the Russians. If the
investigation reveals that relatives have given assistance to facilitate escape from France, then severe measures are to be taken'.[35]
Further evidence was revealed in a report by Reichcommissioner
Terboven in Norway:

> I have just received a teleprint from ... Keitel, asking for a regu-
> lation to be issued, making members of the personnel, and, if
> necessary their relatives, collectively responsible for cases of sabo-
> tage occurring in their establishment (joint responsibility of rela-
> tives). This demand serves a purpose and promises success only
> if I am actually allowed to perform executions by firing squads.[36]

Opposite the words in the text referring to execution by firing squad
was a pencil note from Keitel, 'Yes, that is best', confirming official approval and encouragement for the execution of the next of
kin for acts by a member of their family. This practice was codified
by the authorities in France under SS Chief Oberg into the Con-
sanguinity Proclamation of July 1942. According to this Family
Hostage Law, which was 'a brainchild of Himmler'[37] if known saboteurs or assassins did not surrender within ten days, the authorities would shoot any adult male relatives – fathers, brothers, sons,
brothers-in-law and cousins over the age of sixteen – and females
would be deported to labour camps. Repressive measures were also
applied to the families of people who evaded compulsory labour.

Those who volunteered for resistance activities assumed responsibilities which extended far beyond personal risks. Resisters knew that if they were captured and tortured they would be jeopardizing not only their own lives, but those of their family and friends. One's neighbours might be penalized, one's birthplace obliterated. The painful decision to expose one's family and friends to reprisals created an inhuman test which was beyond the endurance of many. The dilemma for the resister lay in the tension between the necessity to fight for freedom and the knowledge that one was likely to add to the sum total of human misery by doing so. When the Germans withdrew from the French town of Mende on 15 August 1944, they murdered all the prisoners held hostage in the jail: 'These were the parents and brothers and sisters of some of the Maquisards... Right in the midst of our elation and celebrations was the grim reminder of all the horrors of the occupation.... the youngest of those murdered... was eighteen.'[38]

An Order from the Chief of the Radom district in Poland, on 20 August 1944, is a typical example of the merging of family and collective responsibility:

> In the case of an assassination of a German, either effected or attempted, or the destruction of public facilities, not only the offenders should be shot, but also their male relatives, while their female relatives aged 16 and over should be put in concentration camps.... The same method should be applied to women [offenders]. Through this procedure we aim at establishing collective responsibility by all the male and female members of the offender's family. In addition, this system strikes most painfully at the family of the political criminal.[39]

The family was the basic unit of European society. It was the moral anchor in the Nazi storm. By targeting the vulnerable and the innocent, the Nazis attacked the weakest link in the anchor's chain. The human impulse to protect one's children or elderly relatives was a morally draining experience. Dutch Jew Etty Hillesum noted:

> I can see in myself the effects of worry about the family. It gnaws at you worse than anything else.[40]
> ... I had to struggle... not to be overwhelmed by pity for my parents since it would paralyze me if I gave in to it.[41]

It was impossible for someone to join the resistance without knowing that he was putting his family or community at deadly risk. Collective family responsibility robbed resistance of any moral grandeur or sense of heroism. It could also lead to involuntary betrayal. The concept of the traitor who is disloyal to his cause or country seems clear and straightforward. The notion becomes more troublesome when we consider how German security targeted and played upon the emotions of resisters in order to turn them into double agents. By threatening family hostages with torture and death, the Germans could induce resisters to act as informers to save their own relatives. Colonel Buckmaster, Head of French Section, SOE, described the strain that had been put upon a resister codenamed *Le Chef*, to make him betray his group, and the ruthlessness required by the resistance to deal with him. The cell leader, 'Roger', questioned Le Chef 'systematically' for six hours; probably a euphemism for torture:

> Le Chef had been a faithful and brave leader until the arrest of his wife. The Germans had threatened to kill her. He loved her. He had agreed to talk. Anyone, he said, would have done the same. The Germans were not satisfied and threatened to rearrest his wife if he did not tell more. He wanted to save the lives of the Resistance, and that was why he had [only] given away the arms dumps. Then they asked for names. They had promised not to kill. Each time, because of his love for his wife, he had believed them.[42]

After discovering the tortured body of a member of the cell,

> Roger was determined that Le Chef should die. His resolution had weakened somewhat . . . as he heard Le Chef's excuses and asked himself what he would have done in the same circumstances. But now he knew he must die; in any case there was nowhere where he could be imprisoned.[43]

Because Le Chef's wife was a security risk she had to be killed as well. 'Nobody felt proud of the day's work, but it had to be done.'[44] The incident illustrates the different circles of hell to which resisters descended in order to wage their struggle.

The German practice of punishing people for actions that they had not committed, and against which there was no appeal, no judicial process, raised the painful question of whether it was right for resisters to endanger the lives of large numbers of innocent people by actions which would bring down extensive reprisals upon their families (if the identities of the perpetrators were known) or the community as a whole. This was an issue which could paralyse the most resolute. It produced more ambivalence, doubt, uncertainty and division than any other subject within resistance movements. Burdened with this terrible guilt – the blood of the innocent – resisters constantly had to balance the benefits of paramilitary action against the certainty of savage retribution. Some resisters were morally torn. SOE agent Bill Jordan reflected on his experience in Greece:

> The practice of taking hostages was one of the cruellest means adopted by the Germans ... to terrorise the civilian population. If we British operators ... carried out any military action, such as the sabotage of communications or an attack on an enemy column, the ... Germans shot a number of Greek hostages as a reprisal. Always we had to weigh the military value of a sabotage operation against the number of hostages we estimated the enemy would murder as a reprisal, and then make the terrible decision of assessing the real military worth of our project. Was it worth so many lives?[45]

As the Germans were preparing to withdraw from Holland, resistance groups drew up lists of known collaborators that they intended to arrest. In one incident the collaborationist Burgomaster in the town of Leersum had been taken prisoner before the Germans had evacuated the area. The SS Commandant made enquiries and discovered that the collaborator had been taken by Mr Van Hoop, a leading resister in the area. The SS interrogated Mrs Van Hoop at her house. After denying any knowledge of the whereabouts of the Burgomaster:

> She was told that if she did not inform the SS where he was, all the men living on the right hand side of the road would be shot ... eventually, unable to contemplate being responsible for the deaths of so many men if the Germans carried out their threatened executions, she told them.[46]

Mrs Van Hoop's house was set on fire, and the governor of a reform school where the collaborator was hidden, was shot. Her husband was taken hostage, and eventually executed in retaliation for the attempted assassination of SS General Rauter in March 1945.

Most works on resistance mention German security policy in passing, as merely one element which we need to take into account when coming to some understanding of how people responded to Nazi rule. However, collective responsibility was the decisive factor in raising doubts about, and shaping opposition to resistance. One of the principal arguments of this book is that collective responsibility has not been sufficiently emphasized in previous studies, or given the prominence it deserves. It needs to be placed in the very centre of the picture as the main focus of attention. The failure to do so results in a distorted perception of what was at stake in the fateful choice between resistance to Nazi rule and collaboration/ co-operation, and seriously underestimates the impact of German security policy upon the civilian population. For example, in 1940 the political leaders of the occupied Czech rump state (Bohemia-Moravia) were threatened that if they refused to sign a declaration of loyalty to the Third Reich, then 2000 hostages would be shot – this after 8000 leading Czech figures had already been sent to concentration camps after 1 September 1939. Faced with this choice, they had little option but to agree to sign the oath. There is no one single, causal explanation of collaboration, but given the widespread spontaneous displays of resentment and symbolic resistance soon after German occupation, the failure to convert this into a mass movement is to a significant degree attributable to the success of German security policy in developing a psychological climate which thrived on fear. Collective responsibility is the key to a proper understanding of the relatively small amount of armed resistance in the occupied territories.

German security policy was built around the simple but effective psychological strategy of exploiting the moral qualms of those under their control. Collective responsibility illustrated the hopelessness of wrestling with moral problems against an amoral enemy, and the impossibility of avoiding those problems. Lacking moral scruples themselves, and without misgivings, the Nazis readily played upon the misgivings of the potential resister in order to bring about a Hamlet-like state of paralysing indecision; crippling their opponents by artificially creating a conflict of conscience from which it was impossible for the scrupulous to escape without feeling guilt. The resister's mind became a battleground as an internal debate raged between colliding duties. This had the hallmarks of authentic tragedy: the tension inherent in the necessity to resist in conflict with the need to protect the innocent. German security policy aimed to undermine the moral resistance and resolve of the occupied population. It was predicated on the assumption that inner conflicts weakened the resister and made him at odds with himself. The collision of duties between individual responsibility to resist and collective responsibility to refrain resulted in the paralysis of an inexorably hopeless choice.

People living under German occupation would be damned if they resisted, and damned if they co-operated. The Germans wished to impale them on the horns of an impossible dilemma – either physical or moral destruction; either the bodily death of their fellow countrymen, or the spiritual death of their own country. The resister confronted a regime which murdered bodies while it tortured souls. Thus the practice of collective responsibility was the most important obstacle to the growth of widespread resistance. It deliberately exploited humane feelings in order to turn them into a weakness, because if resisters allowed the threat of reprisals to determine or limit their course of action, then the war terrorism of the Nazis had succeeded. They dictated the terms of the struggle. All the Germans had to do was to take hostages or threaten reprisals, knowing that civilized people would be inhibited from resorting to strikes, sabotage, assassination of German soldiers if the blood price was paid in innocent lives.

The major moral dilemma that the resister had to wrestle with was whether he had the right to jeopardize the lives of countless innocent fellow citizens because he was willing to risk his own life; or to the extent that he was prepared for others to pay that price, he became less humane, less civilized, and more hard-hearted, like the enemy against whom he fought. Starting off by defending human rights against the inhumane philosophy of Nazism, the resister could easily end by regarding human beings, his fellow countrymen, as expendable pawns in order to secure victory.

The option of limited co-operation with the Nazi authorities was largely conditioned by considerations of the consequences of disobeying German security policy. To that extent state terrorism worked; it successfully deterred possible opposition for lengthy periods of the occupation. The aim was not so much the punishment of culprits as the intimidation of potential opponents. The mere threat of force was sufficient to induce many a would-be resister to conform to the rules of the occupation.

COLLECTIVE RESPONSIBILITY IN THE CAMPS

Collective responsibility was also employed extensively by the German authorities in the transit, labour and concentration camps as a simple but devastatingly effective method of deterring escapes and acts of defiance. Lawrence Langer summarizes the testimony of one concentration camp inmate:

> If a Gestapo man were abusing his father, he could vent his anger. But the punishment meted out to him would be negligible compared to the knowledge that he would be causing the death of ten innocent men. Going to his father's defence, he insists, viewed from the premises established by the Nazis . . . would not be resistance but a 'foolish act'

Langer refers to this as 'the diminished self' . . . trying to come to terms with memories of the need to act and the simultaneous inability to do so.

> . . . even when resistance and sabotage occurred, they could not be acclaimed, and rarely were, by the actors themselves, as gestures of heroic defiance.[47]

One young man broke down when told of the death of his family. He decided to take revenge by attacking an SS officer. This would have cost the lives of all 400 men in his barracks. After his fellow prisoners had failed to persuade him not to commit the act they arranged for his transfer to the camp hospital, where he 'disappeared', presumably killed by the resistance movement in the hospital.[48]

Polish resister Josef Garlinski describes the effects of the system of collective punishment in Auschwitz:

> From the very beginning collective responsibility had been imposed; now it was stepped up. Several times, in retaliation for the escape of individual prisoners, the Camp Commandant or another SS officer picked a number of prisoners out of the Block in which the escapee had lived and sent them to the bunker, where they were left without food and water to die of starvation.[49]

This barbaric practice was reinforced by the threat of collective family responsibility – the parents, wife, brothers or sisters of the escapee might be arrested in his stead. This caused the underground movement in Auschwitz to abandon escapes as a form of resistance, contrary to popular preconception and countless Hollywood film images. The leader of the resistance movement, Witold Pilecki, wrote:

> At that time we, as an organisation, took up a definitely negative attitude to escapes. We did not organize any escapes and we condemned any step in this direction as a sign of extreme selfishness until the position altered fundamentally in this respect. For the time being all escapes were 'wild-cat' affairs and had nothing to do with our organisation.[50]

Similarly, Eugen Kogon, a devout Catholic who survived seven years of incarceration in Buchenwald, testifies that:

> Every prisoner was dependent on his fellow prisoners, utterly at their mercy. . . . There were . . . outstanding examples of solidarity to the death, of the unfaltering assumption of responsibility for the whole group down to the last. When political prisoners permitted themselves to be led to execution without offering resistance, this was done with patent consideration for the fellows they left behind. Had such doomed groups defended themselves in order at least to die fighting, they would instantly have been branded as mutinous and the fiercest reprisals would have been visited on the whole camp. This question was again and again discussed in camp.[51]

In his harrowing memoir, 'The Death Brigade', Leon Wells, a Lvov Jew whose assignment was to obliterate all traces of mass execution sites, tells how the German overseer extolled his workers to be 'clean':

> By clean he means clean in conscience . . . because if one of us tries to escape, they will shoot twenty inmates. Thus the inmate who will cause the death of his comrades will not be clean.[52]

Etty Hillesum, in her *Letters from Westerbork* transit camp, relates an incident in which a terrified young boy escaped from a transport:

His fellow Jews had to hunt him down – if they didn't find him, scores of others would be put on the transport in his place. He was caught soon enough, hiding in a tent, but 'notwithstanding' ... 'notwithstanding', all those others had to go on transport anyway, as a deterrent, they said. And so, many good friends were dragged away by that boy. Fifty victims for one moment of insanity.[53]

Etty says of this incident: 'will the boy be able to live with himself, once it dawns on him exactly what he's been the cause of'.[54] She further observes:

If you are a Jew you may not run away, may not allow yourself to be stricken with panic. The commandant is remorseless. As a reprisal, and without warning, scores of others are being sent on the transport with the boy, including quite a few who had thought they were firmly at anchor here. This system happens to believe in collective punishment.[55]

The Nazis had succeeded in perfecting a system in which each person was a hostage for the 'good' behaviour of everyone else. Primo Levi laconically records the roll-call prior to departure from his Italian holding camp, to Auschwitz: 'For every person missing ... ten would be shot'.[56]

Collective responsibility as a mechanism of control was used in a planned manner throughout the ghettos and slave labour camps of eastern Europe. A poster in the Vilna ghetto warned the population:

Six Jews ran away from the Bialewaker Camp. The German Command ordered 10 Jews shot in the same camp for each runaway; that is, 60 adults, not counting children. The punishment was meted out: 60 adults and 7 children were shot there.

A similar punishment awaits the population of the Vilna ghetto for a similar occurrence.[57]

Dr Moshe Beisky, a witness at the trial of Adolf Eichmann, was a young inmate of the Plaszow labour camp. He was asked in the witness box at Eichmann's trial:

You were fifteen thousand prisoners, facing tens, even hundreds, of policemen. Why didn't you attack them? Why didn't you revolt?[58]

Beisky had the opportunity to escape, but refused because collective punishment, almost certainly by hanging, would be imposed upon his entire block of two hundred people.

DECIMATION

The camp authorities also employed the practice of 'tentling' or 'decimation'. After an act of defiance or a failed escape attempt, a whole section of the concentration camp would be assembled for a roll-call, and every tenth man in a line would be selected for execution. Chaim E was in a detail of ten Jews sent to work in a wood outside Sobibor. The workers killed their Ukrainian guards and escaped.

> The remaining working Jews in the camp were lined up, and every tenth man was selected for a similar death, as a punishment and warning. 'I happened to be number nine', Chaim E dryly reports, brusquely deromanticizing the will to survive that surfaces so often in Holocaust commentary.[59]

Thirteen-year old Hungarian Jew, Elli Friedmann, relates how after an allegation of sabotage in Plaszow, the SS announced that her group of workers were to be subject to punishment.

> We shall be decimated at dawn.... We have heard of decimation. The Polish inmates have mentioned the word frequently enough. In earlier years, the entire camp or a barrack or a commando would be decimated for every minor infraction. The inmates of the guilty group would be lined up at dawn facing a firing squad, and at the count of an S.S. soldier, every tenth would be shot. No-one knew until the moment . . . Sometimes they would start counting in the middle of the row. Sometimes at the end, then switch directions. You never knew if you would be the tenth. Not until the moment of shooting.[60]

In order to increase the unbearable psychological terror, the SS would sometimes announce the punishment, but then not enforce it for days.

The Germans would do this in order to torture the guilty even more. They would do this for a week sometimes. Every evening the decimation would be announced for the following dawn then postponed, unannounced, for another day.[61]

Even the humanitarian impulse of protecting an invalid, someone who had fallen ill, counted as sabotage, and block leaders had to report the sick to the SS or risk a further decimation.

Although this book examines moral choices in Hitler's Europe, it is important to acknowledge that frequently *chance, not choice*, ruled in this arbitrary universe. Life and death were often determined by caprice: a person's fate was sealed because he happened to be in the wrong place at the wrong time – on the street closed off by German troops for the selection of a hundred hostages. One's individual identity was unimportant as long as the quota was filled. The practice of 'tentling' or 'decimation' depended upon the random choice of a guard who decided that every 5th, 15th and 25th man in a row, rather than every 7th, 17th and 27th man, was to be executed. Lawrence Langer argues that the notion of a moral world: 'founders on the capricious essence of Auschwitz and the Holocaust'.[62]

The individual was the plaything of circumstance, his life depended on the whim of his captors. Choice, and the ability to shape one's destiny, was denied to concentration camp prisoners. Elie Wiesel writes:

The choice had not been theirs. Intelligence, education, intuition, experience, courage – nothing had counted. Everything had been arranged by chance, only chance. A step towards the right or the left, a movement begun too early or too late, a change in mood of a particular overseer, and their fate would have been different.[63]

The brutal reality of this is conveyed by Tadeusz Borowski, a Polish inmate at Auschwitz who describes taking part in a football match with some fellow prisoners:

Between two throw-ins in a soccer game, right behind my back, three thousand people had been put to death.[64]

On arrival at a concentration camp, mothers who did not want to be separated from their children unknowingly chose the path which led to death. Even the distinction between the fit and the unfit was not always followed, and on occasion both doors of a railway wagon were opened:

> Those who by chance climbed down on one side of the convoy entered the camp; the others went to the gas chamber.[65]

NON-VIOLENT RESISTANCE AND COLLECTIVE RESPONSIBILITY

Wars are not won with the methods of the Salvation Army.[66]

Hitler

The Nazi occupation of Europe was the supreme challenge, the acid test, for the pacifist strategy of non-violent resistance as an alternative to war. Could anything less than force have prevailed against Nazism? Could a strategy based upon moral force and civil resistance have been an effective alternative to waging war? Could the force of argument prevail against a regime that recognized only the argument of force?

Against the criticism that the failure to resist evil is to acquiesce in evil, pacifists reply by denying that they are 'passive' in the face of evil. They argue that non-violence is not synonymous with non-resistance. Faced by the threat of Hitler, many pacifists advocated a policy of non-violent action, including a nation-wide campaign of civil disobedience, in order to deny the invading army the fruits of victory. In the long run the invader could be defeated through the frustration of his aims. Strikes, demonstrations, the non-payment of taxes, boycotts, non-violent sabotage, obstruction and the 'go-slow' at the workplace, would paralyse the operation and make it uneconomical.

During the 1930s British pacifists made a number of assumptions about Nazism, and the most effective method of resisting a German occupation of one's country. If there was no military opposition then the invading army would be small, and would behave reasonably, with restraint. Confronted by unarmed people, the soldier is in an unusual position, and is easily disconcerted and thrown off-balance. Canon Dick Sheppard, the founder of the Peace Pledge Union, found it 'impossible to believe' that enemy soldiers would bring themselves 'to gas, to bomb, to shoot, to crush and conquer' defenceless civilians, and they would refuse to obey their dictator's orders. Donald Soper, the Methodist leader, thought it important:

> to face the worst . . . though there is little chance that its women and children will be butchered, the people of any country might have their lives seriously restricted and their outward freedom denied them. That is I think a real prospect if such an invasion were to come. I cannot believe that it would involve any loss of life.[67]

Another prominent pacifist, Wilfred Wellock, wrote in 1937:

> An invading army being greeted with kindliness and hospitality . . . would be wholly unable to continue shooting down their hosts.[68]

Bertrand Russell speculated about the prospects of confronting a German invasion during the First World War with non-violent resistance:

> All the existing officials would refuse to co-operate . . . the Germans would have to dismiss them all. The dismissed officials could not all be imprisoned or shot: since no fighting would have occurred, such wholesale brutality would be out of the question. Whatever edicts they might issue would be quietly ignored by the population.[69]

The crucial question that needs to be addressed is: does this strategy work? Non-violent resistance is possible, but arguably only under certain conditions. It assumes that the occupiers will act with self-restraint and abide by the laws of war in not harming civilians. As Michael Walzer observes:

> The success of non-violent resistance requires that soldiers . . . refuse to carry out or support a terrorist strategy. . . . Non-violent defence depends upon non-combatant immunity. . . . When one wages a 'war without weapons' one appeals for restraint from men with weapons.[70]

The Nazi occupation of Europe provides valuable lessons about the strategy of non-violence. The few German pacifists were sent to concentration camps as a matter of course, and most were executed for their refusal to comply with conscription. Beheading was the method of execution reserved for this shameful dereliction of one's patriotic duty. Any pacifists who tried to persuade others to refuse to comply with conscription were prosecuted under special military laws which dealt with the subversion of the armed forces. Hitler told Lord Halifax, the British Foreign Secretary, in 1937:

> All you have to do is shoot Gandhi: if necessary some more Congress leaders. You will be surprised how quickly the trouble will die down.[71]

If Gandhi had been under a totalitarian system he would have simply disappeared overnight. Gandhi's use of the hunger strike as a means of exerting moral pressure upon government would have had no influence upon a regime which deliberately used starvation and the withholding of food as a weapon to crush its enemies.

In the light of Europe's experience of Hitler's rule, the assumptions underlying the views of Sheppard, Soper, Wellock and Russell read like the bitterest of jokes. They totally underestimated the preparedness of the Nazis to go to any lengths to impose their will upon the subject population. The grim reality of Hitler's Europe exposed the insularity and limited mental horizon of much British pacifist thinking and the inability to comprehend the crushing effects of collective responsibility. Far from being 'out of the question' as Russell phrased it, 'wholesale brutality' was the Germans' normal response to any opposition. A nation-wide campaign of civil disobedience requires co-ordination and widespread publicity. It cannot be run effectively if the occupying regime imposes a communications blackout, the rounding-up and torture of strike leaders, plus mass killings as a deterrent against future unrest. Non-violent resistance implicitly appeals to a civilized tradition of soldiery which recognizes moral limits set by the soldiers' code of honour and chivalry. Thus, Russell:

> If they ordered that ... young men should undergo military service, the young would simply refuse; after shooting a few, the Germans would have to give up ... in despair ...
>   ... If they tried to take over the railways, there would be a strike of the railway servants. Whatever they touched would ... instantly become paralysed.[72]

Russell's hypothesis was written in 1915, and demonstrates a touching faith in the limits of barbarism. The idea that an invading army will refuse to carry out orders to massacre an unarmed, non-violent population, is sadly refuted by German practice throughout eastern Europe during the Second World War. Civil disobedience and civilian resistance were impossible in Poland and Russia, where moral protests were met with firing squads. Even symbolic gestures often ended in the death penalty. An anti-German slogan daubed on a wall could result in the destruction of the nearest house and the death or deportation of its inhabitants. The slightest infraction of military occupation rules was deemed to be sabotage. A 16-year-old Russian girl was shot for singing a patriotic song. In the village of Zielonka, near Warsaw, a handmade poster proclaimed the words of a Polish writer: 'No German will spit in our faces or make Germans of our children.' As a collective punishment German soldiers killed nine people, including three boy scouts.[73] One of Hitler's orders for the occupation of the USSR stated:

> The whole vast area ... must be pacified as quickly as possible – and the best way to do that is to shoot anyone who so much as looks like giving trouble.[74]

Pacifists also advocated the strike weapon both to protest against and to halt the deportation of Jews within Nazi-occupied Europe. However, the devastating impact of collective responsibility invalidated this strategy, as was demonstrated by a protest strike which took place in Holland. During a raid in Amsterdam's Jewish quarter, a single gunshot was fired by a Jew. In reprisal 425 Jews aged between 20 and 35 were snatched off the streets and deported to Buchenwald. In a spontaneous display of solidarity thousands of Amsterdam workers went on strike on 25 February 1941. It escalated into a general strike.

This strike is significant because it was the first, and in fact the only sympathy strike against the deportation of Jews in Nazi-occupied Europe, and it has been widely and rightly regarded as one of the most heroic episodes in Dutch history. At first it took the Germans completely by surprise, but they soon crushed it. A state of emergency was declared, and martial law was imposed. Soldiers in armoured cars fired indiscriminately into crowds, killing nine and wounding 40. A thousand strikers were arrested, and 60 deported to concentration camps; over 100 leaders of the Communist party were arrested, severely weakening the most militant resistance group. A total of 390 Jewish hostages were seized and sent to Mauthausen, where only one survived. An ultimatum was given to the leaders of the Jewish community: to persuade the strike leaders to abandon the strike, otherwise additional Jews would be deported. The mayor of Amsterdam was forced to sack striking municipal workers, in an economic climate where no work meant no food. A heavy fine was imposed upon Amsterdam and two other strike centres. Within two days the strike was crushed.

The incident illustrates the difficulty of applying the strike weapon under the conditions of collective responsibility. Unlike other forms of non-violent resistance which would be disguised and carried out in a clandestine manner, strikes were a public, open act of defiance. The names and addresses of the workers were registered and available to the Germans. This exposed not only the vulnerability of individual strikers, but also the flaws and limitations of the strike as a weapon. It also underestimated the brutality of an enemy which did not feel constrained by a moral code governing the treatment of civilians. The combination of a display of ruthless force coupled with economic sanctions, demonstrated the inherent weakness of a strategy of confronting evil with public disobedience and peaceful persuasion. Open defiance was not feasible against unlimited state terror. Non-violent resistance exposed innocent people to reprisals, and this caused anguished soul-searching among those who believed in the sanctity of life.

Despite its admirable intentions the February strike failed to halt the persecution of Dutch Jews, and gave the Germans another excuse for intensifying anti-Jewish measures. The historian of the destruction of Dutch Jewry, Dr J. Presser, observes, perhaps rather harshly:

> It has been alleged, particularly by Jews, that the February strike must be called a fiasco, since far from forcing the Germans to stop the persecution of Dutch Jewry, it convinced them that machine-guns and threats sufficed to overcome any resistance to anti-semitic excesses.[75]

After this incident there were no further major demonstrations against anti-Jewish policies.

In other parts of Europe, wherever strikes occurred, the same pattern of protest and repression was repeated. Thus, on 2 October 1942 workers in the Renault factories in Paris stopped work for three hours, and only returned after a German threat to shoot 50 hostages. In Holland in April 1943 the Germans decided to re-intern Dutch prisoners-of-war who had been released in 1940. Strikes spread through Holland, and farmers refused to supply the Germans with food. As a collective punishment 150 Dutchmen were shot, and all radio receivers were confiscated. In some armaments factories gallows were erected to deter industrial action. Executing strike leaders was the normal response. It is surprising that strikes were used at all, given the dangers involved in organizing and participating in industrial action under the terms dictated by collective responsibility.[76]

If collective responsibility was a pervasive feature of German control throughout occupied Europe, there was no uniformity in the responses it evoked in resistance circles. German security policy revealed and exploited profound disagreements within and between different resistance groups, not merely over tactics, but over basic moral perceptions of what was, or was not, permissible to inflict upon one's fellow countrymen. It is to that theme that we turn next.

6 Collective Responsibility and the Responsibility of the Resistance

> A brave man may decide to risk his death and the many cruel ways of his own dying. Decided. Done. And then? What of the others who do not so decide, but die nonetheless out of his decision? His, not theirs. How many innocent unconsulted lives does a man earn the right to endanger because he is willing to risk his own?
>
> Michael Elkins[1]

The most agonizing moral dilemmas facing resisters concerned the human cost of violent resistance. This was a subject constantly debated by scrupulous resisters; a subject laden with emotion, doubt and confusion. The fundamental question for resisters everywhere was how best to respond to the officially declared German security policy of enforcing collective punishments for individual crimes against the occupation forces. The varied answers to this question revealed profound philosophical, moral and practical divisions within and between resistance groups – and primarily exposed a division and mistrust between Communist and non-communist resisters. There were also important differences of opinion over the diverse forms of violent resistance.

ASSASSINATIONS

The question of whether or not to kill individual German soldiers was a major source of tension between Communist and non-Communist resistance groups. Until the German invasion of the Soviet Union, no German soldiers had been assassinated in western Europe. After June 1941, however, there was a sudden upsurge in violence with the entry of the Communist Party into the ranks of the resistance. Bringing with them all their organizational skills in clandestine activity, the Communists became the only group to adopt an official policy of targeting individual German soldiers and officials. In political terms it demonstrated solidarity with the Soviet Union. In purely military terms the random killing of German soldiers was of limited nuisance value: at most it produced a climate of tension among soldiers who were foreigners in a hostile country living under constant strain. It also diverted some troops and resources from the eastern front. But such isolated, unco-ordinated executions could hardly, in themselves, weaken the German Army, or hasten the defeat of the Third Reich.

The main purpose of the Communist policy was a calculated, and critics would say a cynical, strategy of deliberately provoking the German authorities into taking harsh reprisal actions against the civilian population. Until the invasion of Russia, German rule in western Europe had been 'correct' and relatively lenient. Knowing that the Germans would not hesitate to shoot hostages, Communist policy was based upon the assumption that the civilian population would be shaken out of its apathy and acquiescence by German over-reaction. Public opinion would turn against the Germans out of a sense of revulsion at their disproportionate and barbaric revenge. The execution of innocent hostages would rouse the people and be beneficial to the Communist cause. This was summed up in a Communist slogan curiously reminiscent of the early Christian martyrs:

> The blood which stains our paving stones is the seed of future harvests.[2]

By acts of provocation, the Germans were to be goaded into repressive measures, resulting in arbitrary injustices. The Germans duly rose to the bait. After the first killing of a young naval cadet in Paris in August 1941, the following warning was issued in the notorious red and black posters which struck terror throughout Europe:

> On the morning of the twenty-first of August, a member of the German Army was murdered in Paris. Consequently, by order:
>
> (1) Beginning on the twenty-third of August, all Frenchmen who have been arrested by the German authorities in France . . . will be considered as hostages.
> (2) In case such an act should happen again, a number of hostages corresponding to the gravity of the crime will be shot.[3]

Despite this threat to shoot hostages, or rather precisely because of it, assassination attempts increased. The day after this warning was issued, two German officers were killed in Lille, and the following day two soldiers were executed near the Belgian border, resulting in the death of eight hostages. Thus began a cycle of violent resistance answered by reprisal.

The official hostage quota for France was set at 10:1, but when the German Military Commandant was shot at Nantes on 10th October 1941, 50 hostages were killed, and an additional 50 were arrested in order to enhance the deterrent effect, and to impress the French people with the might of German security. The Military Commander in charge of France, Von Stulpnagel, issued the following proclamation:

> In expiation of this crime, I have already ordered that fifty hostages be shot.
>
> Given the gravity of the crime, fifty more hostages will be shot if the guilty parties are not arrested by midnight, October 23, 1941.
>
> I offer an award totalling fifteen million francs to those citizens who contribute to the discovery of the guilty parties[4]

As the perpetrators were not caught, one hundred hostages perished. The day after the Nantes killing, a German major was assassinated in Bordeaux, and an identical threat was made. Another hundred hostages died.

Thus, according to the logic of Communist strategy, the very severity of German repression would alienate public opinion, win over waverers, produce a more militant attitude, and thereby swell the ranks of the resistance. Faced with the cold arithmetic of a policy which anticipated and actively invited reprisals as a method of recruiting new members, many resisters – including Communist Party veterans – hesitated before they decided whether they should continue this form of resistance. Confronted with the publication of the red and black death lists, posted prominently in all towns, the weight of individual moral responsibility became enormous.

Colonel Rol, a Communist militant who was later in charge of the Paris Resistance at the Liberation, described his feelings:

> We went through agonizing hours ... we were tormented by scruples, self-questioning, anguish.

But he concluded that:

> Even at the price of this precious blood of hostages, France could not afford to be presented to the world as a passive prostrate country without will to resist and react . . . The price had to be paid . . . bitter as it was.[5]

The deep ethical consideration which presented itself to the resister was that it was one thing to risk one's own life, but what if the consequence of resistance resulted in the execution of neighbours or one's fellow countrymen?

Roderick Kedward provides compelling evidence of the deep rift between Communist and non-communist resisters, in his series of oral testimonies of ex-resisters in southern France. François Rouan was a Trotskyist member of the militant Maquis Bir-Hakeim. He acknowledged that:

> German reprisals were atrocious. I'm still affected by the memory of Les Crottes where all the population was massacred, including the very young. We had confronted a German force nearby, but were able to withdraw after inflicting considerable losses. They then turned on the village. . . . We couldn't have allowed for this; it was war, and ambushes had to be carried out suddenly when the information announcing a convoy arrived. We had no time to weigh up the possible consequences.[6]

Despite this claim, the consequences were predictable and followed established German procedure in response to guerrilla ambushes. Other resistance groups in the area utterly rejected such tactics. According to resister Jean Pujadas:

> The Maquis Bir-Hakeim came into our area briefly. They were crazy. You couldn't take on the Germans like that: they left the villages open to reprisals.[7]

Another resister confirmed: 'Our policy was not to endanger the local people'.[8]

Personal scruples about individual guilt and responsibility confronted many resisters with the choice: whether to refrain from provocative forms of resistance when faced with inevitable reprisals, or to accept the terms and conditions of collective responsibility, and to pay for their country's honour by the blood sacrifice of its innocent sons and daughters.

SHOULD RESISTERS SURRENDER?

Another constant question eating away at the conscience of scrupulous resisters was whether they should give themselves up in order to save the lives of innocent people. Some resisters felt that they could not let 50 or 100 innocent people die on their behalf, but others tried to talk them out of this course of action because it could endanger the entire resistance group. If the Germans got hold of the resister, they would almost invariably interrogate and torture him to find out the identities, hiding places and arms' caches of the rest of his cell.

In Yugoslavia, a 28-year-old night watchman called Milorad Stosich performed the ultimate act of self-sacrifice for his fellow countrymen. In his home town of Kranj, in Upper Slovenia, a German civilian had been killed. The Germans randomly selected 10 men from the town as hostages, and announced that they would be hanged unless the individual responsible for the killing gave himself up within the next 24 hours. Shortly before the expiry time, Milorad Stosich walked into German headquarters and confessed to the crime. The 10 hostages were released, and Stosich was hanged in the marketplace, where his body was left on the gallows for a week as a warning to the local population. It soon transpired that Stosich had nothing to do with the assassination, but had given his life to save the lives of the hostages. The Germans discovered this, and ordered the re-arrest of the hostages. However, they had fled to the mountains to form a partisan group, known as the Milorad Stosich Brigade. Unfortunately, other villagers were taken and executed in their stead.[9]

Some individual Communists were reluctant to carry out the official Party policy, and at Nantes, one official recommended that the assassin of a German officer should hand himself over to the authorities in order to prevent the shooting of hostages.[10] In another incident in Italy, a Communist resister betrayed a priest who had sabotaged a German freight train. The authorities threatened to kill 20 hostages a day until the saboteur surrendered. But the priest refused to do so because he was the only person available to offer absolution for his parishioners' souls. After three days, the Communist – who obviously put no faith in the doctrine of the resurrection or eschatological verification – decided that those who attacked the body were a more immediate threat than those who attacked the soul, and informed on the priest in order to stop any further loss of innocent life.[11] Nevertheless, these examples were exceptions to the Communists' official policy. In France it was even thought that a more militant attitude could reverse the German ratio of 10:1, by increased violence. The French Communist Party declared:

> For every Frenchman, ten Germans or creatures of the Germans calling themselves Frenchmen will be executed without hesitation.[12]

This was a piece of bravado which never came close to realization, and in fact the opposite occurred. The Germans were true to their word and never promised what they could not deliver.

The assassination of ordinary German conscripts and high-ranking officers provoked passionate controversy within resistance groups. It was widely condemned by the public and by non-Communist resisters, who called for restraint in view of the unacceptably high, suicidal, casualty rate among the civilian population. Thus it is important to stress the fact that resisters themselves cautioned against quixotic gestures which resulted in unnecessary sacrifices. The rejection of routine assassination by non-Communist resisters was based upon a more modest and arguably more realistic appraisal of the limits of resistance, and a recognition that the benefits of killing German soldiers were usually outweighed by the disadvantages. Many resisters were deeply ambivalent about waging such a one-sided war in which the losses were totally disproportionate to the gains. The French Resistance veteran Henri Michel voiced the prevailing scepticism over Communist methods:

> It seems questionable whether acts of resistance liable to be punished by such violent reprisals are necessary or even useful. Their effect is purely moral and the enemy's strength remains intact . . . It may also be thought that a population which needs to be shaken out of its apathy by such methods, has no great predilection for clandestine work.[13]

The killing of individual soldiers was also condemned by the governments-in-exile: the leadership of the external resistance. On

23rd October 1941, coinciding with the assassinations at Nantes and Bordeaux, General De Gaulle declared in a radio broadcast to France:

> It is absolutely natural and right that Germans should be killed by Frenchmen. If the Germans did not wish to receive death at our hands, they had only to stay at home ... but there are tactics in war. War must be conducted by those entrusted with the task ... for the moment, my orders to those in occupied territory are NOT to kill Germans there openly. This is for one reason only: at present, it is too easy for the enemy to retaliate by massacring our fighters, who are, for the time being, disarmed.[14]

Similarly, the Dutch government-in-exile officially signalled its disapproval of assassinations in a broadcast in February 1943, warning patriots not to take justice into their own hands.[15]

In purely military terms assassinations were meaningless, indeed counter-productive, because increased German security searches often netted valuable resistance members. In his war-time memoirs, Henri Frenay, the creator of one of the first French resistance groups, *Combat*, articulated the uneasiness that many resisters felt about the Communist line – the futility of routine assassinations and the preparedness to sacrifice so many lives for speculative advantages.

> We were familiar with the Communist belief that, since war inevitably involves the death of innocent persons, the execution of hostages had an essentially positive effect in that it aroused the hatred of the people against the occupier. They insisted that ten volunteers would rise up to replace every hostage that was shot.
>
> Though I understood this viewpoint, I could not share it. That war kills innocent people is of course only too true. But that I, of my own free will, should sign what would in effect be somebody else's death warrant, for the sole reason that it might instil a greater combative ardour in the people (and this without any serious damage to the enemy) – no, I could never have consented to such a policy!
>
> Between the Communists who held this 'utilitarian' point of view and those who thought as I did, the quarrel was of a philosophical or religious nature and hence without any practical solution. And yet their cold determination compelled my respect, for it never flinched, even when the hostages themselves were party members.[16]

As a senior resistance figure, Frenay's considered opinion could not be easily dismissed. His view represented the sentiment of many within resistance circles. The divisions between Communist and non-Communist resisters were fully exposed in an incident in Italy in 1944.

THE ARDEATINE CAVES MASSACRE

On 23 March 1944, the 25th anniversary of the founding of Italian Fascism, a Communist-led organization – the Gappists ('Groups for Patriotic Action') – exploded a bomb hidden in a dustcart in a narrow street, the Via Rasella, in Rome. The bomb killed 33 SS troops, and in addition 10 Italian civilians, including six children. Although the resisters gave some warnings to passers-by, it would not have been possible to evacuate the resident population of this densely populated area without arousing the Germans' suspicions. Other resistance groups disclaimed any responsibility for the attack, and condemned the act as militarily useless. Furthermore, given the Nazis' track record of reprisals, critics argued that the Communists should have anticipated that a major atrocity like the Ardeatine Caves massacre was bound to follow, and therefore should have refrained from this needlessly provocative act.

According to a report from the High Command of the Wehrmacht, Hitler's immediate reaction was to demand that an entire quarter of Rome, the working-class districts of San Lorenzo, Tiburtino and Testaccio, should be blown up, including everyone who lived there, and for 50 Italians to be shot for every German death: a total of 1650 reprisal victims. Eventually the German commanders in Rome, including Lt Colonel Kappler, the head of the SD, agreed that the Führer's demands were not feasible, and reduced the reprisal ratio to 10:1. 330 people were officially designated for execution in the Ardeatine Caves, south of Rome. 280 were political prisoners and Jews taken from Rome's jails, the remainder were randomly rounded up from the streets. In their haste to execute the order, the Germans miscounted, and an additional five victims were also killed. Of the 335 victims, the youngest was 15 years old; the oldest was 74. Six members of the Di Consiglio family were among those murdered. SOE and the British authorities approved the Via Rasella bombing, and a BBC radio broadcast to Italy described the partisans who carried out the action as 'Italian patriots.'[17]

The Roman Catholic Church, articulating the views of many non-Catholics as well as Catholics, denounced both the resistance act and the subsequent German reprisal. A Vatican communiqué proclaimed:

> In the face of such deeds every honest heart is left profoundly grieved in the name of humanity and Christian sentiment [for] persons sacrificed for the guilty parties who escaped arrest.... We call upon the irresponsible elements to respect human life, which they can never have the right to sacrifice, to respect the innocence of those who are their fatal victims.[18]

Defenders of the attack argue that to refrain from violent resistance out of fear of reprisals 'leads to submission and finally to abject surrender to all forms of tyranny and intimidation.... This is the equivalent of a rejection of armed resistance to armed aggression.'[19] Though this argument has some merit as a general point about the problems of confronting evil, it fails to address questions concerning the specific circumstances and timing of the bombing, the partisan party-political considerations which motivated the bombers, and the fact that non-communist resistance groups, who could not be accused of passivity and abject surrender, distanced themselves from the act and failed to condone or support it. With the Allied armies advancing through southern Italy, and soon to liberate Rome on 4 June 1944, questions can be raised about the military necessity and advisability of the Via Rasella attack, particularly in view of the imminence of a German withdrawal. The act cannot be regarded as a desperate last resort. In placing their political objectives above humanitarian considerations, Communist resisters exhibited too little concern for, or sensitivity towards, the level of human suffering, which was predictable and followed the established German pattern. The controversy surrounding the bombing caused continuing division in Italy after the war, with neo-Fascist groups exploiting the grief of the relatives of the victims in order to tarnish the reputation of the resistance as a whole.

COMMUNIST GUERRILLA WARFARE

> I think the most important [concept] was that marxism-leninism was for us the only scientific world outlook. Everybody else in

the world, the social democrats, the liberals, the conservatives, had their opinion, but we, the marxist-leninists, we had a scientific world outlook. A science that was applicable to nature, to human beings, to social affairs, to all countries and all nations of the world.

It was a concept that gave a scientific answer to what was going to happen ... we knew the fundamental answer to the riddle of the past, present and future for all nations and for all countries.[20]

Wolfgang Leonard

Communist resistance during the Second World War has to be seen in the perspective of the Communist Party's teleological view of history as a movement progressing inexorably towards the goal of the future society. The Party alone possessed the correct map of history. Historical self-awareness, and the need to direct and shape life towards the goal, also prompted a confidence that Nazism was only a temporary relapse into barbarism – the death-rattle of capitalism. Armed with this faith, and seeing themselves as the instruments of fate, the executioners of historical destiny, Communists felt empowered to use any means to achieve their goal, and to remove any obstacle that lay in the path of the locomotive of history. Believing in their exclusive right to lead, many Communists were ready to commit appallingly cruel acts in the name of freedom, without moral reservation and regardless of the losses and suffering among their own people. This was the Communist version of Manifest Destiny. Because of their understanding of the immutable laws of historical development, Communists were absolved from pity and guilt. Thousands, probably hundreds of thousands of people, paid with their lives because Communist resisters believed in the infallibility and inexorability of their cause. In the name of Communism and the future generation, everything was permitted, including torture and reprisals against ordinary people in this generation. Many Communist resisters attempted to achieve their aim at any cost, feeling themselves freed from normal ethical constraints, or moral responsibility for the effects of their actions, by the historical process which guaranteed them inevitable victory. All conventional moral rules were subordinate to the iron laws of history. Perhaps this is an old-fashioned form of Marxism that many contemporary Marxists would reject, but it was the type of Marxism which underpinned, and gave meaning and purpose to, the actions of leading Communist resisters. Resistance to Nazism, and the expulsion of the German army of occupation, was not an end in itself, but a means to the goal of the future society. Resistance was a transition on the road to revolution. Resistance and revolution were an extension of politics by other means for 'the armed strug gle against the occupation strengthened the Communists'.[21] Lead ing Yugoslav resister Milovan Djilas wrote of how 'the historically predetermined role of the avant-garde' meant that 'Communists identified the destiny of the people with the role of the party'.[22] Djilas articulated the vital importance of ideology for Communist guerrilla warfare:

> No-one before us Communists was ever so scientifically convinced that they were not only transforming a given state of affairs, but giving men and nations an ultimate and unalterable direction. All development and movement were seen as the self-fulfilment of the ideology and the party.[23]

Anyone who questioned the Party's methods, or the human cost of achieving the goal, was regarded as aiding the enemy. As in Stalin's Russia, anyone who was captured by the enemy, or who surrendered, was seen as a traitor. Djilas records that 'The Party Committee had passed a decision that every party member who surrendered should be executed, and carried out that decision re gardless of circumstances.'[24] A peasant pointedly asked Djilas: 'If you treat your own people like that, what can we expect?'[25] The short answer to this question is that the peasant population were regarded as expendable pawns in the struggle.

ASSASSINATIONS IN PARTISAN WARFARE

> Their feet run to evil, and they make haste to shed innocent blood.
>
> Isaiah, 59:7

Assassinations were a routine, indeed inseparable, feature of par tisan warfare in eastern and south-eastern Europe. The killing of German soldiers under the conditions of guerrilla warfare – and in areas where Nazi racial doctrines resulted in the brutalization of everyday life for the 'sub-human' Slavs – raises many wider ques tions than the isolated executions of soldiers in the more settled conditions of western and northern Europe. But one common – Communist – element was the tactic employed by both Soviet and Yugoslav partisans, of deliberately engineering reprisals as a method of recruiting new members, and turning the populace against the occupiers. One Soviet saboteur spelled out the logic of actively inviting:

> The most drastic repressions upon the peaceful populations in order to stir their animosity and hatred for the Germans. . . . We would choose the quietest settlement, with a population loyal to the occupants. Then we would kill a German soldier, or we would mine the railroads in the vicinity; and the Germans would retaliate upon the whole village and the peasantry learned a cruel lesson.[26]

Another Belorussian guerrilla described the provocation of German reprisals as a highly effective technique of recruitment. His band:

> would spy out one or two German soldiers, . . . mutilate and kill them, then freeze the corpses, often in the posture of the Nazi salute, and stand them at road intersections. The enraged SS would seek revenge on the nearby villages. . . . Like lightning the news spread all over the region. . . . Seized with panic people fled to the woods. There the Soviet agents would find them, curse the Germans with them, and tell them that Comrade Stalin knew their misfortunes and would not leave them without food, medical help, and arms to defend themselves. . . . Then, at night, a Soviet plane would drop a few medical kits. . . .[27]

Similarly:

> Several German or other Axis soldiers would be captured, mutilated and killed. Their bodies would then be left in a place where the Germans would surely find them, often next to villages sympathetic to the invaders or neutral in their political sympathies. When the bodies were found, German security troops would take revenge on all the villages in the area by killing everyone they saw, by confiscating all cattle and crops, and by devastating entire sections of land. The survivors fled to the forests where they would be met by the partisans who would sympathise with them and offer help.[28]

Soviet citizens in occupied Russia had to wear a conspicuous identification number to facilitate German security measures. Village chiefs and mayors were instructed to compile registers of all people living in their area. After registration, every house had to display a list of its inhabitants. Strangers had to report to the local authorities on arrival, or else face imprisonment or death. Anyone caught hiding unregistered people would be shot. Special permits were needed to travel outside one's area. With the operation of these pass laws and curfew regulations, people were shot on suspicion in sensitive areas.[29] Mayors and villagers who complied with these regulations were deemed to be collaborators. According to the official Soviet view there was no such thing as a neutral, or a 'wait-and-see' attitude. Those who were not for us were deemed to be against us, and were therefore expendable. Partisans provoked reprisals, partly as punishment for disloyalty, and also to increase animosity towards the Germans. In various areas of occupied Russia, the Germans warned village mayors that they and their families would be executed if there was any partisan activity in the vicinity of their villages. This was exploited by Soviet partisans in order to punish villages deemed to be collaborationist, by carrying out violent incidents in the areas concerned.[30]

The same story can be told for Yugoslavia. The Partisans believed that they would be the beneficiaries of German repression, and therefore embarked upon a strategy designed to maximize the slaughter. Ordinary peasants and villagers were trapped in a vicious circle of terror and counter-terror. The only way out of this circle was to join the Partisans. With their villages burned, their livestock slaughtered, and their families killed in German reprisal raids, homeless and destitute survivors had little option but to take to the mountains or forests. Those who were totally dispossessed had nothing to lose, and often proved to be the best recruits, bent upon revenge. While goading the Germans into retaliation the Communists cynically exploited the emotive propaganda value of German reprisals in order to consolidate their political position. Reprisals were their best recruiting sergeant. Communist resisters did not scruple to sacrifice innocent lives in order to attain their goal.

In Montenegro, because villages had given their support to the more cautious Chetniks, out of fear that their houses would be burned down in German reprisals, Tito authorized counter-terror methods. According to Djilas, Tito reasoned that:

If the peasants realized that if they go over to the invader we will also burn their houses, they will change their minds. This argument seemed logical to me, too, though I did not support it resolutely. Finally Tito made up his mind . . . 'Well, all right, we can burn a house or a village here and there.' Tito issued an order to that effect.[31]

Djilas records the destruction of two villages – Ozrinici and Donji Zagarac – which had 'gone over to the Chetniks'.[32] These villages were burned to the ground, and Djilas notes that such methods 'turned undecided, vacillating peasants into bitter adversaries',[33] and that this was compounded because numerous 'unjustified, executions were being carried out'.[34] Djilas relates how peasants 'come to me with complaints against the excessive, insane executions'.[35]

Tito's closest associate, Edward Kardelj, trained in Stalin's Russia, was a more determined and ruthless advocate of this policy for Yugoslav partisans: actively inciting enemy retaliation.

We must at all costs push the Croatian as well as the Serb villages into the struggle. Some commanders are afraid of reprisals, and that fear prevents the mobilisation of Croat villages. I consider, the reprisals will have the useful result of throwing Croatian villages on the side of Serb villages. In war we must not be frightened of the destruction of whole villages. Terror will bring about armed action.[36]

The moral issues raised by this policy came to a head in the Autumn of 1941 after the notorious massacres at Kraljevo and Kragujevac. The massive scale of German reprisals led to the end of co-operation between Tito's Partisans and Mihailović's Chetniks. On 20 October 1941, after an ambush upon a German convoy had left 30 dead, and numerous others wounded, an estimated 4000 inhabitants of the village of Kraljevo were killed. The following day, in reprisal for the death of 10 German soldiers and 26 wounded, the town nearest the raid, Kragujevac, was subject to the most bloody reprisal of the German occupation. According to the official German hostage quota, 2300 people were executed: 1000 for the ten dead soldiers, and 1300 for the 26 wounded men.

When an NCO informed the major that the 'quota' had already been filled . . . the major ordered the shooting to continue. Then all counting stopped. When the killing was over, the bodies of some 7000 male inhabitants of the town of Kragujevac awaited burial.[37]

These events, which included the death of over 300 schoolchildren in Kragujevac, convinced Mihailović to revert to a more cautious long-term strategy which avoided unnecessary blood-letting – akin to that adopted by De Gaulle: of building an underground network and waiting for more favourable circumstances; with a national rising against the Germans to be co-ordinated with an Allied invasion, in order to bring about a swift liberation of the Balkans at the least cost in human life, rather than to persist in futile attacks upon the German army which would only result in more bloodbaths and risk national annihilation.

The same events convinced the Partisans under Tito to draw the opposite conclusions. Thus Djilas:

> It was evident that the struggle could be continued only by a strong organization able to overcome its own feelings of guilt about enemy reprisals against the people, and able to oppose all vacillation and crush all resistance to the struggle...[38]

Basil Davidson, an SOE officer who was parachuted into Yugoslavia to aid Tito's forces, offers an insight into the morality and values of the Partisans:

> The conditions upon which they accepted to fight the occupying armies were so frightful in the scale of reprisal on the civilian population that weaknesses would have quickly undone their voluntary system and put paid to their movement. And it was clear that they accepted these conditions of reprisal by the enemy as the only alternative to compromise and eventual surrender, and as a necessary moral contribution to the winning of the war.
>
> The notion that they might be open to reproof for entailing their families and the families of their friends in reprisals by an infuriated enemy they emphatically rejected, and on the whole it did not occur to them....
>
> Those from outside who might counsel caution and moderation and the avoidance of action that would 'lead to enemy reprisals' they regarded as soft-hearted fools or partly interested knaves.[39]

Beyond a certain point German reprisals became self-defeating because they played into the Communists hands, and aided their strategy. Even the quiescent, the timid and obedient would be driven to resist because they were no longer sure that their own 'good behaviour' would guarantee their safety. Some German commanders realized that the injustice of punishing innocent people for crimes they did not commit would have an adverse effect upon German pacification policy. One German lieutenant colonel in Belgrade pointed out that the Communists had a desire to create unrest, and that therefore massive reprisals were counter-productive because they stimulated the growth of the partisan movement: 'For their purpose the shooting of people who did not directly participate in the acts of sabotage is actually welcome.'[40]

A German official in the Ministry of the Interior in Belgrade offered a Cassandra-like prophecy concerning the detrimental effects of German reprisals following the death of a German Army captain by Communist guerrillas.

> The consequence . . . will be that a large number of innocent people will be slaughtered and that the Communists in the woods not only will not be exterminated but will increase in numbers. Because many farmers, even entire villages – even though up to now they had no connection with the Communists – will flee into the woods only out of fear and will be received there by the Communists. They will be provided with arms and used for combat and for open revolt against the German armed forces. This insurrection will develop on a large scale and will have incalculable and terrible consequences for the entire population.[41]

After an incident on 5 April 1944 in which Greek Communists killed two German motorcyclists, the village of Klissura, two miles from the attack, was targeted. Knowing what to expect, the male villagers fled to the hills. The rest of the population assumed that their age and sex would protect them. An SS unit threw a cordon around the village, and herded all the remaining old men, women and children into the public square. In the bloodbath that followed 215 people were massacred, including 128 women, and seven men over the age of 80. 72 victims were under 15 years old, including nine children less than one year old; six between one and two years, eight between two and three years, 11 aged three to four, and four between the ages of four and five.

Herman Neubacher, the Foreign Office Plenipotentiary for south east Europe, produced a report on the Klissura massacre which offered a farsighted warning of the catastrophic political consequences of indiscriminate collective punishments:

> It is utter insanity to murder babies, children, women and old men because heavily-armed Red bandits billeted themselves over night, by force, in their houses, and because they killed two German soldiers near the village. The political effect of this senseless bloodbath doubtless by far exceeds the effect of all propaganda efforts in our fight against Communism. . . .
>
> The wonderful result of this heroic deed is that babies are dead. But the partisans continue to live and they will again find quarters by use of submachine guns in completely defenseless villages.[42]

German troops were clearly guilty of a major war crime at Klissura. What degree of responsibility does the resistance share for knowingly engineering such atrocities by goading the Germans into savage reprisals? Calculated acts of provocation were an intrinsic feature of Communist guerrilla warfare.

THE KILLING OF INFORMERS AND COLLABORATORS

A hooded figure stands in a village square, pointing the finger of accusation at a number of men lined up in front of him. The masked informer[43] was a common sight in eastern Europe under Nazi occupation. The assistance of the paid informer was invaluable to the Germans in detecting strangers and Jews. In order to meet the requirements of a constant supply of hostages to fill the hostage pools, village Quislings were recruited by the German security police, the SD. Native collaborators prepared lists of suspects – Communists, Jews, relatives of men who were away from the village without good reason, or people who showed a 'hostile' attitude. Resistance and underground warfare took place in a climate of constant nervous strain and the need to root out and kill traitors.

Both Communist and non-Communist resisters agreed in principle that it was justifiable and necessary to kill important collaborators, and dangerous informers who had a more intimate understanding of the nuances of local conditions than their foreign

paymasters. Prominent national figures and highly placed collaborators epitomized the betrayal of their country and deserved exemplary justice. In addition, the Germans were far less concerned about
the lives of their collaborationist allies than of their own troops,
and usually did not guarantee protection to them. Hostage-taking
as a form of deterrence was the exception rather than the rule.
Nevertheless, the German response was unpredictable. After the
death of a prominent collaborator in Warsaw in March 1941, the
German authorities arrested 200 Poles, 21 of whom were summarily executed, and the rest detained as hostages. As a result, the
Polish government-in-exile forbade the killing of collaborators except in extreme circumstances of self-defence.[44] In Holland, the
Resistance 'National Action' groups faced the same dilemma which
confronted assassins of German soldiers. In a seven-month period
in 1943, they killed over 40 Dutch National Socialists, and a number
of Dutch secret agents who were working for the Germans.

> None of these operations could be described as random or arbi-
> trary acts of political murder. Each attack was carefully discussed,
> often with ministers of religion or representatives of legitimate
> Dutch authorities, and none was approved without a thorough-
> going examination of every conceivable ethical, moral, practical
> and psychological objection.[45]

In retaliation, the German security apparatus launched a com-
pensatory murder programme by death squads upon innocent people,
and in September 1943, instituted an official hostage quota of 3:1
for the death of each Dutch National Socialist. In other parts of
Europe, resisters had to contend with local collaborationist paramilitary police militias, but these groups wreaked their revenge only
arbitrarily and sporadically, and not with the Teutonic efficiency of
the hostage quota system.

In addition to the uncertainties of how the Germans and their
collaborationist allies would respond, the killing of collaborators
and informers caused moral problems, for a number of reasons.
There was the danger of abuse: that some resisters would use patriotism as a cloak to cover their private motives of settling old
scores, or for criminal gain. There was also the perennial problem
of terrorism: the danger of mistakes, and the tendency to hit the
wrong target with tragic consequences. Some resisters who played
a 'double game', working in an administrative capacity for the

Germans in order to gain access to highly important, confidential information, were mistakenly killed as traitors. But the most profound moral issues surrounding the question of how to deal with collaborators centred around the problem of the imitation of Nazi methods. This involved:

1. the adoption of the practice of 'reverse' collective responsibility;
2. the use of torture by the resistance.

Reverse Collective Responsibility

For security reasons, especially the constant fear of betrayal, innocent members of collaborators' families were, on occasions, killed as well: a mirror image of the German doctrine of collective responsibility. In Lyon, a Communist poster urged patriotic citizens to draw up 'dossiers of reprisals' against informers and collaborationist policemen, judges and journalists.

> Informers were threatened with the sentencing to death of five to ten members of their families.[46]

In December 1943 the Communist underground newspaper 'Franc-Tireur' published a warning to the Milice and the Fascist PPF:

> To each new murder that they commit, the *milicien* and the PPF must expect immediate and merciless reprisals... the French Resistance sends a warning – 'For an eye, both eyes; for a tooth, the whole jaw!'[47]

On 20 April 1944 at Voiron, near Grenoble, the Resistance assassinated Jourdan, the head of the local Milice, and in addition they killed his wife, his 82-year old mother, his 10-year old son, and his 15-month old daughter. When the French collaborationist writer Robert Brassilach went into hiding after the liberation, resistance officials raided his mother's apartment and imprisoned her. She was only released after Brassilach gave himself up. After an explosion in the town of Pertuis had killed 30 French resisters, townspeople engaged in a reprisal by taking 37 suspected collaborators as hostages, and threatening to kill them if the culprits did not give themselves up.[48] Less extreme threats of collective punishments were also used against the families of collaborators, in effect making them hostages for their relatives' good behaviour. The National Council of the Resistance in France issued a warning to civil servants.

> If any public employees are killed in the course of service for the enemy, France will feel no moral or financial obligation towards their families – this is reserved for those who defend the country, not those who betray it.[49]

Soviet partisans often killed the families of collaborators, including children, and also anyone who had inadvertently witnessed a partisan action. The risk of betrayal overrode any humanitarian considerations. An 18-year-old guerrilla wrote in his diary:

> Shot a traitor. Morale good! In the evening I went to do the same to his wife. We are sorry that she leaves three children behind. But war is war! Towards traitors any humane consideration is misplaced.[50]

On various occasions Jewish partisans in the forests of eastern Poland and western Russia engaged in collective punishments upon the Germans and native collaborators. One group of Jewish resisters who sheltered other Jews in the woods near Siemiatycze in the Bialystok district, threatened to shoot any Poles who betrayed Jews to the Gestapo. After three Jews had been captured by a Polish peasant, and had been tortured and killed by German security forces, in an act of revenge, and as a warning, the Siematycze group 'murdered not only the peasant but his family'.[51]

The threat of reprisals and collective punishments – burning the houses and farm buildings of informers – coupled with the dire warning that all family members of collaborators would be deemed legitimate targets, was practised most thoroughly and ruthlessly by the Bielski group of Jewish partisans in Belorussia. They exacted grim revenge upon the families of informers and German security police in their theatre of guerrilla war. After one operation they left a large sign attached to the door of a house:

> This family was annihilated because it co-operated with the Germans and pursued Jews, signed The Bielski Company.[52]

They also took action against a large Belorussian family, the

Marciniewskis, who had informed the Germans about Jewish hide-outs. One of the Marciniewski sons became a policeman. He and his brother-in-law, a forester, had regularly caught Jews:

> The Bielski otriad reacted... one day we waited for the police-man to come home. We watched the house. When we returned we killed the entire family... [the] forester and his family were also eliminated.[53]

A similar fate befell the Stichko family, who were shot, with the usual warning notice left to intimidate other potential informers. Many among the native population were so impressed by the effec-tiveness of this Jewish partisan group and so fearful of reprisals that they refrained from denouncing Jews.

Such methods were probably unavoidable given the heavy odds stacked against them by the large numbers of informers, and the genocidal conditions of struggle dictated by the Germans. The Jewish partisans were overwhelmed by circumstances not of their own making. This was the extenuating factor against a ruthless and unprincipled enemy who did not hesitate to use any means to im-pose his will. Nevertheless, the practice of killing entire families was a reflection of the Nazi policy of collective and family responsi-bility, and could not be dismissed simply as a necessity of war. It violated principles of innocence central to just war theory, and raised a moral question mark over partisan operations. It poses a prob-lem for any sanitized or romanticized view of resistance as a mor-ally unblemished activity.

Torture by the Resistance

Prior to execution, suspected informers and collaborators were in-terrogated. This could easily degenerate into a brutal, sadistic form of torture. In a searing personal memoir, Marguerite Duras analy-ses the moral ambiguities of this neglected aspect of the resist-ance, in her description of the interrogation of an informer by a woman called Therese and her resistance comrades. Her account shows how difficult it is to draw a line between interrogation and torture, and just how easy it is to cross it. Gradually the question-ing is accompanied by slaps on the face, and taunting the suspect. This is followed by heavy blows to the body, until he is eventually tormented and tortured.

They hit harder and harder. . . . They hit better and better, more coolly. The more they hit and the more he bleeds, the more it's clear that hitting is necessary, right, just. . . .

Extract the truth this swine has in his gullet. . . . Beat him till he ejaculates his truth, his shame, his fear, the secret of what made him only yesterday all-powerful. . . .[54]

In a new preface to the text, Marguerite Duras reveals that:

Therese is me. The person who tortures the informer is me.[55]

In this disturbing short work, Duras vividly demonstrates the morally disintegrative effect of the Nazi occupation upon even the most idealistic resister. Resisters could easily become tainted by the very evil that they were struggling to overcome. The tortured is no longer a human being, but simply a source of intelligence. The subterranean world of resistance readily lent itself to the mal-treatment of suspects and an escalation of brutality. There was growing indifference to the enemy as a human being. When people are degraded and reduced to the level of 'things', this can lead easily to pitiless butchery, and the descent into evil. Major Bill Jordan, a New Zealander who was sent by SOE to organize resist-ance in Greece and France, provides compelling testimony of this process by which resisters lost sight of suffering and death. In 1944 Jordan was parachuted into the Department of Lozère. He recounts his experience of the Deuxième Bureau (Intelligence Section) of the Maquis at Les Sauvages. Most members of the Deuxième Bu-reau were former policemen; their job was to trap Vichy traitors:

I was given grim evidence of the bitterness of the French strug-gle. A room near mine was used by the Deuxieme Bureau as an 'Interrogatoire'. There the captured traitors were brought for ques-tioning, an ordeal that was as crude and frightening as anything the Nazis had perpetrated. All traitors were shot, but before ex-ecution, they were questioned for every last piece of informa-tion that could be extracted from them by one means or another.

In the yard . . . was a small, portable forge. Coals would be lighted in the forge. . . . Pieces of iron were then brought to red heat and taken into the Interrogatoire to persuade the traitors to cough the last dreg of their sordid information. One night, as I lay in bed, I could hear the blows, the screams and groans of a man under interrogation. After some ear-splitting screams I was suddenly sickened by the odour of burning flesh.

Poulain, a doctor who was one of the leaders of the Maquis group, and the senior medical officer with the Resistance in Southern France, informed Jordan that:

> the man they had tortured the night before was in a bad way. They had put a red hot iron up his rectum. He had to treat the terrible wound that morning and was nearly overcome in doing so.[56]

The doctor's sense of revulsion is mixed with his own sense of shared responsibility as a member of the group. He had participated in the system of torture by performing deeds abhorrent to him, and was thus an accomplice.

Two young women who had tried to infiltrate the group were also interrogated, tortured and shot. Jordan recounts the atmosphere of moral unease:

> We received a visit from a superior FFI officer about this time, and one of the matters he brought up concerned the Deuxieme Bureau torture and execution of Vichy traitors ... he was uneasy over the whole matter.
>
> One of the young resisters 'stopped me in the grounds of Les Sauvages and said that it was not right to torture and execute women ... they thought it was wrong to treat women or girls like that. They asked my opinion. This was a French affair and, no matter what I thought, the Maquis would carry on as they pleased. I told them I didn't agree with them. To me the question was not should we torture women and execute them, but should we torture and execute at all.
>
> There was a silence. I went on to say that if it was right to torture and execute at all, it was not right to distinguish between male and female traitors. Such deep moral questions are easily solved by a moralist in the remote safety and comfort of a peace-time study; to the Resistance leaders faced with denunciation by traitorous fellow citizens, ethical niceties seemed academic and remote. Take for instance the member of the Deuxieme Bureau who usually worked the mobile forge at Les Sauvages to heat the torturing irons. When I remarked that he seemed to derive pleasure from his task, the others quickly turned on me and said

that this man's whole family had been wiped out by Nazis after a Vichy traitor had told the Germans that they were assisting the FFI.

Jordan was plagued by doubts about the effectiveness of torture and beset by moral qualms concerning its intrinsic evil.

Suppose they tortured the innocent? The visiting officer brought up that question and received the reply that every Vichy agent brought to Les Sauvages had been arrested only after he had been watched in his city or town over a period. All were seen to pay regular visits to Gestapo headquarters. Some had been trapped as a result of letters written by other Vichy agents already captured.

Besides, it was pointed out, valuable information had been obtained from all of them after they had undergone torture. There was one exception, the man who had the red-hot iron inserted in his rectum. He had told the Maquis nothing.

Was he innocent? I shall never know. But it is a terrible matter to ponder.

The usual method of inducing the victims to talk with the aid of hot irons was to poke one iron into the stomach, while another interrogator standing behind the victim placed a hot iron hard against his back, giving him the impression that the iron pressed in his stomach had penetrated right through his body.[57]

The indication from this passage is that torture was not an exceptional measure, but a standard procedure, and a routine method of extracting information. Captured Germans were also held prisoner at Les Sauvages. According to Jordan, 'Members of the Gestapo we captured were shot, after as much information as could be tortured out of them had been obtained.'[58]

Many accounts of resistance have economized with the truth and have wrapped themselves in silence over the morally outrageous aspects of the resistance struggle – and this in itself is an indictment of such methods. It is possible to learn a great deal by examining what histories of resistance do not say. Nevertheless, the failure to acknowledge the existence of this more hideous side of resistance is a serious omission and a distortion of the historical record. Significantly, the passages cited above from Duras and Jordan are not referred to, or cited, in any general history of resistance, nor is the taboo subject of torture by the resistance alluded to. Up to a point this is understandable, because the torturers virtually never wrote about their activities. Therefore, it is difficult to gauge just how widespread the use of torture was – given the clandestinity which surrounded it, and the natural reticence to admit personal participation in it, after the war had ended. Whether the experience of Duras and Jordan was typical or representative remains open. Nevertheless, the use of torture seems to have been more commonplace than has previously been imagined or acknowledged and cannot be dismissed as mere episodic excess or isolated aberration. These chilling accounts of torture by the Resistance should prompt reflection, so that we rest under no illusion about the nature of the underground struggle. As Bill Jordan put it, 'This was war at its dirtiest and bitterest. . . . Dirty, stinking, treacherous war . . .'.[59] He concluded, 'I had seen enough in France to last me a lifetime.'[60]

Taken together, the admission of personal involvement in torture by Duras, and the eye-witness evidence of Jordan, who later became a Roman Catholic priest, requires us to call for a reassessment, a need to demythologize the resistance experience, and to acknowledge its darker side. What is perhaps most disturbing is the ease with which some resisters had become coarsened, injured to cruelty and brutalized by their participation in the infliction of pain. Resisters could be brutal beyond measure in their absence of feeling for the despised traitor who had become dehumanized into an abstraction: 'the enemy'. Resistance to Nazism prided itself on its humanitarian goals, and its defence of civilized values. Resisters passed implicit judgement on themselves by overstepping the limits and restrictions which are the hallmark of the just war tradition and by violating the basic human rights which they proclaimed Jean-Paul Sartre's words, in condemning French torture in Algeria are also a tacit judgement by a former resister upon the resistance

> In 1943, in the Rue Lauriston [the Gestapo headquarters in Paris Frenchmen were screaming in agony and pain: all France could hear them . . . one thing seemed impossible in any circumstances that one day men should be made to scream by those acting in our name.[61]

By waging war without restraint, by resorting to the torture of suspected informers and collaborators, and the mutilation and torture of captured German soldiers, the resistance sacrificed something of its own moral case. A hitherto unbreachable moral barrier had been overcome. If the moral code which forbids torture is removed, what barriers are left? If torture goes, then what is left to prohibit? Even in the midst of a savage, atrocity-filled war, was torture justifiable? Could it be defended by arguments of military necessity, or even military convenience? Or was this an attempt to excuse the inexcusable? Are some means impermissible even when employed in an overwhelmingly just cause?

The conflict between the Allies and the Axis was a moral as well as a military conflict, and these methods of resistance meant losing some of the moral standing to which the resisters' cause would otherwise have been entitled. The war against the Nazi occupation was a struggle to defend certain basic values, yet the prosecution of that war witnessed the crumbling of resistance standards. To the Allies' shame, civilized constraints, considerations of morality rooted in the just war tradition, were abandoned. The resistance doctor at Les Sauvages who had to treat the tortured informers, reflected on the moral problems raised by torture, and the French Resistance's policy of executing German prisoners as a reprisal for the killing of resisters: 'all the war would have done to them would be to have reduced Frenchman to the barbaric level of the Germans'.[62] This was the considered judgement of a man who had himself been tortured by the Gestapo. The employment of torture against the enemy grievously disfigured the resistance's own image and defaced its humanistic ideals. By resorting to the degrading treatment of the enemy, they had degraded themselves. By the use of torture, and by adopting the German doctrine of collective responsibility in killing the families of collaborators, resisters had employed the very same intimidatory and terrorist tactics that they condemned in the Nazis. Such methods were a blot on the resistance record, and remain a serious query against the conduct of underground warfare. By steeling themselves to the immoral consequences of their own acts, did resisters risk destroying what they were fighting for – respect for the dignity and value of a single human life? By crossing the line and committing those deeds, had they destroyed something, not just in the enemy, but in themselves: the thing that they valued more than life itself – the reason for resistance?

SABOTAGE

Whereas the justification of assassinations was a persistently controversial question, sabotage was commonly acknowledged to be a legitimate measure, particularly when directed against strategically important targets such as munitions dumps, submarine bases, aircraft factories and troop trains. The cumulative effect of repeated sabotage, it was argued, would seriously weaken the German war effort.

It was impossible for the Germans to superintend the whole of occupied Europe's vast network of industry, transport and communications. It was relatively easy to engage in unattributable acts of small-scale sabotage that were hard to recognize, making them look like human error, or normal wear and tear – draining oil from a gearbox; loosening bolts on a railway track; fraying a cable; throwing the wrong switch, or switching labels. These forms of industrial sabotage were easier to disguise and more effective than the assassination of troops. More substantial acts of sabotage, however, raised urgent moral questions for those who wanted to fight as cleanly as possible.

The dilemma for resisters consisted in balancing the damage inflicted upon the German war machine against the inevitability of collective punishment. But this could not be measured or calculated in any precise way because of the unpredictability and inconsistency of the German response to various forms of sabotage. Whereas the assassination of German personnel operated according to fixed tariffs and penalties, sabotage was not governed by exact quotas, and thus there was no clear correlation between an act of sabotage, the extent of damage, and the scale of reprisal. All that resisters could anticipate was that sabotage would bring severe retaliation, and that in virtually every act of violence, they endangered the lives of others. The general guideline to the German Army stipulated that:

> For an attack against important war installations, up to 100 hostages are to be shot to death, according to the seriousness of the case.[63]

This left considerable discretion for commanders in the field to determine the seriousness of a given act of sabotage, and how many hostage victims to select. The arbitrary judgement of German officers made it difficult, if not impossible, for resisters to gauge their

likely response. For an attack upon a relatively unimportant rail-
road patrol in Serbia, 125 hostages were shot and the population
of two villages deported, but for the destruction of the strategically important Gorgopotomos viaduct in Greece, 'only' 13 hostages were shot.

In Denmark the Germans exercised self-restraint. According to
the testimony of Jodl at Nuremberg, Hitler had stipulated that:

If a Danish factory working for Germany is blown up . . . then a
factory working solely for the Danes will be blown up also.[64]

By contrast, when gypsies were herded into Jewish ghettos,
Himmler, who saw them as born agitators and a potential source
of sabotage, ordered ten gypsy lives for every arson incident:

You will discover that the Gypsies . . . will be the best firemen
you ever had.[65]

In eastern Europe and the Balkans, the scale of reprisal often
bore no relationship to the level of sabotage. Disproportionate
reprisals were, however, commonplace. In one incident from the
grim catalogue of war crimes in Poland, the theft of a rifle and an
act of anti-German vandalism resulted in the execution of 10 hostages.[66] In Greece, an attempt to sabotage a searchlight resulted in
the death of 18 hostages, and in reprisal for the destruction of 16
aircraft by Greek saboteurs, 50 hostages were shot.[67] As a fitting
punishment for the destruction of twelve telegraph poles outside
the Greek town of Arta, twelve men were hanged in public: a life
for each telegraph pole.[68] In July 1943, 50 Greeks were shot at
Melaxa for destroying some cable lines. An additional 40 hostages
were arrested and the population notified that for every additional
act of cable sabotage, ten hostages would be shot. For an attack
upon railway lines near Litochoron, 50 Communists were shot and
four villages burned down. In general, hostage and reprisal killings
for railway sabotage were out of all proportion to the nature of
the offence.

In the Soviet Union, the scale and savagery of German retribution almost defies belief. Because of repeated sabotage in the city
of Kiev, local commanders were given extreme discretion in their
anti-guerrilla struggle. After some acts of arson in November 1941,
the 454th Security Division reported:

A total of 800 inhabitants were shot as a reprisal measure for acts of sabotage.[69]

Shortly afterwards the mayor of Kiev issued a 'Public Notice' following another act of sabotage:

> In Kiev a communication installation was maliciously damaged. Since the perpetrators could not be traced, 400 Kiev citizens were shot.[70]

Before retreating, the partisans engaged in the extensive laying of mines in towns. The response of German security was to threaten capital punishment for any inhabitant who failed to report any information about the existence of explosives. In the Crimean town of Simferopol the authorities declared:

> For every building in the town of Simferopol which is scheduled to be blown up, and which has not been reported to the mine reporting agency, ONE HUNDRED inhabitants, each of the town of Simferopol, WILL BE SHOT as a reprisal measure on the part of the German occupation troops.[71]

The most extreme punishment was the execution of 1300 Russians in January 1943 as a reprisal for a partisan attack upon the Crimean town of Eupatoria.

THE USE OF HUMAN SHIELDS: PROPHYLACTIC REPRISALS

Given the key role of communications and transportation in modern warfare, the destruction of the enemy's transport system – derailing or blowing up troop trains and supply trains, bridges, cutting telegraph and telephone wires – was a vitally important part of resistance sabotage. In order to counter this threat, German security policy reverted to an ingenious method of protection which originated in the Franco-Prussian War of 1870–71: *prophylactic reprisals*. In that war, attempts to wreck trains in north-eastern France became so common that the Prussian authorities issued an order that the trains should:

be accompanied by inhabitants who are well known and generally respected, and *who should be placed upon the locomotive*, so that it may be made known that every accident caused by the hostility of the inhabitants will, in the first place, injure their countrymen.[72]

In addition to this practice of exposing civilian hostages to danger as a form of preventative retaliation, the Prussians published warnings that wherever trains or adjoining telegraph lines were sabotaged, ten men from the nearest town or village would be shot. This policy was completely successful, and no sabotage occurred on trains which carried local notables.

More recently, the practice of using civilians as human shields was adopted in the Boer War by the British, who cited the successful precedent set by the Prussians as a justification for their own anti-guerrilla campaign. As a preventative measure, Kitchener and Lord Roberts sanctioned the use of civilian hostages – usually selected from prominent Boer citizens, coupled with the publication of lists of prospective hostages, drawn up in order to establish a pool of hostages who would travel in rotation on various lines. These 'free excursion tickets' as they were known at the time, varied in their method of implementation: on some trains prominent burghers were given first-class accommodation and rations, on the other trains they were placed on open trucks in front of the engine. In the Second World War, the practice of using prophylactic reprisals was revived with further variations. On occasion, the Germans chained civilian hostages to the outside of locomotives, but more commonly they resorted to a 'hostage cage': a low-sided open wagon covered in barbed wire, and attached to the front of the engine, as a deterrent measure. These steel cages were used extensively in Greece, in order to prevent train sabotage. Even in the relatively 'mild' occupation conditions of Denmark, the High Command of the Wehrmacht ordered captured saboteurs and important public figures to ride as hostages to guarantee their troop trains. In the event of sabotage, they would be shot on the spot.[73] Railway sabotage reached such proportions in Luxembourg that the German Gauleiter Simon ordered all troop trains to be preceded at a short distance by a train carrying Luxembourg civilians, in order that it would absorb the impact of any explosive charges detonated by the Resistance.

Thus the ruthless ingenuity of German security posed the most cruel dilemma for resisters: whether to blow up a train in order to secure a military advantage, however minor, or to spare the lives of innocent people by giving in to terror tactics. In the event of sabotaging the tracks or water towers instead of the train, the lives of the hostages would still be forfeited. Motorized convoys operating in the mountains of Greece and Yugoslavia employed the same technique, on occasions, by strapping hostages onto the bonnets of vehicles. In France in June 1944, the *Das Reich* SS armoured division was constantly delayed by resistance units. In order to counteract this threat, they used:

> eighty prisoners tied to the front of the tanks as hostages to deter maquis attacks.[74]

A Wehrmacht General Order of 17 August 1944 declared:

> to make an end, act brutally and with no consideration whatever; for instance, place women in the front of vehicles when crossing country infested with [guerrilla] bands.[75]

Poles captured by the Germans were frequently used as human screens for German tanks attacking insurgent positions, or to dismantle barricades and remove Germans killed and injured under fire.[76] During the 1944 Warsaw Uprising, German troops used children and teenagers as human barricades, and rows of hostages were forced to run in front of German tanks as a shield for attacking Panzer units. 'Women and children were commonly roped to the hulls of German tanks as a precaution against ambushes.'[77] In one street, German soldiers advanced behind civilians who had been tied to a horizontally placed ladder as cover. The Polish Home Army commander ordered his men to fire, even though many of his innocent fellow countrymen died as well as German soldiers. He justified his action by arguing that the failure to do so would have been taken as a sign of weakness, and would have encouraged the Germans to resort to this tactic throughout Warsaw.

Equally severe security measures were adopted in occupied Russia in order to counteract the partisan threat to German supplies and communications in the 'Battle of the Rails'. With very few roads in European Russia, and many of those impassable from late autumn to spring, the safe-guarding of the railway system was essential to the German war effort. The local population was to be made answerable for the safety and protection of rail links in areas of partisan activity behind German lines:

hostages are to be seized and it is to be made known to the inhabitants that for every assault against the railway a number of the hostages are to be shot. This measure is to be ruthlessly enforced. [78]

A typical German rear areas' security report against surprise attacks states:

> It is vital that such acts are countered with ruthless reprisal measures.
>
> In future hostages are to be seized ON ALL stretches of railway and military tracks that are to be secured. For every successful attack at least 5 hostages are TO BE HANGED AT THE PLACE WHERE THE ATTACK OCCURRED. The hostages, without regard to gender, are to be seized from the localities in the vicinity of the threatened stretches and from areas sympathetic to the partisans.[79]

With blockhouses containing large numbers of security troops established at regular intervals, and armoured trains, the German Army was taking no chances. Forests, villages and huts were cleared in the immediate vicinity of railway lines, and a no-man's-land was created: a security zone 300 yards wide on both sides of the track. Security forces operated a shoot-on-sight policy for any unauthorized personnel.

Large numbers of Russian civilians were employed as forced labour on the railways, and Russians were also used to guard the track, with their families taken as hostages to ensure compliance:

> Russians were recruited to serve as voice-alarm sentries. Posted at intervals along the line, they were to warn the nearest German guard-post by shouting whenever they spotted partisans, and then take cover. Theirs was an unenviable position, for they and their families were subject to reprisals by the partisans if they did their job well, and to rigorous punishment by the Germans if they did not.[80]

The German Commander of Army Group South ordered that:

> in case of sabotage to railway tracks, hostages were to be strung up from poles along the lines as a reminder of the consequences of such action....[81]

One commander stipulated:

> In case of sabotage of telephone lines, railway lines, etc, sentries
> will be posted selected from the civilian population. In case of
> repetition, the sentry on whose beat the sabotage was committed
> will be shot. Suitable as sentries are only those people who have
> a family who can be apprehended in case the sentry escapes.[82]

The Germans also considered the use of human shields in areas of
occupied France which were particularly exposed to RAF bombing
raids. General Warlimont asked the Commander-in-Chief of the
German Army in Western Europe to examine the possibility of
reprisal measures against the relatives of French resisters in London, and relatives of well-known French resisters in hiding.

> We might . . . study the question of whether these families should
> be interned in regions particularly exposed to air attacks; for
> instance in the vicinity of dams, or in industrial regions which
> are bombed often.[83]

In Holland, 460 prominent Dutchmen were taken as hostages in
order to put pressure on the Dutch government-in-exile to stop its
BBC propaganda broadcasts.

GUERRILLA WAR, THE LAWS OF WAR AND THE CIVILIAN POPULATION

> But peasants are a silent people, without a literary voice, nor do
> they write complaints or memoirs.
>
> Alexander Solzhenitsyn[84]

> The Russians have now ordered partisan warfare behind our front.
> This partisan war has some advantages for us; it enables us to
> eradicate everyone who opposes us.[85]
>
> Hitler

What is most striking in this brief study of guerrilla war is the
manner in which the struggle between the partisans and German
anti-guerrilla security forces was waged with complete disregard
for the life and suffering of the ordinary civilian population. In

Minsk, German security foiled a partisan plan to poison the city's water supply, which would have killed large numbers of unsuspecting Soviet citizens, as well as German troops. Similarly, in Kharkov the partisans attempted to create an epidemic by polluting the water supply, but again the plan failed.[86] In occupied Russia civilians were: 'caught between the Soviet hammer and the Nazi anvil'.[87] The same could be said of the mass of peasantry throughout occupied eastern Europe: trapped between the guerrillas and the anti-guerrilla forces. The war was conducted with a maximum of cruelty and a minimum of humanity, and civilians caught between the opposing forces suffered the most.

The essence of partisan war is that the guerrillas are invisible: they hide in the countryside concealed among, and indistinguishable from, the civilian population. Guerrilla war has no battle-fronts; its aim is not direct confrontation with the uniformed enemy in set-piece battle, but rather hit-and-run raids, or 'shoot-and-scoot' warfare. It is a form of war without fronts and rear areas, fought by an evasive enemy which employs the methods of surprise attacks, sudden ambush by apparent civilians, concealment, sniper fire and booby-trap mines in order to harass and hamper the enemy's supply lines and communications. Partisans use intimidation and coercion as a political weapon to establish control over villages and areas which do not show sufficient zeal or commitment to the national cause. Djilas described how the Communists treated any denial of their authority 'as an aid to the enemy'.[88] Thus, the indigenous civilian population is coerced into providing food, temporary shelter and 'safe houses' to store weapons and equipment, and is threatened with punishment for non-cooperation. When the guerrillas evacuate an area, the villagers are left to face the questions and suspicions of the enemy army. They are terrorized by the partisans because their prudence and caution is perceived as passive collaboration. They are terrorized by the enemy army because their caution is taken as a sign of passive resistance, or 'hidden cooperation' with the partisans. In many villages German troops lined up women and children on one side of the street, and men and boys on the other. The women were informed that unless they identified the perpetrators of attacks, the men would be killed and the village burned. Usually partisans had no connection with the village, so the inhabitants were powerless to prevent slaughter and the reduction of their village to rubble and ashes. In Yugoslavia, German security forces warned the inhabitants that unless they volunteered information concerning the location of partisan bands, the number of men missing from the village, and the names of strangers, drastic measures would be taken – including hostages from the male population. Nuremberg Trial documents reveal:

> The pattern of terror and intimidation was simple. . . . When there were no volunteers, priests . . . teachers . . . farmers . . . sometimes just every third, fifth, or tenth man – were called out of ranks and loaded in lorries for shipment to the division's hostage camp. . . . Whether to save one's husband, father, or son by re-vealing that a neighbour's brother had joined the bands or was absent from the village, was a difficult choice for those who re-mained. Sometimes men or women weakened.[89]

Villagers were subject to German reprisals for non-cooperation, and guerrilla counter-reprisals for co-operation with the enemy. 'In most areas a man had no choice but to join either a guerrilla or an anti-guerrilla group. The decision was fathered by necessity . . . supporting the Germans or the guerrillas was largely a matter of expediency, since it was not possible to protect oneself from both at the same time.'[90] Djilas describes the slaughter of the popula-tion of the village of Hurije – men, women and children:

> The village was Serbian and 'guilty' in the sense that our units had spent the night there, despite the villagers' protests that they might have to suffer for it.[91]

In some areas of the Balkans and eastern Europe, the exploita-tion and blackmail of the civilian population was supplemented by torture. This was fairly common among Greek Communist parti-sans. Bill Jordan describes the ruthless methods of Aris, one of the leaders of the Greek Communists:

> To him, if a Greek was not a Communist, he was an enemy. If a prominent Greek refused to join him, Aris had him either flogged or executed.

Jordan had spoken to several witnesses who confirmed that 'Aris had had several patriotic Greeks executed on trumped-up charges of collaboration' because they had pursued the wrong politics.[92] One of Jordan's fellow resisters described:

how he had seen Aris torture a Greek woman who refused to work for the Communists. He cut gashes in the woman's body, then had boiling oil poured into the wounds. Finally, he cut off her breasts. The woman died.[93]

British soldiers in Greece in 1945 entered one village freed from ELAS occupation and discovered a well 'containing the bodies of one hundred and fifty slaughtered women and children – the women almost invariably with their breasts amputated'.[94] Although this form of terrorist warfare was repugnant to most civilians, it could achieve its intended effect by immobilizing the population and making them responsive to the guerrillas demands, and unresponsive to the Germans' requests for co-operation, until they too employed such methods. Both sides played upon civilian insecurity rather than attempting to win the hearts and minds of the people. 'Between the violence and extortion of both occupants there was little to choose.'[95]

In Communist-controlled areas of Greece, levies were imposed on each village to supply ELAS with food and oil. Stocks of food had been severely depleted by the German occupation. In the village of Xeromerou, a peasant called Leonidas protested against Communist forced requisitions, and tried to save the village food supplies:

> The Communists dragged him into the street and felled him with rifle butts. In full view of the villagers . . . they clubbed . . . Leonidas to death . . . smashing his skull to pulp in as savage and cruel a crime as any they had committed in Greece. The horrified villagers were powerless to do anything to stop the atrocity; to intervene would have meant death. This was a bitter time for the Greek people. Over the years of the Axis occupation, they had become accustomed to the thieving raids of the enemy . . . now they had to submit to similar treatment from the Communists . . . the villagers could run away from the Germans . . . but from fellow Greeks there was nowhere to run; they were not safe anywhere. Villagers dared not congregate in groups in a Communist-occupied village for fear of being arrested for 'plotting against The People's Government'.[96]

Partisan war jeopardizes the most elementary principle of the laws of war: the guarantee of protection for civilians under the concept of non-combatant immunity. The laws of war – embodied in the Hague and Geneva Conventions – attempt to regulate and restrain warfare, and to limit violence and control its destructive effects in order to reduce the evils inherent in war. The aim of these restrictions is to prevent war from lapsing into barbarism, vengeance, uncontrolled destruction and indiscriminate killing. The central theme of the just war tradition is that war is evil, there is a moral presumption against war, and that is why waging war needs special justification.

In particular, the laws of war place a series of restrictions and prohibitions on what is, and what is not, a legitimate target for enemy attack; and they legally codify the moral principle which distinguishes between the killing of soldiers or combatants, and the killing of civilians or non-combatants. Civilians are immune from enemy attack. However, with the direct participation of irregular civilian warriors, which is characteristic of partisan warfare, the concepts of combatant and non-combatant become hopelessly blurred. It becomes almost impossible for uniformed, regular soldiers fighting against guerrillas, to tell friend from foe. Guerrillas do not carry arms openly. When they conceal themselves among the population, and apparent civilians are disguised combatants, this creates a climate which is especially conducive to atrocities by nervous, frustrated and trigger-happy troops. German captain Helmut Tausend described an incident in France after the armistice:

> A platoon of ours was walking on the outskirts of Clermont-Ferrand, they were passing a group of workers, some twenty or so . . . digging potatoes. Suddenly, these workers throw down their tools, grab for rifles, and shoot down fourteen of our men in a second. You call that 'partisan' resistance? I don't. Partisans for me are men that can be identified, men who wear a special armbank or a cap, something with which to recognize them. What happened in that potato field was murder . . . with these sorts of things happening . . . you've got to admit we had to take harsh measures.[97]

A moment's hesitation might lead to death, and therefore anti-partisan security forces are likely to shoot first and ask questions later. Insecurity is answered by resorting to terror, with the civilian population paying a heavy price for any damage that the guerrillas inflict.

The moral problem for this form of resistance is that for the guerrillas to succeed, they rely upon and presume that their uniformed opponents will respect the principle of non-combatant immunity: that civilians (for example peasants digging potatoes) should not be targeted or attacked. Indeed, there would be no point in hiding among civilians for safety if this were not the case. Guerrillas deliberately use and abuse their non-combatant status as a cloak to cover their military operations. But the whole nature of partisan war and the adoption of civilian disguise is such as to undermine the principle of non-combatant immunity which offers protection for innocent civilians. This leads to the problem that if the partisans do not respect or adhere to this crucial feature of the laws of war, but simply exploit it for their own military advantage by using civilian clothing as a disguise or ruse, then:

> If the partisans don't maintain the distinction of soldiers and civilians, why should they?[98]

This was precisely the view that the Germans took. Guerrilla war was incompatible with the restraints on battle built into the laws of war, and the partisans failed to meet the requirements of lawful belligerency. The German army of occupation in the Balkans and the USSR argued that because the enemy was invisible, then they could not be sure who the enemy combatants were, and therefore they could not restrain themselves in fighting against the partisans, and those who might be helping them. They saw terrorists in every civilian. Fear of reprisal was the only deterrent to ensure compliance with the laws of war. An affidavit from a German officer, Klaus Goernandt, at the Nuremberg Trials, encapsulated the frustration of regular troops about irregular warfare:

> Hardly any distinction could be made between combatants and non-combatants, since the combatants lacked any standard uniform. . . .
>   The army was bitter because it had to fight in the dark against an enemy who claimed the rights of a non-combatant in civilian clothes when the situation became critical.[99]

The Hague Convention works to the advantage of the population of a country under occupation, by guaranteeing protection for non-combatants. From the German perspective, however, if the civilian population supported, or directly engaged in, irregular warfare, then they must be subject to the irregular punishments which fell outside the provisions of the Hague Convention. The prevailing German view was that wars should be fought between legitimate, uniformed, trained national armies. 'Civilians should be spectators, not participants.'[100] War is a fight between states. Guerrilla war was not war in the strictest sense of the word, but banditry. This encapsulates a widespread belief throughout the German Army that partisan warfare was an insidious, uncivilized, illegal form of violence conducted by 'terrorists' or 'francs-tireurs'. Extraordinary measures such as hostage-taking, reprisal killings, the use of human shields, were justified, both as an insurance policy or deterrent, and as a punishment. It was a basic principle of German military justice that retribution and reprisals should be the answer to banditry:

> From the Fuhrer in Berlin to the lowliest infantryman in Serbia or Southern France, the Germans considered guerrilla warfare to be simple murder.[101]

PRISONERS OF WAR

Reprisals against prisoners of war are expressly forbidden by the 1929 Geneva Convention. However, it is common practice in guerrilla war for no prisoners to be taken alive, and for wounded soldiers who fall into enemy hands to be slaughtered. Because the Germans regarded the partisans as bandits and not legitimate fighters, they were not accorded prisoner-of-war status. Because partisans have no permanent base for detaining enemy troops they too are invariably killed. Djilas records how

> the Partisans gave the Germans measure for measure and killed their prisoners . . . nor could we in the leadership come up with any reason to oppose this.[102]

On another occasion, Communist Partisans negotiated a safe surrender of rival Serbian Chetnik troops with 'promises that they would be tried after the war. . . . Twenty-three Chetniks surrendered, and the Partisans shot them all'.[103] Djilas felt moral qualms out of 'an inherited respect for one's word of honour', but he added 'What else could you have done? You had no prison. You could hardly have dragged them along with you for months in the hills.'[104] Djilas adds 'we decided to deal severely with the Chetniks: to burn down their houses and take no prisoners'.[105]

A 1943 directive from the First Bosnian Partisan Corps sanctioned mass murder against the civilian population in pro-Chetnik areas:

> Often the confiscation of property is not a sufficient punishment against regions attached to the Chetniks. There are cases when it is necessary to burn whole villages and destroy the populations.[106]

The partisans imitated the Nazis' arithmetical calculations and decreed that ten 'traitors' – anti-Communists – were to be killed for the loss of each partisan. Towards the end of the war 700 White Guard collaborationist troops had taken refuge in the castle of Turjak in Slovenia. The guerrillas stormed the castle, and then, according to Djilas, 'the Partisans wiped out all the Turjak prisoners'. Djilas asked Kardelj whether this was necessary:

> 'But why did you have to kill them all?'
> 'That ought to demoralize them!' Kardelj replied with a knowing smile.[107]

Prior to the infamous massacre of an estimated 1830 Italians in the commune of Marzabotto, 15 miles south of Bologna, in September 1944, repeated partisan attacks in the area of Monte Sole had resulted in a number of atrocities against German soldiers and collaborators. One alleged informer 'was buried to his shoulders in a cornfield and kicked like a soccer ball until his head tore loose from his body'.[108] In one incident, partisans attacked a German truck, killed the driver and left another soldier for dead. When another group of partisans reached the scene they found a local doctor treating the injured German:

> 'Is there any chance he will live?' one of the partisans asked.
> 'I think he will', the doctor said.
> The partisans emptied their Sten guns into the patient.[109]

At the same time two other German soldiers were captured by a patrol of partisans in a nearby village.

While the Germans were holding their hands in the air in surrender, one of them was shot down. The other was taken to a
partisan encampment where he pulled out his wallet, showed
pictures of his wife and babies, and begged for mercy. He was
strung up on a pole, head down, his hands pinned to the ground
by knives, and left to die in the sun.[110]

It was in this context of reciprocated savagery and provocation that
the Marzabotto murders took place. 'Soon the whole area of Monte
Sole had become involved in a dialogue of death and torture.'[111]
The shadow war was undeniably savage and yielded a harvest of
hatred. In places the severed heads of slaughtered German prisoners were booby-trapped, and fixed on stakes in such a manner that
if they were touched they would trigger hidden land-mines.[112] In
France the Communist 'Francs-Tireurs-et-Partisans' (FTP) frequently
shot captured German troops out of hand. At Vannes a number of
German prisoners were executed by the Resistance.[113] After the
surrender of Waffen SS troops at Tulle on 9th June 1944 the FTP
executed and mutilated a large number of prisoners in retaliation
for the previous German reprisal in the town. Although there was
a tendency to dismiss these atrocity stories as Nazi propaganda, a
leading member of the Secret Army in the Correze region confirmed that the allegations were true.[114] After the Germans had
shot 80 captured partisans whom they did not recognize as legitimate prisoners-of-war, the French Resistance at Annency in southern
France shot 80 German prisoners who had surrendered, as a reprisal
measure, in August 1944.[115] The Resistance had publicly announced
that the 3000 Germans captured in the area would be protected as
prisoners-of-war in conformity with the 1929 Geneva Convention.
Although an understandable retaliation, the killing of the 80 Germans
was unlawful, and in flagrant violation of the Convention, which
strictly prohibits reprisals against prisoners-of-war. The International
Committee of the Red Cross condemned the French for treating
the soldiers as political hostages, and for carrying out illegal reprisals. General De Gaulle had previously discussed the question
of prisoners-of-war with Professor Burckhardt of the Red Cross:

> The leader of Free France had affirmed, and had repeated it in
> the presence of the Red Cross representative, that he was going
> to shoot 10 Germans captured by his troops for each of his own
> men captured whom the Nazis would dare to touch.[116]

At Les Sauvages, captured Germans were executed in reprisal for Maquis prisoners. The German Commandant in the capital of the Lozere Department was given a letter 'explaining why . . . two men had been executed, and threatening that for every Frenchman shot, two Germans would face a firing squad'.[117] In December 1943 Greek Communist partisans in the interior of the Peloponnese captured 80 German soldiers, and pushed them over a mountain precipice. German retribution for this action was the destruction of the village of Kalavryta. The entire male population, 511 men, were machine-gunned or burned to death in reprisal, and a further 24 villages in the mountains around Kalavryta were destroyed. After the war 1200 graves of reprisal victims were discovered.

DOUBLE STANDARDS AND RESISTANCE

Actions are held to be good or bad, not on their own merits but according to who does them, and there is almost no outrage – torture, the use of hostages, forced labour . . . imprisonment without trial . . . assassination, the bombing of civilians – which does not change its moral colour when it is committed by 'our' side. . . .

The nationalist not only does not disapprove of atrocities committed by his own side, but he has a remarkable capacity for not even hearing about them.

There is no crime, absolutely none, that cannot be condoned when 'our' side commits it . . . even if one knows that it is exactly the same crime as one has condemned in some other case.

George Orwell[118]

Guerrilla war is the antithesis of war based upon moral limitations grounded in just war theory. In guerrilla war, restraint is discarded by both sides as a matter of course. Ruthless slaughter and merciless execution, reprisals, counter-reprisals, atrocities and hostage-killings become routine occurrences, inseparable from the essence of guerrilla warfare. The partisans were as little bound by the Hague and Geneva Conventions, or by qualms over non-combatant immunity, as the Germans. Both sides waged unlimited, lawless war, refused to give quarter, and resorted to any and every means to secure their goal. Both sides exhibited double standards in the propaganda war, accusing each other of atrocities and war crimes, while turning a blind eye to their own violations of the laws of war. What each said about the other was usually true. Each relied on the other's crimes to justify themselves. The Germans wanted all the rights which protected them from attack by guerrillas, but did not feel bound themselves to adhere to their obligation to protect the civilian population, enshrined in Article 50 of the 1907 Hague Convention, which expressly prohibits collective punishments for individual acts. The primary responsibility rests with the Nazi regime, and ultimately with Hitler, for removing all restrictions on battle on the eastern front. But the greater crime does not excuse the lesser. Partisans conducted the war with great inhumanity and committed acts which were contrary to the rules of engagement and were in blatant disregard for the usages and customs of war. The issue of serious violations of the laws of war by partisans cannot be ignored. It is important to avoid glossing over the more questionable aspects of partisan war and to confront inconvenient facts. This allows us to form a less romantic, more realistic picture of resistance. In the pervasive atmosphere of insecurity the real losers were the hapless civilian, peasant population. The morally corrosive and destructive quality of partisan war must be acknowledged.

What is surprising is not the Germans' indifference to the lives of foreigners and 'sub-humans', but the unconcern of the partisans for the lives of their own fellow-countrymen, and the profligacy with which they deliberately provoked the Germans into massive reprisals against innocent civilians. The Germans widely publicized the fact that if they were fired upon from any village, the village would be burned down. By carrying the war into the villages, and embedding themselves in dense civilian areas disguised as non-combatants, the partisans knowingly exposed the population to grave harm. A report from a German Brigade Commander on the atrocities of an SS unit at Popovaca village in Bosnia after it had been attacked by the partisans illustrates the erosion of non-combatant immunity:

> The unit commander reported . . . that when he had to retreat, he had killed all persons who were in the open because he had no chance to distinguish between the loyal population and the partisans. He himself said that he killed about a hundred persons in this incident.[119]

n addition to violating the principle of civilian immunity, the ratio
of innocent bystanders to combatants was also incompatible with
he principle of proportionality. Moral blame must be attached to
he guerrillas for enlarging the area of civilian death and damage.
The fundamental flaw in the doctrine of collective responsibility as
a deterrent lay in the fact that the perpetrators might not suffer at
all, and might be completely indifferent to the suffering of those
on whom the punishment fell. It is difficult to avoid the conclusion
that Communist partisans did not particularly care what happened
to their own people as long as they could inflict damage on the
Germans and further their own political objectives.

There has been a reluctance to discuss resistance crimes, and a
willingness to keep silent about atrocities committed by the partisans. The French resister Albert Camus pointed to the dangers of
moral amnesia and 'the art of forgetting . . . must we really be willing to forget all that is bad on one side to fight what is worse on
the other?'[120] It is necessary to avoid selective moral indignation
whereby our attitude is determined not by what happens but by
who does it. It is important to apply the same stringent standards
of international humanitarian law consistently, and to avoid con-
niving at terror and human rights' violations by our own side. Justice Jackson, the Chief Prosecutor for the United States at the
Nuremberg Trials, articulated the fundamental principle that the
record by which we judged the Germans is the record by which
history will judge us:

> If certain acts . . . are crimes, they are crimes whether the United
> States does them or whether Germany does them. We are not
> prepared to lay down a rule of criminal conduct against others
> which we would not be willing to have invoked against us.[121]

This surely is the yardstick by which resistance must be measured.
There cannot be a different benchmark for the partisans and for
German anti-partisan forces. Murder, torture, unspeakable mutilations, the execution of defenceless prisoners-of-war, the taking and
killing of hostages, are war crimes whether committed by the Nazis
or by the Resistance. Above all, it is important to avoid the double
standard of judging the partisans solely by their ends, and the
Germans by their means. The idea that all was permitted against
Nazism dehumanized the enemy, and also removed the crucial just
war protection of the need to avoid wanton destruction, unnecessary

bloodshed and prohibitive casualties among one's own population
The cumulative effect of guerrilla warfare was to engender more
barbarism and bestiality, and to further erode the elementary protection offered by the laws of war. Partisans progressively discarded
humanitarian restraints, imitated the methods of the enemy, and added to the inhumanity the Resistance had committed itself to oppose
Resistance means were often incompatible with resistance ends.

7 Jewish Resistance/Jewish 'Collaboration'

Most of the many discussions of Jewish resistance appear as a mixture of folly and obscenity.[1]

Emil Fackenheim

When the Jews were being murdered, the world was indifferent. Now it asks why the Jews did not fight.[2]

Elie Wiesel

I believe that no-one is authorized to judge them, not even those who lived through the experience of the Lager [concentration camp] and even less those who did not live through it. I would invite anyone who dares pass judgment to carry out upon himself, with sincerity, a conceptual experiment: let him imagine, if he can, that he has lived for months or years in a ghetto, tormented by chronic hunger, fatigue ... and humiliation; that he has seen die around him, one-by-one, his beloved; that he is cut off from the world, unable to receive or transmit news; that finally, he is loaded on to a train, eighty or a hundred persons to a boxcar, that he travels towards the unknown, blindly, for sleepless days and nights; and that he is at last flung inside the walls of an indecipherable inferno. [He is then offered] a rigid either/or, immediate obedience or death.[3]

Primo Levi

The moral issues surrounding Jewish resistance and 'collaboration' during the Holocaust are infinitely complex and controversial. At the heart of the controversy is the often reiterated, but insensitive question: why did the Jews go like sheep to the slaughter? Why did they do so little to prevent their own destruction? This question hangs over the subject, dominates the discussion and sets the tone for the detailed analysis of Jewish Resistance. Following on from the charge of passivity, there is the allegation that the leaders of the Jewish Councils, or *Judenrate*, collaborated with the Nazis, and thus participated in their own people's destruction. The charge of collaboration cannot be discussed in isolation, it has to be examined simultaneously with its alternative: resistance.

In January 1942 in the Vilna Ghetto in Lithuania, a young poet called Abba Kovner issued a call for resistance which was full of biblical symbolism. It declared:

> Let us not be led like sheep to the slaughter.[4]

Since then that famous phrase 'like sheep to the slaughter' has been taken out of its immediate, original context, and used as a coded message to indicate a stereotype of Jewish behaviour – namely passivity, fatalistic resignation and acquiescence in the face of Nazism. Kovner himself has stated that the phrase 'haunts me wherever I go'[5] because it has become distorted and twisted into something he did not intend when he coined it in early 1942. Kovner's declaration has been turned into a loaded question which points the finger of accusation at Jews themselves: Why did the victims become passive accomplices in their own destruction?

RAUL HILBERG AND JEWISH 'PASSIVITY'

The image of Jewish passivity was painted most clearly in the work of one of the leading Jewish scholars of the Holocaust – Raul Hilberg's *The Destruction of the European Jews*. Hilberg reinforced the stereotype of the 'mass inertia'[6] of the Jews in response to the Nazi onslaught. In a strongly worded but highly controversial passage, he wrote:

> The reaction pattern of Jews is characterized by almost complete lack of resistance.... On a Europeanwide scale the Jews had no resistance organization, no blueprint for armed action, no plan even for psychological warfare. They were completely unprepared.... The Jews were not oriented toward resistance.[7]

Hilberg cited an interview that the Commandant of Treblinka, Franz Stangl, gave while serving in prison after the war. When asked about his reaction to the Jews, he said that:

> only recently he had read a book about lemmings. It reminded him of Treblinka.[8]

Hilberg interpreted Jewish behaviour during the Holocaust as a fatal symptom of Jewish history. Living as a minority in Christian Europe, Jews had to adapt to a hostile environment. In order to survive they had to compromise and to refrain from resistance. Lacking their own territory, Jews had learned that they could avert destruction by placating the rulers and peoples in whose lands they lived as unwelcome guests. Through the long history of Christian anti-semitism Jews had been persecuted, yet had endured. Their past experience had conditioned them to bend with the wind, and to ride out the present storm of persecution. Individuals, sometimes whole groups, perished, but the Jewish community had not been annihilated.

According to Hilberg, the Jewish response of accommodation and appeasement was so ingrained that by the time the Nazis were ready to implement the Final Solution, the Jews were 'caught in the straitjacket of their history'.[9] Jews were prepared for, and knew how to cope with, old-style European pogroms and persecution. But they were totally unprepared for the unprecedented conditions of Nazi domination. To summarize Hilberg's thesis: Jews were the prisoners of their past – a history of 2000 years of persecution answered by propitiation. Jews had no tradition of armed revolt, and this complete lack of physical resistance which had been a major strength in the past, was their major weakness when faced with the present Nazi extermination policy. The fate of Europe's Jews was sealed because they could not adjust to vastly changed circumstances.

A 2000-year-old lesson could not be unlearned; the Jews could not make the switch. They were helpless.[10]

Hilberg also argued that the extent of Jewish resistance was negligible. Because of the cult of martyrology which emerged after the Holocaust, and the desire not to offend the memory of the victims, there was a tendency on the part of Jewish writers to exaggerate or inflate the amount of armed resistance, and to avoid unpleasant facts. Nevertheless, the weight of evidence led Hilberg to the compelling conclusion:

Jews of all regions and all classes failed to resist in significant measure throughout the destruction process. Much as we would want to have it otherwise, we cannot increase the skirmishing to battle proportions without losing sight of reality.[11]

Outbreaks of Jewish resistance were infrequent, insignificant and inconsequential. In military terms Jewish resistance was ineffective and useless.

> Measured in German casualties, Jewish armed opposition shrinks into insignificance. . . . It is doubtful that the Germans and their collaborators lost more than a few hundred men, dead and wounded, in the course of the destruction process. . . . The Jewish resistance effort could not seriously impede or retard the progress of destructive operations. The Germans brushed that resistance aside as a minor obstacle, and in the totality of the destruction process it was of no consequence.[12]

Hilberg's analysis relied very heavily upon official German documents. These sources conformed to the stereotypical Nazi image of the docile, cringing, servile Jew, and, to put it mildly, did not paint a flattering portrait of Jewish behaviour under German control. Since the publication of the first edition of Hilberg's book in 1961, a great deal of new evidence has come to light which shows that the extent of Jewish armed resistance was considerably more widespread than Hilberg had assumed (although he remains convinced of his thesis, and has re-stated it in the revised, updated 1985 edition of the book). Numerous historians have progressively revised Hilberg's account and have offered a more qualified understanding of Jewish fighting resistance. A very different picture emerges when we examine Jewish, as opposed to German, documents from the same period.

It should be added that the question 'Why did Jews go like sheep to the slaughter?' was pondered by Jews themselves during the Nazi occupation. Thus Emmanuel Ringelblum, in his diary entry for October 15th 1942, asked:

> Why didn't we resist when they began to resettle 300,000 Jews from Warsaw? Why did we allow ourselves to be led like sheep to the slaughter? Why did everything come so easy to the enemy?[13]

Other ghetto diarists asked the same question. Thus it is not illegitimate *in itself* for Hilberg and for later generations to raise the question. Indeed, Hilberg quotes the passage from Ringelblum in support of his thesis of Jewish passivity.[14] However, Hilberg fails to cite Ringelblum's subsequent comment in which he rejects the option of armed resistance as 'no answer' because of the threat of collective responsibility. Thus, what for Ringelblum was a 'rhetorical question without an answer, a cry of despair over the utter hopelessness of their position', was turned after the war into an accusation. It was transformed into a caricature of the truth, into a bitter and harsh judgement upon the resignation of the victims, from the comfortable vantage point of personal immunity from the consequences of Nazi terror. It is dangerously easy to say that Jews should have resorted to armed struggle, and to romanticize violence at a safe distance – to engage in the vicarious pleasure of armchair resistance free from the consequences of collective responsibility, and free from the ravages of hunger which drove men and women on the verge of death to the deportation train in order to obtain the bread and marmalade promised by the German authorities.

Again, we have the gift of hindsight, and we should be aware of the perennial methodological problem of being wise after the event. We have to try to divest ourselves of this inestimable benefit – to peel away the accumulated layers of our historical knowledge of the full extent of the Holocaust – and to understand events as they emerged chronologically from mid-1941 onwards, and most crucially of all, *as they were seen at the time.*

What Jews experienced in some ghettos was radically different from other places. There seemed to be no clear pattern to German killings. For example, the speed of the Holocaust in Lithuania in 1941 contrasted with working ghettos, such as Bialystok which remained an oasis until mid-1943, and Lodz, which survived until the summer of 1944. Again, even where large numbers of Jews had been killed, so too had large numbers of Polish, Russian and Serb civilians. The distinctive nature of the Jewish Holocaust was partially obscured by widespread Nazi mass killings and reprisal measures against other occupied populations. What Jews lacked in many ghettos, until it was too late, was an accurate overall understanding of Nazi intentions. They did not have a clear appreciation of the full extent of the Final Solution. All that Jews knew with absolute certainty was that if they disobeyed any Nazi decrees, or if they resisted overtly, then fierce and disproportionate reprisals and punishments would be imposed. While Jews harboured the hope of an Allied victory in time to liberate them, armed resistance was rejected as a form of induced collective suicide. Where there was hope there was life. Thus Abraham Lewin wrote in his diary on June 5th 1942:

One of the most remarkable ... phenomena seen in the presen
war is the clinging to life, the almost complete cessation o
suicides ... people do not try to escape from life. In fact jus
the contrary: people are bound to life body and soul and wan
to survive the war at any price ... everybody ... wants to live to
see the outcome of this giant struggle. ... Old men have only
one wish: to live to see the end and to survive Hitler.[15]

The ghettos were rife with rumours, wild swings of mood from
hope to despair. Starved of accurate news, they fed on rumours o
German military reverses. 'Rumour is our daily food',[16] said
Emmanuel Ringelblum. Even the normally cautious Abraham Lewin
was prey to these illusions. On 26 May 1942, he wrote:

In the last few days I have become more and more certain that
the war will end this year – 1942 – by the time winter comes ...
    my clairvoyance is based on a sober appraisal of the facts. I
consider it a certainty that the Anglo-American invasion of Europe ... must come to fruition in the near future.[17]

While these hopes persisted, most Jews believed in the need to
avoid any incitement or provocation to the Germans; hence what
Ringelblum defined as the 'mute life instinct of the masses': each
extra day brought liberation closer. To survive was a victory over
Nazism, and thus:

not to act, not to lift a hand against the Germans, has become
the quiet, passive heroism of the common Jew.[18]

Under extreme circumstances, even self-restraint and the dogged
determination to survive, to outlast their persecutors, could be interpreted as a form of resistance.
    This leads on to the wider conceptual problem of definition. The
question arises: what do we include in, and exclude from, our definition of resistance? Hilberg offers a very narrow definition, limit-
ing Jewish resistance to *armed* resistance. 'Resistance is opposition
to the perpetrator.'[19] He equates resistance with physical force intended to stem the Nazi advance. But does only armed resistance
count as resistance? He excludes food smuggling, which many would
classify as economic resistance, and escape, and the struggle to stay
alive: 'to me, these evasion and alleviation reactions are not resist-

ance.'[20] Thus for Hilberg resistance means armed resistance, and the absence of armed resistance is taken to mean the absence of resistance as such, and therefore implies acquiescence to German rule. But a less restrictive definition would have to encompass non-violent dimensions of opposition, especially when these incurred the risk of punishment. The smuggling of food into the ghettos, often by Jewish children who were shot on the spot if caught, must be recognized and classified as a form of economic resistance. The Nazis prohibited the importation of any food into the ghettos other than the insufficient official rations. Smuggling preserved life and obstructed the Nazis' aims. Without the activities of smugglers, starvation would have succeeded in reducing the population much more rapidly.[21] In his diary Abraham Lewin wrote:

> Each piece of bread that we buy . . . is soaked with Jewish blood. . . .
> Under the present conditions smuggling is life's imperative.[22]

CULTURAL RESISTANCE

> to the last syllable of recorded time.
>
> Macbeth, Act 5, Scene 3

> I don't know whether anyone else is recording daily events. . . .
> Anyone who keeps a record endangers his life, but this does not frighten me. I sense within me the magnitude of this hour, and my responsibility towards it, and I have an inner awareness that I am fulfilling a national obligation, a historic obligation that I am not free to relinquish. . . . My record will serve as source material for the future historian.
> . . . a strange idea has stuck in my head since the war broke out – that it is a duty I must perform. This idea is like a flame imprisoned in my bones, burning within me, screaming: Record! Perhaps I am the only one engaged in this work, and that strengthens and encourages me.[23]
>
> Chaim A. Kaplan

Given that the Nazis regarded the Jews as sub-human, and routinely treated them in the most degrading ways, any cultural activities which affirmed their human dignity and their individual identity were forms of resistance to the dehumanizing techniques of the

Nazis. To perform whatever was forbidden was an act of resistance. Where there was no scope for peaceful methods of persuasion or protest, or for legal dissent, or for civil disobedience, then any opposition became resistance. Thus it is important to recognize the continuation of education and cultural life as examples of Jewish resistance. In his Warsaw Diary entry for 12 August 1940, Chaim Kaplan wrote:

> Public prayer in these dangerous times is a forbidden act. Anyone caught in this crime is doomed to severe punishment. If you will, it is even sabotage, and anyone engaging in sabotage is subject to execution. But this does not deter us.[24]

Kaplan's entry for 15 February 1941 reads:

> Jewish children learn in secret . . . to educate them is forbidden. In time of danger the children learn to hide their books.[25]

Where the synagogue was outlawed and education banned, attendance at religious services and illegal schools was resistance. Precisely because the Nazis prohibited the expression of Jewish culture, then the schools and underground university classes in the ghettos which taught Yiddish and Hebrew, and also transmitted the values of Jewish history and religion to the younger generation, were engaging in cultural resistance. The Nazis themselves classified all punishable acts as forms of resistance. Thus, any acts which were aimed at frustration, foiling or thwarting the enemy's plans, were acts of resistance. In a world where books were banned, the illegal writing, printing and dissemination of ideas was resistance. Where bookshops were forbidden, secret lending libraries became a form of resistance.

It should also be borne in mind that the Nazis wanted not only to eradicate the Jews, but also to expunge the Jews from the collective memory of European history; to re-write history by wiping out the traces of Jewish influence on European culture. The assiduous documentation of life and death in the ghettos, in the hope that their memory would endure, was a form of resistance which required determination and ingenuity. To bear witness was a moral and historical imperative. We now have a large number of ghetto diaries, memoirs, documents, paintings and photographs, as an indispensable record of Jewish life in the most appalling conditions.

The most extensive collection is the clandestine archive of the *Oneg Shabbat* (The Joy of the Sabbath) – a code name for the secret operation organized by Emmanuel Ringelblum in the Warsaw Ghetto. Under no illusion that they would survive as individuals, members of the Oneg Shabbat buried their archive documents in milk churns and other sealed containers for future generations to discover and understand. In the Kovno ghetto, Hirsh Kadushin committed himself to become the photographic chronicler of ghetto life. He began his work after a dying neighbour drew a message on the ground with his blood: 'Yiddin Nekana!' (Jews, Revenge!) Kadushin felt that he had been summoned. 'I don't have a gun', he said. 'The murderers are gone. My camera will be my revenge'.[26] Kadushin succeeded in making a visual record of all aspects of ghetto life for posterity.

It is important to stress the point that Jews were expressly forbidden to keep diaries and records, to paint or take photographs of ghetto life, and anyone caught in possession of such material during a house search would be subject to instant death. It is a humbling experience to examine these documents today, and it is difficult for us to realize just how important these records were for people being slowly starved to death, and working continually under the threat of a death sentence. Although he had not eaten for five days, Chaim Kaplan wrote feverishly about the terrible events that he had witnessed: the unfolding tragedy of the deportations, and the need to record:

> I feel that continuing this diary to the very end of my physical and spiritual strength is a historical mission which must not be abandoned.[27]
>
> ... My utmost concern is for hiding my diary so that it will be preserved for future generations. As long as my pulse beats I shall continue my sacred task.[28]

The last recorded words in the diary of Chaim Kaplan before he was deported to Treblinka capture the sense of anguish at being abandoned by the world, and the desperate need not to become a forgotten footprint in the sands of time:

> If my life ends – what will become of my diary?[29]

This obsession to document the everyday life and death of the ghetto, down to 'the last syllable of recorded time', was a persistent feature of the moral resistance of the diarists. What is remarkable is that exactly the same thoughts, the same moral compulsion to record, occurred to people writing in total isolation and solitary confinement, and with no contact with their kindred spirits in other ghettos. Thus Avraham Tory, composing what he thought was his 'Last Will and Testament', wrote at the end of December 1942:

> Driven by a force within me, and out of fear that no remnant of the Jewish community of Kovno will survive to tell of its final death agony under Nazi rule, I have continued to record my diary.
>   ... I overcame the fear of death which is directly connected with the very fact of writing each page of my diary, and with the very collection and hiding of the documentary material.
>   Had the slightest part of any of this been discovered, my fate would have been sealed.
>   With awe and reverence, I am hiding in this crate what I have written, noted, and collected, with thrill and anxiety, so that it may serve as material evidence ... when the Day of Judgment comes, and with it the day of revenge and the day of reckoning, the calling to account.[30]

Though many of the ghetto diarists were killed, their voices were not stifled, their message not silenced. To read the diaries today is a haunting, yet immensely moving experience.

Abba Kovner recounts an incident in the Vilna ghetto which encapsulates this urgent need to record, and the moral obligation of remembrance. After a raid by Lithuanian police to remove Jews for execution, Kovner entered what he thought was an empty room in a deserted house.

> There sat a man pushing the treadle of a sewing machine, under whose empty needle was a piece of white paper, punctuated by the needle's incision of the pattern of stitch holes.
>   'What are you doing here?' Kovner asked.
>   'I am writing the history of the ghetto', the man replied.
>   'You are writing the history of the ghetto on paper on a sewing machine without thread?'
>   'When the war is over', the man replied, 'there will be time to pull through the thread'.[31]

These examples of remarkable resilience against overwhelming odds are clear testimony to the existence and power of cultural resistance, rather than passivity, in the face of evil. Against a regime that routinely treated Jews with indignity, which daily denied them elementary human rights, and which attempted to strip them of their human image, any act by Jews which affirmed their human worth was resistance. Because the Nazis decreed death for anyone who performed or participated in a Jewish wedding ceremony, marriage became an act of resistance. In many ghettos pregnancy was prohibited. Thus on July 14th 1942, in the Kovno ghetto:

> The Gestapo issued an order: pregnancy in the Ghetto is forbidden. Every pregnancy must be terminated. . . .
> Pregnant women will be put to death.[32]

The Germans declared that from September 1942, giving birth was 'strictly forbidden', and the Jewish Council was forced to issue an announcement on September 8th 1942:

> From now on . . . any pregnant woman will be killed on the spot.[33]

Similarly, in the concentration camps, unreported pregnancies resulted in the death of mother and child. Because of these Herodian decrees, concealed pregnancy was an act of resistance. Because the Nazis decreed death for Jews, any act conducive to survival was resistance. As Chaim Kaplan noted: 'Whatever we do we do illegally; legally we don't even have permission to exist.'[34] Because the Nazis attempted not only to kill Jews, but also to degrade them and to extinguish their human spirit, we need a broader definition of resistance than one based exclusively upon armed revolt. It is difficult to disagree with Abraham Foxman:

> Attempting to stay alive was passive resistance. Escaping, hiding, or giving birth to a child in the ghetto was resistance. Praying in congregation, singing, or studying the Bible was resistance.[35]

JEWISH 'COLLABORATION' AND THE HANNAH ARENDT THESIS

> Fierce discussions and debates took place in newspapers, magazines. . . . Why the Judenrate? Why a Jewish police? Why Jewish kapos? Why did the victims march to the slaughter-house like

cattle? . . . The height of irony and cruelty: the dead victims needed
to be defended, while the killers, dead and alive, were left alone.[36]

Elie Wiesel

The publication in 1963 of Hannah Arendt's book, *Eichmann in
Jerusalem* was the beginning of a controversial new chapter in the
study of the Holocaust. Arendt was a German-Jewish political philosopher who had covered the trial of Adolf Eichmann for a New
York newspaper. The effect of her book was to put the leaders of
the Jewish ghettos on trial for complicity in the Final Solution –
diverting attention away from the killers, while turning the victims
into the accused. Hannah Arendt built upon Hilberg's thesis of
Jewish passivity. Hilberg had argued that the result of the Diaspora
mentality of submissiveness was that Jews had 'unlearned the art
of resistance'. This mental attitude was an essential element in the
'role of the Jews in their own destruction'.[37] Whereas Hilberg offered a deterministic, fatalistic analysis of the logic of events – with
Jews being trapped as the prisoners of their past history – Hannah
Arendt took his thesis one step further by arguing that Jewish leaders
made *active choices* which aided and abetted the Nazis. Not only
did the Jews not resist, but their leaders actively collaborated with
the Germans. Her main thesis was to accuse the Jewish Councils
of co-operation with the Nazis in their own people's destruction.

This culpability and complicity of the Jewish leaders had been overlooked or ignored in previous studies, although it had been brought
out into the open during Eichmann's trial. Hannah Arendt saw the
collaboration of the Judenrate as the missing piece in the jigsaw puz-
zle, the vital factor which needed to be put in place in order to
understand the complete picture of how so many Jews could have
been killed in such a short time. The Nazis faced manpower shortages, and without help from the recognized leaders of the Jewish
communities in deporting Jews, the number of victims would have
been considerably fewer than the six million people who did die.

The Jewish Councils of Elders were informed by Eichmann or
his men of how many Jews were needed to fill each train, and
they made out the list of deportees. The Jews registered, filled
out innumerable forms, answered pages and pages of questionnaires regarding their property so that it could be seized the
more easily; they then assembled at the collection points and
boarded the trains. The few who tried to hide or to escape were

rounded up by a special Jewish police force. As far as Eichmann could see, no-one protested, no-one refused to co-operate.[38]

Without Jewish help in administrative and police work . . . there would have been either complete chaos or an impossibly severe drain on German manpower.[39]

So the very existence of the Jewish Councils contributed to the Holocaust, and the leaders should not have agreed to the funcioning of the Councils in the first place, or to serve on them.

Wherever Jews lived, there were recognised Jewish leaders, and this leadership, almost without exception, co-operated in one way or another, for one reason or another with the Nazis. The whole truth was that if the Jewish people had really been unorganised and leaderless there would have been chaos and plenty of misery but the total number of victims would hardly have been between four and a half and six million people.[40]

Without the appeasement and co-operation of the Jewish leadership, the extermination of six million Jews would not have been possible, and thus the victims in complying with the Nazis' orders, contributed significantly to the Final Solution.

To a Jew this role of the Jewish leaders in the destruction of their own people is undoubtedly the darkest chapter of the whole dark story.[41]

Arendt's indictment of the Jewish Councils for their responsibility in facilitating the Holocaust provoked a bitter and acrimonious debate. She was criticized for a variety of reasons and upon a number of grounds. It is possible to isolate three key areas of criticism:

1) Methodological problems arising from her use of empirical evidence.
2) Her failure to make allowance for the conditions under which the Judenrate functioned – the historical setting.
3) Her insensitivity to the very real dilemmas that the Councils had to face.

1. *Arendt's methodology.*   The main charge against Hannah Arendt was levelled by the American Jewish historian Lucy Dawidowicz,

who argued that Arendt's thesis derived from 'total ignorance of the historical evidence' and was based upon 'disdain for historical evidence'.[42] She accused Arendt of being very cavalier in her use of facts, which were selectively chosen in order to support a dubious conclusion that she had arrived at before studying all the empirical evidence. Arendt had reversed the normal methods of historical scholarship. 'Miss Arendt began with grand generalizations and sweeping moral judgments'.[43] Above all, Hannah Arendt had committed the methodological sin of making hasty and incorrect generalizations based upon insufficient evidence. These sweeping generalizations were largely derived from secondary sources, 'some of which were lamentably ill-informed about the Judenrate'.[44] These unsupported accusations of Jewish collaboration were far harsher than any charges levelled by survivors from the ghettos; and were written in a tone that one of her friends described as 'heartless, frequently almost sneering, and malicious'.[45]

Thus the book was a moral tract rather than a work of objective historical research, and if her historical method was so casual and faulty, then Hannah Arendt's moral lessons about how Jews should have behaved during the Holocaust lose much of their force, and must be called into question. In short, bad history produces poor moral philosophy. For example, Arendt's claim that fewer Jews would have died if there had not been any Jewish leadership does not stand up to the evidence. The clearest and most convincing factual refutation of her main argument is the case of the Soviet and Baltic Jews, where there were no Jewish Councils. The Einsatzgrüppen, the SS roving death squads, killed approximately one and a half million Soviet and Baltic Jews in a very short space of time in areas where Jewish community structures had been wiped out previously by Stalin's regime. The percentage of Jewish losses was not any lower despite the lack of 'assistance' by Jewish leaders.

B. The historical setting. Hannah Arendt failed to take into account the historical conditions in which the Jewish Councils operated. The Judenrate *were not* voluntary bodies. They were *imposed* upon the Jews by the SS under an order of Heydrich's dated 21 September 1939:

1. In each Jewish community a Council of Jewish Elders is to be set up. . . . The Council is to be composed of 24 male Jews. . . . It is to be made FULLY RESPONSIBLE (in the literal sense of the word) for the exact execution . . . of all instructions.

2. In case of sabotage of such instructions, the Councils are to be warned of severest measures.[46]

Thus a large degree of forced co-operation with the Germans was unavoidable and inescapable. The leaders of the Councils – and their families – were to serve as a hostage group for the good behaviour of the ghetto, and in order to prevent the sabotaging of German orders. Under the principle of collective family responsibility, the leaders and their families were subject to the death penalty for failure to comply. Many Council members paid with their lives for disobedience. The Judenrate had responsibility without real power, and the German authorities deliberately exploited the situation, in the full realization that Jewish annoyance and hatred would be directed at their fellow Jews and not at the authors of their misery. As Heinz Auerswald, the German Commissar of the Warsaw Ghetto, wrote:

When there is suffering . . . the Jews' wrath is directed primarily against the Jewish authorities, and not against the German supervising authorities.[47]

It is also important to recognize the ratchet effect of German demands. The Nazis were psychologically astute in adopting a step-by-step approach, gradually increasing their demands and familiarizing the Jewish leaders with the need to obey. Through the steady escalation of orders, and through the power of habit, Jewish leaders were conditioned to become gradually more submissive and pliable. Starting off with seemingly innocuous tasks, they proceeded to more difficult and unpleasant tasks, and then to invidious tasks, and eventually were asked to perform impossible tasks. The German vice tightened gradually, inch by inch. There were four stages in the process of accommodation:

a) conducting a census, an accurate register of all Jews within the ghetto;
b) providing money, property and personal possessions;
c) providing a workforce, with the Judenrate having the responsibility for carrying out out selections for labour;
d) carrying out selections for deportation.

The first stage, the gathering of a body of information, led on to the second stage: the gathering of a body of material goods; then to the gathering of bodies for labour, and finally to the gathering of bodies. It is this last stage, Jewish co-operation in the process of deportation, which has caused the most controversy. It is important to bear in mind two crucial factors:

(i) Nazi deception: in the early stages of deportation, Jewish leaders did not know what the Nazis' ultimate plans were. The Germans resorted to an elaborate process of deception through the use of lies and euphemistic, bureaucratic language such as 'resettlement', and the 'transfer of the population to the east', and so on in order to disguise their real aims, and to create a false sense of security. Also the complete annihilation of an entire race did not make sense to rational people. Leaving aside its intrinsic immorality, it was impractical and served no rational or utilitarian purpose. The Germans faced acute manpower shortages. So the Nazi explanation that Jews were being resettled on labour reservations in the vast territories of the East initially seemed plausible. Jews were not naive. From the outset of the Second World War they feared the worst. But the worst they could conceive was slavery. In a perceptive analysis, the French historian Alain Finkelkraut makes the point that:

> It is true that they were deceived, but deceived in the first place by their own pessimism.
> What they are promised is forced labor. Isn't this perspective absolutely terrifying in itself? . . .
> . . . But Hitler did not give them what they expected: he gave them worse than the worst.[48]

This interpretation is confirmed by the Kovno ghetto diarist Avraham Tory. In a memoir note written in the spring of 1945, he looked back over the unfolding tragedy of his people:

> We feared for the fate of the men if they fell into the hands of the Germans, but we never imagined that they would murder women, children and the elderly; and so far as the men were concerned, we never expected mass murder. The worst thing we could possibly conceive of was that men would be drafted as slave laborers.[49]

It must be borne in mind that nobody in 1939 or 1940 could

have envisaged Birkenau or Treblinka. Not even the deepest pessi-
nists imagined the complete physical extermination of European
Jewry. That was inconceivable and without precedent. The enormity of the crime was beyond comprehension. Thus, when trying
to come to some understanding of the dilemmas of the Jewish
Councils, it is vital to take into account the level of understanding
of *individual* Jewish Councils, and the *extent* of their knowledge of
the Nazis' real aims. Above all, there is the essential difference
between assisting the Nazis out of belief that those being deported
were going to be resettled, and assisting the Nazis when it was
clear that those being deported were being sent to their deaths in
an extermination camp. In some ghettos, young and healthy workers
were the *first* to be deported because Judenrate leaders believed
that the old should be exempted from the hardships of deportation,
and that the journey to the east would be too strenuous for them.[50]

(ii) *Collective responsibility*: if the Jewish Councils failed to co-operate
with any Nazi orders, or if there was any overt resistance or sabotage within the ghetto, reprisals and collective punishments would
be imposed. In a number of ghettos, Jewish Council leaders instituted a policy of labour selections as a more humane alternative
to a German round-up, in which Jews were caught at random on
the streets, and treated in a brutal manner. The Councils under-
took to look after the welfare of the labourers and their depend-
ants, and to organize labour in a just and reasonable way.

If the Councils refused to co-operate with deportation orders,
deportations would be speeded up, and their numbers increased.
The Councils operated under the constant and very real threat that
the Germans would do the job themselves, but in a far more cruel
and brutal manner. Also, as part of a hostage group, any leaders
who refused to carry out an order were either shot on the spot, or
deported to an extermination camp. The same fate automatically
applied to their families. In Zdunska Woła, the leader of the
Judenrate, Dr Jacob Lemberg, was ordered to draw up a list of ten
innocent Jews to be executed in reprisal for the infraction of German rules. If he refused, Dr Lemberg was threatened with the hanging
of himself, his wife and two children. 'These four names you mentioned are the only names you will get through me', he replied.[51]
As a result of this act of defiance, the entire Lemberg family was
murdered, plus ten Jews randomly selected. Similar stories can be
told from various other communities.

On arrival in a town, the Germans arrested prominent members of the Jewish community and detained them as hostages in order to deter opposition. Theo Richmond describes the initial sense of unreality and dislocation amongst 14 Jewish hostages in the small Polish town of Konin, 'worrying about their families, brooding about their own fate'. The pattern of German terror was clear and intended to strike fear into every Jewish family. The 14 men were released after a day. 'Other men were promptly arrested to take the place of those freed, and every 24 hours they in turn were replaced with other hostages.'[52] Prior to the first great deportation from the Warsaw Ghetto in July 1942, 40 administrators working for the Jewish Council were taken as hostages. In addition, the wife of Adam Czerniakow, the head of the Judenrate, was also held hostage. The Judenrate was to be responsible for delivering 6000 Jews each day to the deportation centre, the Umschlagplatz. If the Jewish Council failed to comply entirely, the Germans warned, 'an appropriate number of hostages will be shot in each instance'.[53]

Non-compliance was a one-way ticket to death. In the Lechatov Ghetto, eight successive Jewish Councils were liquidated for refusal to obey Nazi decrees. Similarly, in Mlana, every member of the Council was hanged for not carrying out orders. Collective responsibility acted as a major deterrent to the growth of Jewish armed resistance. Massive reprisals were the invariable answer to any act of physical resistance. The Nazis widely publicized this security policy, and there were examples of whole communities perishing in this way – for example, the disappearance of the Jews of Lublin.

In the light of all these conditions, Hannah Arendt could be criticized for failing to consider the question: *what was the alternative to compliance*? While the hope of survival lasted, armed physical resistance, against hopeless odds, was seen as a form of collective suicide. The full tragedy of the ghetto Jews was that every road led to death. Resistance led to immediate and certain death, whereas the policy of the Jewish Councils appeared to delay or postpone the inevitable. Compliance seemed to offer the best chance for survival for the largest number of Jews. The policy of the Jewish Councils was dictated by extreme necessity – by the lack of any feasible alternatives.

Hannah Arendt did not address the question: *was forced co-operation – co-operation at gunpoint – collaboration?* Is compliance under duress to be judged by the same standards as the voluntary ideological collaboration of neo-Nazis in occupied countries? To regard the Council leaders, with all their personal failings and weaknesses, as Quislings, is to distort the nature and the complexity of the choice open to them. Most Judenrate leaders invoked the strategy of 'rescue through work' as a means of lessening the evils of Nazi rule. Their aim was to play for time, buying time for an Allied victory, by making their communities economically useful to the German war effort, and squeezing tactical concessions from the Germans in order to make life as bearable as possible. The basis of Jewish Council policy was to hold on, to persevere and to survive until the Nazis were defeated. This was their life insurance policy in the absence of any viable alternatives. That this policy also failed should be grounds for lamentation, not recrimination. Critics argue that it is inaccurate to accuse the Judenrate officials of 'collaboration' because they were coerced by German terror methods to submit: 'To say that they ... "collaborated" with the Germans is semantic confusion and historical misrepresentation'.[54] At no point did Jews consent to their captivity, befriend the enemy, or will a Nazi victory.

C. Hannah Arendt's insensitivity. The major ground for criticizing Hannah Arendt lies in her insensitivity to the unbearable plight that the Jewish Councils faced, and her lack of imaginative understanding of the historical setting in which the Judenrate operated. It is significant that she does not mention German reprisals, let alone examine in detail the constraints which collective responsibility imposed upon Jewish communities.

We need to place Jewish behaviour in the ghettos in the context of the most excruciating and tragic moral dilemmas that human beings have ever had to face, in conditions of appalling brutality. This point cannot be emphasized too strongly: the Jewish Council leaders confronted agonizing, unprecedented and unparalleled choices. In order to save Jews, they reluctantly had to participate in the destruction of Jews. Arendt does not examine these dilemmas. Instead, she side-steps the issue by referring to the desire for power among Council leaders. 'We still can sense how they enjoyed their new power.'[55] But this analysis is unconvincing, and fails to grasp the nature of the unbearably painful and solemn choices that the Judenrate leaders had to address. This failure of historical imagination – of empathy – is all the more puzzling because as a political philosopher concerned with the power of the state and the limits of freedom, Hannah Arendt had previously written a large book in 1950 on *The Origins of Totalitarianism* in which she pointed out that one of the most cunning and devilish features of totalitarian government was *precisely* its ability to create conditions of impossible choices, and to make the victims inevitable accomplices in the crimes of the regime. This totalitarian technique diverted attention and blame away from the guilty instigators, and projected it onto the victims themselves. Thus, surprisingly, the most telling critique of the Hannah Arendt thesis of Judenrate collaboration comes from the pen of Hannah Arendt herself:

> Totalitarian terror achieved its most terrible triumph when it succeeded in . . . making the decisions of conscience absolutely questionable and equivocal. When a man is faced with the alternative of betraying and thus murdering his friends or of sending his wife and children, for whom he is in every sense responsible, to their death; when even suicide would mean the immediate murder of his own family – how is he to decide? The alternative is no longer between good and evil, but between murder and murder. Who could solve the moral dilemma of the Greek mother, who was allowed by the Nazis to choose which of her three children should be killed?
>
> Through the creation of conditions under which conscience ceases to be adequate, and to do good becomes utterly impossible, the consciously organized complicity of all men in the crimes of totalitarian regimes is extended to the victims and thus made really total. The SS implicated concentration camp inmates . . . in their crimes by making them responsible for a large part of administration, thus confronting them with the hopeless dilemma whether to send their friends to their death or to help murder other men who happened to be strangers. . . .
>
> The point is not only that hatred is diverted from those who are guilty . . . but that the distinguishing line between persecutor and persecuted, between the murderer and his victim is constantly blurred.[56]

Hannah Arendt cites the real life 'Sophie's Choice' of a Greek mother who had to choose which one of her three children should be killed in order to save the other two. The paradox in her theory is that Arendt unfortunately forgot to apply her own powerful insights, or to draw the appropriate lessons from them when it came to the equally crushing dilemmas and 'choiceless choices' that had to be faced by the Judenrate leaders.

Hannah Arendt is very unfair in taking the actions of the Councils out of historical context, and in under-stating the desperate and harrowing conditions in which they worked. It is also unfair to single out the Judenrate officials for a high level of blame and re-sponsibility when in a sense they were powerless, and when the decisive factor was always German power.

Arendt drew very heavily upon Hilberg's account of Jewish ap-peasement. They both portray Jewish co-operation with the Nazi occupation authorities as *voluntary*. At all stages Jews complied – from registration to deportation. As Arendt put it:

As far as Eichmann could see, no-one protested, no-one refused to co-operate.[57]

As Eichmann told it, the most potent factor in the soothing of his own conscience was the simple fact that he could see no-one, no-one at all, who actually was against the Final Solution.[58]

In a similar vein, Hilberg wrote that:

Throughout Poland the great bulk of the Jews presented them-selves voluntarily at the collecting points and boarded the trains for transport to killing centres.[59]

He quotes a German official in support of his thesis:

Without resistance and in submission they marched by the hun-dreds in long columns to railway stations and filed into the trains. Only very few gendarmes were supervising the operations; it would have been easy to flee.[60]

It does not require much mental effort to accept Hilberg's and Arendt's thesis – all that one needs to do is to suspend one's criti-cal faculties and one's imagination and to forget the barbed wire and the high walls which surrounded the ghettos; the watch towers with searchlights; the SS guards with machine guns; the Alsatian dogs – the *hundestaffel* – trained to kill; the constant security pa-trols of rear-areas' troops, and the assistance of ethnic German auxiliaries and native collaborators. When Arendt quoted Eichmann's claim that no-one protested, no-one refused to co-operate, in sup-port of her thesis of Jewish complicity, she ignored the disingenuous, self-serving nature of his defence. Arendt failed to point out that Eichmann's testimony invalidated itself because he failed to specify the price of protest, the human cost in refusal to co-operate. No Jews were 'actually against the Final Solution' because its workings were carefully disguised until the last deportations. Hilberg invalidated his own argument about the sheep-like submissiveness of the Jews by admitting that when Jews had an accurate understanding of German intentions, that they were not being resettled, but exterminated, they tried every method to dodge evacuation.

> As ... the awareness of death increased ... towards the end of the operations increasing numbers of Jews hesitated to move out.[61]

Again, the notion that Jews 'volunteered' cannot be left unqualified. It constitutes a new usage of the term with which most of us are unfamiliar. There is no mention – or understanding – of the way in which the Germans used food as a coercive weapon. The withholding of food supplies was a key form of collective punishment; the Germans sapped the strength of the Jews by starving them, and then offered them food as an inducement for deportation. Hunger stalked the ghettos. In his Warsaw Ghetto diary entry for 2 August 1942, Abraham Lewin wrote:

> A new proclamation. . . . All those who are not employed ... have to report voluntarily on 2, 3 and 4 August and they will receive 3 kg of bread and 1 kg of jam. . . . *Hunger haunts us*.[62]

Marek Edelman, one of the resistance fighters in the Warsaw Ghetto, spelled out this point:

> Listen ... Do you have any idea what bread meant at that time in the ghetto? Because if you don't, you will never understand how thousands of people could voluntarily come for bread and go with this bread to the camp at Treblinka. Nobody has understood it thus far.[63]

The price of a human life was cheap. People sold themselves for a small sum. A Jewish life was worth three loaves of bread and a half pot of jam. While ordinary Jews hungered for ordinary food, Hannah Arendt portrayed the Judenrate leaders as power-hungry individuals who 'enjoyed their new power'.[64] She justifiably mocked the pretentious airs and graces of Chaim Rumkowski, the leader, or dictator, of the Lodz ghetto, with his 'rumkies', the bank notes which carried his signature, and the postage stamps engraved with his portrait. But she failed to point out that for all his megalomania, Rumkowski's strategy for Jewish survival nearly worked. The Lodz ghetto was the last large ghetto to be liquidated. His 'rescue through work strategy' kept Lodz in existence for 1–2 years longer than many other ghettos, and nearly succeeded in rescuing over 70 000 Jews. If the Red Army had not halted its westward advance on the River Vistula in July 1944, 70 miles from Lodz, perhaps Rumkowski's dictatorial methods would have been partially vindicated. As Jacob Robinson has argued, 'It is only by accident of military history that a considerable part of Lodz Jews did not survive.'[65]

Arendt failed to disentangle Rumkowski's personal qualities from his policy. There were other ghetto leaders who were far more modest than Rumkowski, but who made essentially the same decisions to rescue a remnant of the Jewish population, even if this entailed bargaining with the devil. Dr Elkes in the Kovno Ghetto had the opposite character traits: he was a humble, self-effacing man. In some ghettos lots had to be drawn to choose members of the Jewish Council because of the lack of volunteers. Thus, one should be cautious of making generalizations about ghetto leaders' hunger for power on the basis of one or two individuals.

The one good thing to come out of Hannah Arendt's work was the massive controversy which it sparked off, leading to the publication in 1972 of Isaiah Trunk's comprehensive study, *Judenrat*, which painted a far more accurate picture of the diversity of the Councils, and the substantial differences between them, and the need to avoid easy generalizations which don't fit the facts. The Councils endeavoured in every way to turn German demands to Jewish advantage. Even the act of conducting a census and drawing up a card index registration could be exploited in the desperate struggle to save lives. The census returns could be distorted in order to hide 'superfluous' people. For example, in March 1943, the Gestapo wanted to know how many people were left in the Kovno ghetto after their deportation 'actions'. According to their calculations only 14 000 Jews should have been left. The Council massaged the registration in order to conceal the existence of an additional 3000 people.

We were afraid to disclose that there were more people in the ghetto; perhaps the Gestapo had orders to leave only a certain number of people and would carry out a new slaughter. . . .

However, we could not hold out long, because we received food rations according to the number of people we said lived in the ghetto. As a result, nearly 3000 people were left without food. What did we do? We distributed three to four food rations a week instead of seven.[66]

In addition to this policy of equality of misery, and sharing their meagre rations, the Council bided its time, waited for the danger to pass, and then informed the Germans that they had made a mistake in their calculations, and that there were 16 000 people in the ghetto. This sleight of hand gained extra food rations and also allowed the Council to hide the additional 1000 very old and very young Jews who, according to the Germans, should not have been in the ghetto. This example illustrates the complex manoeuvres of the Councils to preserve life, and the error, indeed absurdity, of categorical allegations of Judenrate 'collaboration'. Far from engaging in what Hilberg defined as 'anticipatory compliance' the Councils tried wherever possible to anticipate German demands in order to subvert and reduce the scope of vicious orders. The Judenrate in the Kovno ghetto even suppressed information about contagious diseases in the ghetto, and placed affected patients in special isolation wards.

Officially, there are no people suffering from contagious diseases in the Ghetto. Should . . . such news reach the Germans, they would resort to severe measures at the expense of the entire community. . . . This is the crux of the problem. The Germans are capable of 'erasing' whole neighbourhoods, even the entire Ghetto: if they as much as sniff the existence of contagious diseases in the Ghetto . . . we are overcrowded in the Ghetto; but when need arises, we always manage to find a necessary space.[67]

A further example, from the Lodz ghetto, illustrates the tireless efforts of Jewish leaders to lessen the evils of Nazi occupation. In May 1941 an unknown sniper fired shots from inside the ghetto at a German guard post. Although no one was hurt, and the identity of the attacker was not discovered, the Gestapo demanded as a collective punishment that 25 Jews be selected by *Rumkowski* for summary execution. After much negotiation, Rumkowski succeeded in softening the punishment. The Germans demanded a list of 25 Jews for flogging. Rumkowski temporized and then rejected this oo as unacceptable, and when the authorities insisted on carrying out this punishment, Rumkowski presented himself for the public ashing, but refused to provide others. The Germans persisted in heir demands, and finally Rumkowski proposed as an alternative punishment for the whole ghetto, a curfew. To his surprise, the Gestapo agreed.[68]

In her characteristically harsh judgement, Hannah Arendt referred o 'the haunting specter of universal cooperation'.[69] by the Jewish Councils. Similarly, Hilberg refers to how 'the impotent machinery of the Judenrate responded mechanically to German command.'[70] We are entitled to ask how Hilberg and Arendt would have responded to German commands. But this incident again illustrates that Judenrate leaders, including the despised Rumkowski, did *not* automatically comply with German demands, but tried by every means within their power(lessness) and ingenuity to salvage what could be rescued from the wreckage of their community life.

MILEHAIM, MILAMOVET: WHO SHALL LIVE, WHO SHALL DIE?

Let us do evil, that good may come

Romans, 3: 8

He that toucheth pitch shall be defiled therewith

Ecclesiasticus (Apocrypha), 13: 1

The Yom Kippur prayer, 'Milehaim, Milamovet' – the eternal prayer, 'Who is to live, Who is to die' – raises the central moral question which confronted the Judenrate . The Jewish Councils aimed to keep as many Jews as possible alive until the end of the war by marking time – gaining a breathing-space by playing off the military needs of the Wehrmacht and German industry for skilled labour, against those in the Nazi and SS hierarchy who favoured the immediate killing of all Jews. But in attempting to alleviate suffering and in order to minimize the effects of vicious decrees, the Councils found themselves in an invidious, and eventually, an impossible position. For if Jews could be rescued through work, what was to happen to those who could not work – the children, the aged, the sick and infirm, the 'useless mouths'? *Productive* Jews could only be saved at the expense of handing over *unproductive*

Jews to fill the deportation quotas demanded by the authorities. If the Jewish Council did not co-operate in providing the required number of Jews for deportation at the specified time, collective responsibility would be imposed – entailing the certain death of a large number of Jews, and the distinct possibility that the whole ghetto might be liquidated. If it was not to perish all at once, the community had to live and die by the quota system. This was the fundamental dilemma which racked and tortured the Jewish Councils. As Henry Feingold has written:

> The paradox inherent in the Jewish condition under the Nazi heel was that the same organization could serve both life and death.[71]

The Nazi system of rule in the ghettos was deliberately designed as a moral maze from which there was no escape. It was created in order to exploit the moral sentiments of its victims, to cripple them with moral doubts and to burden them with impossible choices. Inside this ethical labyrinth, whichever path they chose led to humiliation, and ultimately, death.

The most important criticism of Hannah Arendt is that she fails to put herself in the position of Judenrate members: she does not ask herself what she would have done if she had to confront the invidious choices that they had to face. Imagine yourself in Chaim Rumkowski's position. On 1 September 1942, German soldiers entered the Jewish hospital and killed many sick patients. Consider his famous speech delivered before a large crowd in the Lodz ghetto three days later on the eve of an 'action' – a selection for deportation – against the children, sick and elderly, on 4 September 1942:

> I was given an order yesterday evening to deport some 20 000 Jews out of the ghetto. [I was told that] if I refused, 'We shall do it ourselves'. The question arose: Should we comply and do it, or should we leave it for others to do? We were not, however, motivated by the thought of how many would be lost, but by the consideration of how many it would be possible to save. We all . . . have come to the conclusion that despite the horrible responsibility, we have to accept the evil order. I have to perform this bloody operation myself; I simply must cut off limbs to save the body! I have to take away the children, because other-

wise others will also be taken; God forbid (a terrible outcry from the assembled people followed these words)

... I did not come to console you today ... but to reveal to you the whole woeful, torturing truth. I came like a robber to rob your dearest ones from your very hearts! With all my might I strove to repeal this evil order. And as it has been impossible to rescind it, I have tried to make it milder. Only yesterday, I ordered the registration of children of nine years of age, because I have endeavoured to save children of at least this single age group from nine to ten. But they did not relent, and I have succeeded only in saving the ten-year-olds ...

We have in the ghetto many persons sick with tuberculosis, whose lives are numbered in days, perhaps in weeks. I do not know – perhaps it is a satanic idea ... but I cannot restrain myself from mentioning it. Deliver to me those sick ones and it may be possible to save the healthy ones instead. I am well aware how dear the sick are to everyone. . . . But in times of disaster one has to weigh and measure who is to be saved, who can and should be saved. To my mind, those are to be spared in the first place who have any chance of survival, not those who cannot survive anyway.[72]

To read these words is a chastening experience. The anguish in his speech is so deep, and the alternatives so heart-rending that we shrink from the consequences of its faultless logic. The mind reels at the contemplation of the inhuman alternatives – surrendering the unproductive in order to save the productive, or risking incalculable reprisals for disobedience. How can parents be expected to follow the logic of relinquishing their children? How does one understand what is at stake here? How does one assimilate this speech to normal moral discourse? How does one contemplate a choice deprived of all choice except that of sacrificing all children under ten in order to save the lives of their parents; sacrificing those who are an economic burden in order to guarantee the economic efficiency and salvation of the ghetto; sacrificing the unfit to save the fit; sacrificing the few to save the many?

Rumkowski did not attempt to hide the stark reality of the dilemma he faced. It is stated in the boldest and baldest terms. The Germans had originally demanded 24 000 people for deportation. Rumkowski had managed to reduce the figure to 20 000, but only by being prepared to participate in the selection process. The failure to participate could mean that the remaining population of 90 000 Jews would be annihilated.

During August 1942 the Jewish Council in Kielce refused to carry out a German request for help during a deportation 'action'. They were given 24 hours to reconsider. After the deadline expired they still declined to co-operate. All the Judenrate members and Jewish police were murdered, and around 1000 Jews were massacred. The rest of the population, some 21 000 people, were deported to Treblinka for immediate extermination.[73] The horrors of the Kielce, Lublin and Warsaw ghettos were before Rumkowski's eyes as precedents of Nazi brutality. Previously, in January 1942, Rumkowski had succeeded in reducing the number of people deported from 20 000 to 10 000, although at that time he did not know that they were being deported to Chelmno death camp.

As a director of a children's orphanage before the war, Rumkowski had a particular love of children. Because he feared that more deportations of the unproductive might come, he tried to protect the children in the ghetto by making them go to work in the factories and workshops. On 20 July 1942, he ordered all children over the age of ten to work. About 13 900 were found work. Approximately 20 per cent of the labour force was comprised of children under the age of seventeen.[74] What goes almost unnoticed in this life-saving tactic is that Rumkowski had to resort to a barbaric practice – child labour – which the enlightened world had outlawed in order to protect children. However, in early September 1942 the German Commandant Hans Biebow issued a warning that if all children under the age of ten were not handed over, the whole ghetto would be deported to a death camp. Rumkowski attempted unsuccessfully to save the nine-year-old children, on the grounds that they were productive members of the ghetto. Consider also Jacob Gens' speech in the Vilna ghetto in October 1942:

> Many Jews regard me as a traitor . . . I, Gens, lead you to death and I, Gens, want to rescue Jews from death. I, Gens, order the uncovering of *malinas* [hiding places] and I, Gens, try to get more food and more work and more certificates for the ghetto. I cast my accounts with Jewish blood and not with Jewish respect. If they ask me for a thousand Jews, I give them because if the Germans themselves came, they would take with violence not a thousand but thousands and thousands and the whole ghetto would be finished. With a hundred I save a thousand; with a thousand

I save ten thousand. You're people of spirituality and letters. You keep away from such dirty doings in our ghetto. You'll go out clean . . . but if I survive, I'll go out covered with filth and blood will run from my hands. Nevertheless, I'd be willing to stand at the bar of judgment before Jews. I'd say I did everything to rescue as many Jews as I could and I tried to lead them to freedom. And in order to save even a small part of the Jewish people, I alone had to lead others to their deaths. And in order to ensure that you go out with clear consciences I had to forget mine and wallow in filth.[75]

Some leaders, like Czerniakow in Warsaw, committed suicide rather than step over the moral barrier of participating in selections for deportation. But deportations continued apace.

Faced with this unprecedented moral predicament, Gens and Rumkowski arrived at the fateful conclusion that it was necessary and unavoidable to sacrifice some to save others. Rightly or wrongly they believed they had to partake in the crime to avert an even greater catastrophe. Like Rumkowski, Gens used his position to negotiate with the Germans. In June 1942 after the violation of some German rules, including acts of smuggling, the Nazi authorities demanded 300 Jews for execution. Gens bargained with the Germans, and managed to get the number of victims reduced to 80. At the end of October 1942, the Judenrat and the Vilna Jewish police force participated in the deportation and transportation of 400 Jews to Ozmania, an execution site. The Germans had originally intended to shoot 2000 victims, but Gens had succeeded in reducing the figure to 400. He said of this participation:

It is true that our hands are smeared with the blood of our brethren, but we had to accept this horrible task. We are innocent before history. We shall be on the alert to preserve the remnants. . . . We shall give only the sick and the old. We shall not give the children, they are our future. We shall not give young women. A demand has been made to deliver workers. My answer was, 'We shall not give them, for we need them here ourselves.'[76]

One ghetto diarist, Zelig Kalmanovich, reflected the ambivalent feelings that many had about Gens' policy. In connection with the Ozmania incident he wrote:

It is horrible, perhaps the worst of all predicaments, still there is no other way. Blessed be the God of Israel, who sent us this man [Gens] . . .

The young people . . . have accepted this dreadful duty. . . . The result: over 400 souls have perished – elderly people, the weak and ill, retarded children. However, 1500 women and children were saved. If this had been the work of strangers, 2000 people would have perished, God forbid.[77]

A purely factual, narrative description of these events cannot penetrate to the inner meaning of what is at stake here. Moral and historical understanding of these speeches requires a strenuous effort on our part to *imagine* historically. There is a saying from the Talmud, 'Judge not thy neighbour until thou art come into his place.' What would *you* have done if you had to face the decisions and grim alternatives that Gens and Rumkowski had to address? Rumkowski had asked this question of his people, admitting that a 'broken Jew stands before you':

One needs the heart of a bandit to ask from you what I am asking. But put yourself in my place, think logically, and you'll reach the conclusion that I cannot proceed any other way. The part that can be saved is much larger than the part that must be given away.[78]

A decision has to be made – either to co-operate with German deportation orders, or to refuse to do so. You are faced with the following stark choice:

(i)   You have received an order from the German authorities to draw up a list of 10 000 Jews for 'resettlement', and you know that this means death.
(ii) The list must be ready in four days. You have to decide, because 'the decision not to decide'[79] is also a positive act, for the refusal to comply with Nazi demands will entail the certain death of 10 000 people selected by the Germans themselves, plus the certain death of an additional, but unspecified, number of people as a punishment for disobedience, and as a reprisal for sabotaging orders. Two thousand, perhaps ten thousand people, might be killed as an exemplary punishment. As Lang observes, 'not to engage in that act is also . . . a way of

engaging in the act.'[80] Whatever decision is arrived at there will be moral violations.

(iii) If the list is drawn up and delivered, it might be possible to get concessions, and to reduce the number to 8000. The order cannot be undone, but it could be reduced. By compiling the list yourself, it would be possible to select those with little or no chance of survival: the very old or sick who are going to die soon in any case. By propitiating the Nazi Moloch, it would provide a breathing-space, a reprieve, for the healthy young men and women who would have a better chance of survival until the end of the war.

If you carry out the order, are you guilty of collaboration? Have you become an accomplice of the Nazis? If you refuse to carry out the demand, are you responsible for the massive reprisals which will inevitably follow? In the inescapability of this choice we reach the culmination, the crowning point of the practice of collective responsibility. The Germans had succeeded in devising a method which inevitably incriminated its victims, turning them into accessories to Nazi crimes. The unavoidable conclusion of the principle of collective responsibility was that Jews were conscripted to oppress their fellow Jews. Survival dictated severe choices and drastic answers to unanswerable questions. By attempting to minimize suffering, and in order to prolong the life of the ghetto, the Jewish Councils became tainted by guilt, besmirched by the very evil that they were trying desperately to overcome. But the point that is missed by critics who make easy retrospective accusations of 'collaboration' is that it was not possible for the Jewish Councils to step out of the flow of history. As the author of a philosophical treatise on *The Human Condition* Hannah Arendt failed to appreciate that the Judenrate did not have the moral freedom to escape from the cruel necessities of their *inhuman* condition. As Lucy Dawidowicz wrote in criticism of Arendt:

> One would have expected . . . that the expert on totalitarian terror in its philosophic aspect would have recognized the phenomenon of totalitarian terror in its historical reality.[81]

The diminished selves of the Council leaders, gnawed by doubt and remorse, were trapped by the logic of destruction and the destruction of logic. The deadly logic of collective responsibility did not leave open any way of escape. The victims *had* to make a choice but in whatever they chose, they incurred guilt.

It is difficult to disagree with the sagacious judgement of Lawrence Langer:

> The more we immerse ourselves in the daily ordeal of the ghetto residents, leaders ... the more we see that they were all faced with a choice between impossibilities – no meaningful choice at all.[82]

In no area of ghetto life was the choice between impossibilities more evident or more acute than in the role of the Jewish police, who had to carry the logic of selection to its deadly conclusion, having to put it into practice by actively participating in the round-up of the sick and the senile, the young and the old.

THE JEWISH POLICE

Jews were forced by decree to live in ghettos. They were compelled to establish a Judenrat. However, the Germans deliberately left the internal government and administration of the ghettos to Jews themselves, in the full knowledge that self-regulation would lead inevitably to Jews oppressing other Jews, doing the Germans' dirty work for them, and thus leading to deeper and deeper divisions within the ghettos.

The establishment of a Jewish police force within the ghettos was a logical concomitant of the existence of the Jewish councils. The whole *raison d'être* of the Jewish police was to act as the executive arm of the Judenrat, to enforce its policy. This put the Jewish police in the forefront of co-operation with the German authorities, and placed them in a precarious position in relation to their fellow Jews. The Jewish police had to make a number of impossible compromises with their Nazi oppressors. Not unnaturally, they were extremely disliked within the ghettos, especially given the opportunities to exploit their position for bribery, corruption and favours in return for benefits. A recurring theme in the writings of many of the ghetto diarists is their undisguised hatred and contempt for the Jewish police, for their venality and corruption. Isaiah Trunk has written that:

They were burdened with the most inhuman tasks anyone ever carried out against his own brethren: to help the German enemy tighten the noose around the necks of Jewish victims.[83]

The tasks performed by the Jewish police included:

(1) the collection of taxes, and the arrest of tax-evaders;
(2) guarding against the smuggling of food and other goods, and the handing over of smugglers to the German police. Smuggling was an offence punishable by death;
(3) the enforcement of labour quotas demanded by the Germans. If any labourers evaded their 'duty' the Jewish police was required to round-up others in order to fill the quota. In some cases requisitioned workers were rounded-up for labour outside the ghetto when it was almost certain that they would be worked to death.
(4) the collection of fellow Jews for deportation.

Frequently the Jewish police, in association with the Judenrat, had to resort to draconian measures to enforce labour quotas. In February 1944 the Germans demanded 1500 labourers from the Lodz ghetto. The workers went into hiding (erroneously) thinking that they were about to be deported to a death camp. The *Chronicle of the Lodz Ghetto* describes the efforts of Rumkowski to avert serious action by the Germans if the requisition order was not fulfilled:

> It is obvious that the authorities would intervene if the Jewish leadership lost control of the situation. The populace is being assured repeatedly that this is not a resettlement action after the pattern of earlier days of horror, but simply the providing of available manpower.[84]

The following day, Rumkowski warned of the dangerous consequences that would follow from this evasion of labour duty, and of the mutual responsibility of all Jews within the ghetto to avoid provoking the Germans. Where it was suspected that families hid and fed their fugitive husbands or sons, the family's ration cards were cancelled. Rumkowski:

> Of course it is very fine that a family worried about its son or husband is stinting on provisions and soup in order to feed the

person in hiding: but such families are also in danger, and I must make this explicit because – hard as it is for me – I have no choice. After all, I cannot endanger the entire ghetto for the sake of 1500 men who have to be dispatched for external labour.[85]

The Chronicle entry for 14 February 1944 reads:

Since the families of men in hiding have had all their ration cards invalidated, they will probably find it difficult to get through the next several days.[86]

In many cases, men were forced from their hiding places by their own, and their family's, hunger. The Jewish police patrols methodically combed through their ghettos in order to track down and round-up the evaders. Often the police were inhibited by their personal relationships and ties of friendship with the hunted men. The conflict between personal loyalties and official duties reached breaking point in Jewish police participation in deportations.

The most important test, and the most distressing function of the Jewish police, was the collection of fellow Jews for deportation. They had to take part in German-organized manhunts, searching hiding places, and flushing Jews out of their sanctuaries. As Isaiah Trunk writes, 'Brutal force had to be used.'[87]

The Jewish police were offered extra food rations and the inducement that *their* families would be exempt from deportation if they complied with German orders. However, this was coupled with the threat that if they *failed* to comply, their families would be the first to be deported. In his harrowing memoir of the Lodz ghetto, *Days of Nightmare*, Josef Zelkowicz wrote:

As a reward for their efficient and loyal performance, they have been promised that their own families, ie their children and parents, will be exempt from the edict ...

... But the question is: At whose expense have they been privileged? ... who will be deported in their place?

When the Jewish police take people, they take whoever they can, whoever is there ... If someone is not located, they take another in his place. [to fill their allocated quotas][88]

Often the sick were seized from hospital beds in order to meet the quotas. Doctors, too, actively participated in the rounding-up of the infirm and the senile, sifting the healthy from the unhealthy. David Sierakowiak observed:

> The Jewish Police have addresses.... The entries say, in such and such an apartment is a child who was born at such and such a time. The list tells, in such and such an apartment an old person can be found of such and such an age. A doctor enters the apartment. He examines the occupants, to see who is healthy and who is only trying to appear healthy. He can tell at a glance.
> ... The police must fill their quotas.... If they don't take others will.[89]

In the Warsaw ghetto a similar story can be told. Abraham Lewin referred to the 'sad complicity of the Jewish police. With great respect they are "obliged" to carry out their duties and round-up people.'[90] Lewin's diary entry for 16 August 1942 reads:

> The Jewish police have received an order that each one of them must bring five people to be transported. Since there are 2000 police, they will have to find 10 000 victims. If they do not fulfil their quotas they are liable to the death penalty.[91]

Out of fear of German reprisals for non-cooperation, the Jewish Council and the Jewish police in the Lodz ghetto even resorted to hostage-taking, kidnapping the families of those who failed to turn up when their names were on deportation lists. The *Chronicle of the Lodz Ghetto* for 24 March 1943:

> People here have become very skilled in hiding, and the police, who have been issued strict orders, have no choice but to imprison relatives as hostages.[92]

The entry for 1 September 1943 reads:

> Persons ... who ... had gone into hiding ... would be forced to turn themselves in because members of their families have been taken hostage. A few of these hostages actually had to leave with the transport.[93]

In some ghettos, Jewish policemen appear to have acted with personal cruelty, crossing over the indiscernible dividing line between doing the bare minimum compatible with their already impossible position, and actually *exceeding* German orders. Chaim Kaplan wrote on 16 July 1942:

> The Jewish police, whose cruelty is no less than that of the Nazis, deliver to the 'transfer point' ... more than the quota to which the Judenrate obligated itself. Sometimes there are several thousand people waiting a day or two to be transported because of a shortage of railroad cars.[94]

He added:

> The ghetto has turned into an inferno. Men have become beasts ... people are being hunted down like animals in the forests. It is the Jewish police who are cruellest towards the condemned.[95]

Jewish police forces did not act in a uniform manner. Gratuitous violence was not universal. In many ghettos the Jewish police turned a blind eye whenever they could to food smuggling and other 'misdemeanours'. However, some Jewish policemen carried out German orders to absurd lengths:

> Rumkowski's police rigidly enforced all German orders to the extent of turning over to the German guards a man who was found not wearing the Jewish badge.[96]

The head of the Judenrat in the Bialystok ghetto, Ephraim Barash, purged the police force of corrupt, criminal elements. The diarist of the Kovno ghetto, Avraham Tory, informs us that the Jewish police acted with humanity, resourcefulness and compassion on numerous occasions. During a selection on 28 October 1941:

> The commander of the Jewish police, Kopelman ... succeeded in saving Jews and whole families. The number of such survivors ... reached into the hundreds.[97]

On one occasion the Germans instructed the Jewish police to conduct a thorough search of every empty house in the smaller of Kovno's two ghettos in order to find those in hiding. The Germans believed that the hidden Jews would be lulled into thinking that Yiddish-speaking Jewish police were searchers who had come to

escue them. The Jewish police were alert to this danger, and brought
xtra caps and armbands for the Jews found in the hideouts to
ive them the outward appearance and insignia of Jewish police-
nen. This was at personal risk to themselves and their families.

> This ruse worked. Some 20 Jews were saved in this manner: they
> would have been killed upon being discovered by the Lithua-
> nians or by the Germans.[98]

ome members of the Kovno ghetto police force were secretly in-
olved in the resistance movement, and helped to shield people
vho were wanted by the Gestapo. In areas of eastern Poland and
Belorussia numerous Jewish policemen had links with the underground movements.

Jewish resistance veterans and Holocaust survivors are far less
harsh in their appraisal of the Councils and the Jewish Police than
post-war critics. The leader of the resistance movement in the Warsaw
ghetto, Yitzak Zuckerman, recognized the efforts of Jewish official
representatives to act as a buffer to absorb German blows, as a
shield to protect their own people. But moral contamination was
unavoidable in their contact with the Nazis. As Zuckerman wrote:

> I am not of the opinion that all who took part in these groups
> were traitors and that all who participated in these activities were
> concerned only about their own safety... nor motivated by mal-
> ice. But from a strictly objective point of view, all these institu-
> tions were converted into instruments of evil.[99]

It is important to bear in mind that Jewish armed resistance began not with attacks upon Germans, but with the punishment of
informers and collaborators. What Zuckerman described as 'end-
ing the internal treason',[100] by rooting out and killing informers
was the prelude to anti-Nazi operations. Members of the Judenrate
and the Jewish Police automatically came under suspicion because
of their close working ties with the German authorities. Here, too,
moral considerations based upon individual guilt or innocence were
important, for the resistance did not want to punish innocent people
on the basis of circumstantial evidence, or according to any concept
of collective guilt. The resistance leadership within the Warsaw
Ghetto felt the need to draw distinctions between those who
worked for the Judenrate or the Jewish Police in order to mitigate

the evils of Nazi rule, and those who became Gestapo agents
Zuckerman writes: 'It was hard for us to swallow emotionally that
our war had to begin with the Jewish policemen.'[101] It was import
ant for the morality of resistance actions that Jewish policemen
were attacked *as individuals* who had transgressed the code of Jewish
honour, and had committed some specific crime. 'We didn't apply
collective punishment'.[102] Collective responsibility and collective
punishment were Nazi concepts based upon a violation of age-old
principles of natural justice. The Resistance felt an obligation to
uphold these elementary standards, even under the most trying of
circumstances:

> There were death sentences, and every single detail of every person
> we were about to punish . . . had to be checked carefully.[103]
>
> I was always against collective executions. I didn't think it right
> to turn the ghetto into a battlefield of Jews against Jews. The
> time came when we had to kill, but I wanted to announce it
> openly and to justify it, to say why every killing was carried out.[104]

From the resistance perspective Jewish policemen served the
German occupier, the enemy, even though their motives were often
understandable in trying to save the lives of their own families.
The Germans would have been unable to do their job so thoroughly
without the calming influence of the Jewish police, who reassured
the crowds at the deportation centre by their very presence:

> because the Jews would certainly have run away from the Ger-
> mans, but when they saw a Jewish policeman, it didn't occur to
> them he would lead them to their death.[105]

Zuckerman wrote movingly of the moral weight placed upon the
Resistance: 'The burden was extraordinary, the historical responsibility was tremendous.'[106] Despite his anguish at having to sign the
death warrant of fellow Jews, Zuckerman nevertheless felt that some
Jewish policemen and paid informers had condemned themselves
by their own actions:

> So we started . . . attacking policemen. We didn't slay just any
> policeman, we wanted to find the policemen who played a special
> role at the Umschlagplatz, organizing the transports.[107]

However, although the Resistance had 'no choice' but to execute high-ranking policemen and collaborators who put resistance units in danger, Zuckerman was still beset by moral doubts:

> It took me a long time to get rid of the worm gnawing at my insides. It was a sense of responsibility for a human life. I was forced to accept it.[108]

The Judenrate had a thankless task which fuelled legitimate grievances. The tragedy is that while the underground criticized the Jewish Council's actions, they could not offer an alternative strategy to rescue their communities. Primo Levi asks us to consider how we would have behaved if we were driven by the necessity of the victims:

> We are all mirrored in Rumkowski, his ambiguity is ours.[109]

Levi accepts the 'perversion' and moral corruption of the victims by the Nazi system, but adds:

> The condition of the offended does not exclude culpability... but I know of no human tribunal to which one could delegate the judgment.[110]

If each Jewish Council member carried more than his quota of guilt, nevertheless, how would we begin to measure it or sit in judgement upon it? Significantly neither the Courts of Honour in the Displaced Persons camps, nor the Israeli courts regarded membership of the Jewish Councils or Jewish police forces as reprehensible in itself. In 1950 the Knesset's *Nazis and Nazi Collaborators' Law No. 5710* stated that an individual was not punishable or guilty of collaboration if he 'did or omitted to do an act with intent to avert consequences more serious than those which resulted from the act or omission.'[111]

The plight of the Jewish Councils illustrates the difficulty inherent in applying normal codes of judgement to the abnormal condition of the ghettos, and it raises the problem of determining what moral criteria would be appropriate in evaluating the actions of council members and policemen.

CONCLUSION

The Judenrat, like the ghetto as a whole, had two faces – a Jewish face and a German face. Its split personality, its moral schizophrenia, was the result of trying to preserve Jewish life while aiding the German death machine. Many Jews had initially welcomed ghettoization, despite the cramped, overcrowded conditions, because the ghetto offered a fragile form of safety and shelter, a respite from the prevailing anti-semitism among the local population. It also meant that German security personnel were seen less frequently. A certain amount of autonomy, a breathing-space, existed within the confined walls of the ghetto. Most Jews regarded their communities as a necessary means of alleviating the harsh conditions of life under Nazi domination. However, the ghettos were constructed for German purposes and not for the benefit of Jews. *They were not so much Jewish ghettos as ghettos for Jews*: that is, dumping grounds, transit or holding camps; an ante-chamber to the gas chambers.

The Jewish Councils reflected this anomalous, contradictory position. They tried to serve Jewish interests, but they were instigated by the Germans and inevitably became their unwitting tools. The Jewish Councils frantically tried to turn their ghettos into a life-saving device, but they could not do this while simultaneously obeying the Germans, who only viewed the ghettos as a conveyor belt of slaves and corpses. All the paradoxes, all the moral dilemmas inherent in the contradictory position of the Jewish Councils and the Jewish police are the result of the endless web of impossible choices that the Nazis had spun in order to trap their victims. But there was no way for Jews to disentangle themselves from this trap in which they were ensnared. There was no possibility of transcending their condition, no way of leaping over the walls which literally and metaphorically confined them. As we shall see in the next chapter, armed resistance only hastened death.

The choices facing the Councils would have taxed and defeated the wisdom of a Solomon, or the world's greatest minds working with the luxury of time and in conditions of comfort and plenty. The Judenrate leaders had to make decisions under the crushing burden of German terror, forced starvation and a literal deadline. In the breaking of moral boundaries, the Council leaders were themselves torn asunder. The complexity of the moral problems facing the Jewish Councils was encapsulated in the words of Dr Elkes, a physician who became President of the Kovno ghetto:

Who can find his way in this maze; who can distinguish between truth and fiction, between good and evil?[112]

What Hannah Arendt failed to appreciate was that Jewish communities were inextricably trapped in a vicious circle: they faced an insoluble dilemma. They could not survive *without* co-operation with the Nazis, and yet they could not survive *with* it either. In that sense they faced an intolerable choice between impossibilities. Understanding this gives one a glimpse of the full extent of the Jewish tragedy. For the vast majority of Jews, no methods of survival worked. Neither resistance nor 'collaboration' offered a solution for the Jews, because under the terms of the Final Solution, none existed.

It does not become us – those of us who came after, after Auschwitz, after Treblinka – to speak in an accusatory tone, to engage in supercilious condemnation, to pronounce magisterial, yet facile, judgement. There is something not only insensitive, but indecent about such retrospective certainty. The wisdom conferred by hindsight is not appropriate when trying to come to terms with the plight of the Jewish Councils. We have to struggle to attain imaginative historical understanding, but we who have never known the dread threat of collective responsibility and the constant insecurity and debilitating fear engendered by Nazi terror, we who have never felt the ravages of hunger and starvation, have to acknowledge the limitations of our search. As Holocaust survivor Elie Wiesel stated:

You who were not there will never understand.[113]

But we have to attempt to understand when trying to wrestle with the moral dilemmas which tormented the Jewish Councils. We must confront the question: what would I have done in their place?

Is it for us to judge them, we who were not there? ... In another time, in another place, could or would the noblest of us have done otherwise?[114]

8 Jewish Resistance and the Dilemma of Collective Responsibility

> Knowing how strong family ties are among Jews, and that they would not jeopardize their families, nor the community as a whole, for the sake of saving their own skins, the Nazis practised collective responsibility. They did not shy away from killing children in front of their mothers ... if a Jew were to kill one, two or more Nazis, he would have accomplished nothing, but only exposed others to collective punishment.[1]
>
> Joachim Schoenfeld, Holocaust Survivor

> Inasmuch as the enemy had established collective Jewish responsibility, we could not raise a hand against the Germans, and so bring about the murder of thousands of Jews ... these were psychological hindrances for every Jew. ... These psychological restraints stemmed primarily from the Nazi doctrine of collective responsibility and collective guilt; this weighed down the decision.[2]
>
> Yitzak Zuckerman, Commander of the Jewish Fighting Organisation in the Warsaw Ghetto

The clear and repeated testimony of numerous survivors and Jewish resistance leaders is that collective responsibility was the most important obstacle to the development of Jewish armed resistance, and was the primary reason for forced co-operation with the Nazis. The allegation that Jews were submissive and went 'like sheep to the slaughter' ignores the unique constraints placed upon Jewish communities by German security measures. The question, 'Why did Jews not resist their killers?' is insensitive, is based upon hindsight – upon a clear knowledge of Nazi intentions and policy towards the Jews of Europe – and lacks historical understanding. When we examine the conditions in which Jews were confined, the question which really needs addressing is not why there was so little Jewish resistance, but why there was any resistance at all? As Elie Wiesel observes:

The question is not why all the Jews did not fight, but how so many of them did. Tormented, beaten, starved, where did they find the strength – spiritual and physical – to resist?[3]

The awesome threat of collective responsibility overshadowed every aspect of life in the ghettos – from the feverish debates concerning the appropriate strategy for survival: the choice between co-operation and resistance, to the dilemmas within the resistance movements over the forms and timing of resistance: the questions of where, when and how to resist. The overriding restriction imposed upon Jewish communities was the fear and certainty of collective retribution and vengeance for any disobedience of Nazi rules. An act of resistance would lead to a chain of brutal reprisals upon one's family and the community. One Jewish survivor has written that: 'All this fear kept us disoriented – it didn't occur to us to fight back. The only thing we could feel was the terror that we would soon be dead'.[4] Frequently, however, it required extraordinary self-restraint and self-discipline not to retaliate, not to reply to Nazi taunts and abuse with physical force. Nevertheless, no-one could resist without the certain knowledge that they were putting their family, and possibly the whole ghetto, in deadly peril. After some food smugglers were caught by the Germans in Kovno in October 1942, their entire families were executed: eight adults and five small children. The ghetto diarist Avraham Tory asked:

the most ominous question of all: why did the children have to die for the real or imaginary offences of their parents, or women for the sins of their husbands? . . . and all this because a number of people made a wrong step, not to get rich, but to bring home some flour.[5]

Most ghetto inhabitants accepted that the only viable strategy was the policy of reluctant co-operation with the Nazis, making the ghettos economically productive. The strategy of 'rescue through work' seemed the most sensible course of action to save Jewish lives until the hoped-for Allied victory. Armed resistance, however, was widely regarded as a reckless symbolic gesture which was only guaranteed to endanger the whole community. Most Jews wanted to outlast, not overthrow, the Nazis.

The decision to engage in organized resistance required an accurate understanding of German intentions. Until it was certain that total extermination was the Nazis' aim, the vast majority of Jews supported the Jewish Council policy of making their ghetto useful to the German war effort. Only after the majority in a ghetto had already been deported, and it became clear that the remainder would follow, did Jews legitimize armed resistance. As long as survival was perceived to be a possibility, caution and prudence prevailed and violent resistance was rejected. The overriding fear was that a premature revolt would precipitate a wholesale massacre of Jews in the ghetto, or even throughout the region. It was this sense of community, Jewish solidarity, which prevented Jews from rebelling. Armed resistance would only hasten the liquidation of the ghetto.

In a number of ghettos the pressure of public opinion was exerted to discourage the costly futility of individual acts of violence which only brought collective retribution. The ghetto inhabitants of the town of Radoszkowice in the district of Vilna were so fearful of German reprisals that they tried to intimidate the newly formed underground movement. One member of the underground stated that:

> The Council members tried very hard to persuade us that the plan to join the partisans should be abandoned . . . We were warned that many Jews would be killed because of us. . . . The people threatened to denounce us to the Germans if we did not give up our plan.[6]

In other ghettos, similar threats of denunciation were issued. Far from being seen as heroic defenders or champions of their people's cause, escapers and resisters were widely regarded as rash adventurers who betrayed fellow Jews by endangering their lives. Lucy Dawidowicz makes the important point that while survival seemed a possibility:

> Ghetto Jews regarded the young who planned and plotted armed resistance as irresponsible hotheads who would bring disaster upon the whole ghetto.[7]

Collective responsibility bred the illusion that if Jews did not fight, if they did not resist, then their situation would improve and their security would be assured. Those who opposed armed resistance raised the question of the legitimacy and authority of the partisans: by what right did the resisters claim to represent the Jewish masses when they sought to engage in rebellion? Who authorized or sanctioned their assumed leadership over the Jewish community? It was the old biblical question – 'Who put you as leaders over us?' One of the resistance leaders in the Bialystok ghetto recalls the constant questioning of their strategy by the majority:

'Is it worthwhile? Is it possible? Maybe it is better to save Jews and help them exist? Is it worthwhile for one act of heroism to endanger the whole ghetto?' These were the questions that they always asked in response to our demands.[8]

Without a firm grasp of the debilitating insecurity, the psychological constraints upon resistance imposed by the doctrine of collective responsibility, we cannot begin to understand the way in which the leaders of the Jewish Councils and the leaders of the resistance movements were tormented by an inner struggle over the most painful moral choices that human beings have ever had to face. The whole question of Jewish resistance and 'collaboration' must be viewed in the context of German security policy.

In order to instil fear and to paralyse any opposition, the Germans devised an elaborate system in which the workings of collective responsibility reached down into the smallest details of ghetto life. In addition to the starvation diet and the threat to reduce or withhold food supplies in the event of disobedience, the Germans operated a simple but effective technique of control. Each tenement block had to have a concierge who was responsible for the keeping of house registers containing accurate information about all tenants (including the birth dates of new-born babies). The Jewish Police also had to keep a card index of ghetto residents at police headquarters. An unannounced raid by German security police in which unregistered people were discovered would result in collective punishments, including the concierge's relatives. The absence of a Jew during a house inspection could end in the death of all his neighbours. If a gun was found in a house search, the tenement would be blown up, and 50 people from the apartment would be shot. A solitary act of industrial sabotage could result in the murder of all the factory workers.

In the Kovno ghetto, the leaders of the labour brigades were called to a meeting, and an order from the Gestapo was read out:

It said that labor brigade leaders would be answerable for unau thorized trading and absenteeism from the place of work. If any one is caught committing these offences, his labor brigade leader and the members of his family will be arrested and executed. In more serious cases, several labor brigade leaders will be executed together with their families. The guiding principle is: ALL ARE RESPONSIBLE FOR EVERYONE AND EVERYONE RESPONSIBLE FOR ALL.[9]

In one incident in February 1943, 45 people, including entire families, were killed for deviation from these strict instructions. An anti-German resistance slogan daubed on the wall of a build ing could be sufficient to sign the death warrant of all its inhabi tants. Leni Yahil cites an incident during the first few days of the deportations from the Warsaw Ghetto in the summer of 1942:

Stone splinters hit a car carrying SS men from the unit conduct ing the operation. It was not even clear whether a brick had fallen from the roof of the house or whether the stone had been thrown deliberately. All the inhabitants of the house adjacent to the site of the incident were seized indiscriminately and sent with the next transport to a death camp.[10]

In a similar incident, a piece of glass fell onto the street when some Germans were passing, and all the occupants were removed

Huge numbers of dead at 29 Ogrodowa Street. . . . Shooting all day.[11]

Jews who left the ghetto without official permission were liable to be shot on the spot; ghetto inhabitants who hid fugitive Jews were also subject to instant execution. For both of these offences collective responsibility automatically included the entire family of the offender. In the town of Lida, a girl lost her Jewish armband. She was executed, along with her whole family.[12] In another inci dent in the Warsaw Ghetto in October 1941, 30 Jewish children were drowned by German police as a punishment and a warning for the infraction of rules.[13] Thus any form of disobedience – not only armed resistance, but also non-violent acts – resulted in col lective punishment. The failed attempt by two Jewish food smug glers to resist arrest and inevitable death led to the additional death of 110 people in the Warsaw Ghetto, including 10 Jewish police-men, for failure to carry out their orders to combat smuggling with sufficient zeal. Chaim A. Kaplan noted in his diary:

> And thus the sin is expiated with a hundred civilians and ten policemen.[14]
>
> The Nazis avenged the mutiny of the two porters with a hun-dred and ten Jews. They were put to death for the sins of men who had never laid eyes on them.[15]

ESCAPE AND COLLECTIVE RESPONSIBILITY

Escape as a form of resistance – whether to join the partisans in the forests, or to flee to Palestine, or to hide, if possible, among the gentile population – was fraught with moral as well as prac-tical difficulties. Escape carried with it a human cost for those left behind. Anyone discovered escaping from a ghetto imperilled the lives of family and friends who remained. This gave rise to agoniz-ing misgivings about whether resisters were morally entitled to endanger their fellow Jews, or to put personal survival above loyalty to the group. After six Jews escaped from a labour camp outside Vilna on 29 June 1943, 67 out of the camp's 300 workers were shot immediately.[16]

On 22 July 1943, 21 young people escaped from the Vilna ghetto to join Jewish partisans in a nearby forest. In retaliation the Ge-tapo chief, Neugebauer, issued a decree of collective responsibility, under which the entire families of the escapees were arrested. If an escapee did not have a family, all persons who lived with him in the same room were to be seized. If they were not discovered, all the inhabitants of the building were to be seized. Thirty-two people were shot. In addition, all work parties which left the ghetto were divided into groups of ten. If one Jew escaped, the remaining nine members of the labour gang would be shot. Thus, each was re-sponsible for the behaviour of all.[17]

After this incident, the Vilna ghetto newspaper issued an edi-torial entitled 'Wrath and Grief':

> The responsibility for these deaths falls on those who betrayed our ghetto community and all its serious tasks in the full knowl-edge that they were endangering the existence of our entire ghetto

and the lives of their loved ones in the first place. They are responsible for the spilt blood.[18]

Yitzhak Arad, a leading figure in the Vilna ghetto resistance,
observed that:

> The order concerning collective responsibility rendered the in-
> habitants of the ghetto guardians over one another. People feared
> that they would pay with their lives for the flight of a family
> member, a tenant, a workmate.[19]

Escape was an option for single, unattached young people, but
not for those with large families. A 20-year-old in eastern Poland
could flee to the forests to join the partisans. But whole families
which included the very young, the sick, elderly and infirm, could
not escape. Under the principle of collective responsibility, the
potential resister or escaper had to weigh up the devastating reprisals that the Nazis would visit upon the entire ghetto. Every
young, able-bodied man or woman knew that the fate of infants,
children, the feeble and the old depended upon their decision. Thus,
the system of collective responsibility acted as a powerful restraint
upon resistance and escape. It also raised the question: what was
the primary purpose of Jewish resistance? To kill Germans, and to
wage offensive warfare? Or to save Jewish lives? The forests provided the most suitable terrain, the best prospects, for partisan war.
Yet it required a cool assessment of the harsh reality that it was
impossible to save masses of Jews by escaping to the forests, whereas
it was certain to jeopardize the lives of those who remained. Chaika
Grossman in the Bialystok ghetto recounts that:

> We had to decide what was more worthwhile, what would cause
> the Germans more damage – war in the ghetto or in the forest.

During a debate within her group, one resister called Edek posed
the problem:

> Perhaps in the forest there are better prospects for effective
> warfare. Are we, however, going to be satisfied with that, and
> leave the masses to their fate, to be led ... like sheep to the
> slaughter, so that we may seek effective battle in the forest? ...
> [sabotage and partisan warfare] are very important, but do the

provide an answer to the central question: how do you organize a mass response, how do you bring a whole people's resistance to fruition . . . to keep them from being annihilated? Are we going to fight in the forest and disclaim any responsibility? Will we have done our duty? The forest is a solution for individuals who want to help in the war against Nazism, but where is the collective, national solution? Are we going to desert the . . . ghetto, with its old people, women and children, and say: we have saved our lives? . . . We are being killed as Jews, and it is as Jews that we must fight back, not as individuals but as an organized community.[20]

Similar arguments prevailed amongst those Jewish Councils which were sympathetic to the idea of escape and resistance. Isaiah Rubinstein, Chairman of the Miedryrzec Judenrat, was consulted by a youth group in the ghetto. They confided in him their plan to escape. He replied:

Believe me, I too would have escaped together with you, but how can one abandon the ghetto? You may escape, but next day the Germans will kill everyone, including your families. If all could escape, I would have understood your desire. But even if you rescued yourselves, your parents and all those who remained behind in the ghetto would perish, innocent victims.[21]

The witness to this powerful speech concluded that:

People understood that the responsibility was too great, and that it was a crime to risk the lives of other ghetto inmates. Those were quite weird times. One did not know what was better to do and what was not.[22]

Collective responsibility also burdened the conscience of the solitary fugitive from Nazi 'justice'. Joseph Schupack, a Polish Jew from the town of Radzyn, recounts how his brother was being sought by the Gestapo in connection with an act of sabotage. The brother hid in a barn. The security police left an order at the family house, stating that he must report to the Gestapo office within three days. They then informed the Judenrat that if the order was not obeyed, the entire Judenrat (12 members) and 100 Jews from the town would be shot.

The alternatives we faced were horrible. Either we had to deliver my brother to his murderers or we have the death of 112 men on our consciences, not to mention the suffering of the widows and orphans. Several members of the Judenrat ... came to our house. Some of them implored, some threatened, others pitied us. Friends, relatives, Torah scholars – all of them wanted to help, but none knew how. Nobody doubted the seriousness of the threat.

... it was cruel enough when the Gestapo picked up its victims, but at least one did not have to blame oneself. It was our misfortune to be chosen and thereby punished further when we had to deliver our victims ourselves. The beast did not only want our blood, he wanted to be served as well.[23]

To live with the knowledge that the ultimatum was to expire in 72 hours was the tragedy of this family. Eventually the brother handed himself over to the Gestapo, where he was tortured mercilessly before being shot.

The same method of moral blackmail was used persistently by German security forces in order to exert control. In July 1941, a young Serbian Jewish resister called Almoslino set fire to a German military vehicle in Belgrade. The Jewish male population of the city was ordered to assemble in the main square in the city centre. Every tenth man was ordered to step out, believing that the Germans were organizing a transport for forced labour. After 100 men had been selected, the Germans stated that they would be held hostage, and would be shot if the culprit did not surrender within 48 hours. He did not give himself up, and the hostages were killed. In the Dozhynov ghetto in Lithuania, two young Jews were caught trying to leave the ghetto, but they managed to escape. The Germans informed the Judenrat that if the men did not surrender, the ghetto would be liquidated immediately. The men refused to return:

knowing that they were endangering the lives of hundreds of others. On the morrow the inhabitants of the ghetto were shot. What would we have done in the place of the youngsters?[24]

Should they have surrendered in order to avert the death of innocents?

In the Kovno ghetto, two Jews named Katz and Gelson were

wanted by the Gestapo on a charge of theft. They could not be found, but Gelson's sister lived in the ghetto. The Kovno ghetto diarist noted:

> It is conceivable that the Gestapo will issue an order for her arrest, and even execute her. There is a general consensus that in such a case she would be an innocent victim.
>
> We are racking our brains trying to find a way out of the mess. This is not a theoretical issue but a matter of life and death. The Gestapo ... have set a deadline – eight days from today – for handing Katz over. If within that time Katz is not found, the Chief of the Jewish Police, Kopelman, and the Chief of the Criminal Section of the Jewish Police, Bramson, together with their families, will be taken to the Ninth Fort. [Execution site][25]

Even more severe consequences confronted Jacob Gens, the head of the Vilna Judenrat. A Jewish Communist resister, Yitzhak Vittenberg, had escaped from captivity after his followers had attacked the Lithuanian collaborationist policemen who were guarding him. Vittenberg was being hidden in the Vilna ghetto. Gens was ordered to turn Vittenberg over to the Gestapo within six hours. If he failed to comply, the whole ghetto would be destroyed. The fear that the Germans would indeed liquidate the ghetto was real and plausible. A few days earlier the labour camps at Bezdany and Kena had been liquidated with the murder of thousands of young working Jews. This was at the forefront of the minds of the inhabitants of the Vilna ghetto. Gens convened a meeting with the Jewish resistance movement in the ghetto, and informed them:

> The Gestapo is demanding that Vittenberg be surrendered to them within a few hours. If he is not surrendered, then German tanks and planes will demolish the ghetto by bombing ...
>
> What's to be done now? Shall we become victims because of one man? Or shall we give up this one and save all?[26]

Gens had passed the burden of choice to the resistance itself. Jewish resisters now faced the dilemma of either turning over their leader, or accepting responsibility for the immediate loss of thousands of Jewish lives. Armed resistance was not possible without popular support, and public opinion in the ghetto was firmly against Vittenberg. Although Vittenberg understandably did not want to surrender, it is significant that his own organization, the Communists, demanded that he be handed over in order to avert a massacre. The next morning his body was found in the courtyard of Gestapo headquarters, his hair burned, his eyes gouged out, and his broken arms tied behind his back. The following day, a band of Jewish fighters was ambushed in a forest outside Vilna. The Nazis applied the principle of collective responsibility, killing their families and the brigade foremen from whose labour units the resisters had absconded, 32 people in total.

This series of events clarifies the complex nature of the choices facing both resisters and Jewish Councils. Like some other Judenrate leaders, Gens has been reviled as an 'outright collaborator',[27] the leader of a 'puppet council'[28] which followed a policy of 'abject co-operation'.[29] But this is a gross distortion, a pantomime caricature which ignores the bitter choice which crushed the Councils. Gens was personally incorruptible. He stamped out informers, and unofficial smuggling for personal gain. Gens was ambivalent in his attitude towards resistance. He knew for a long time of the existence of the resistance movement, and some of his closest friends were members of the Underground. He made no attempt to suppress it. But he could not support it, despite his sympathy with its aims. He gambled everything on the Red Army liberating Vilna in time to save a remnant of the Jewish people. Resistance only provoked the Germans, and cost more lives than it saved. Gens was under no illusions. In a conversation with an idealistic young Jewish partisan, he said:

> The ghetto is a death chamber which holds men, women and little children. The death sentence has already been pronounced, but not yet carried out, and the final date is not known. I want to postpone that date, postpone it with all my potential, with all my strength. . . . Who among you dares to hasten that day of liquidation? Who of you has the right to shorten the days and hours of children and women who live in the ghetto? . . . I'm not armed with ideals like you. I'm not armed by visions of honour and a hero's death in the resistance. . . . The only weapon I have is time. I want to avert the end through work. . . . Thanks to that the ghetto exists.[30]

Gens, Elkes, and the other Judenrate leaders who engaged in desperate compromises with the Germans, knew that in the process they became morally compromised. They fully accepted their responsibility, knowing that in an absolute sense their position was morally untenable. But they faced an unprecedented choice in an extreme emergency. They lacked the power to confront or challenge the Nazis directly. To portray them as traitors to their people, as vile lackeys to their German overlords, is to ignore the fact that they were overwhelmed by circumstances which were not of their making, and which were beyond their control.

The Jewish resister Yitzhak Arad, who escaped from the Vilna ghetto and became an active combatant among the partisans in the Belorussian forests, offers a more sympathetic understanding of the complex issues, arguing that the accusations that Jews did not resist, and 'went like sheep to the slaughter'

> are based upon a misunderstanding of the situation of the Jews at the time. . . . The main problem of the Jewish Resistance, then, I would say, was that the way to the forest was open only for young men who could get arms and fight in the forest. For the Jewish masses – women, children, elderly people – there was no way. I was without a family, without children, so it wasn't a question for me. But I ask myself today, 'if I had been twenty-four . . . married, and with two children in the ghetto, what would I have done?' I might have been working in some German factory. That gave us a little security, a way to get food for my family. And I would live like others in the ghetto, hoping that some miracle might happen [a sudden Allied victory, or the death of Hitler]. . . . People lived with some hope. Maybe as a young man I might have possibly escaped to the forest with some guns and left my wife and children behind in order to fight and blow up some German trains. . . . I have asked myself many times, 'What would have been the right thing to do? What does courage mean in this situation?' If you go out to fight and destroy things, you leave your family helpless. At the first selection or first 'aktion' they become immediate victims. Even before that they will suffer from lack of food. If you stay with them you hope you will survive together. Which is the most courageous choice?[31]

Thus the path to the forest was blocked by the inexorable law of collective and family responsibility.

JEWISH ARMED RESISTANCE

> Resistance by force is meaningless. One or two Germans can be
> 'knocked off' but the Ghetto as a whole will bear the conse-
> quences. With just one German heavy machine gun, an entire
> Ghetto quarter can be destroyed; two or three aircraft are enough
> to raze the whole Ghetto to the ground. Armed resistance is of
> no avail. Two or three people can escape but scores of Ghetto
> inmates will suffer.[32]
>
> Avraham Tory, Kovno Ghetto, 4 September 1943

> Lest innocent blood be shed in your land . . . and the guilt of
> bloodshed be upon you.
>
> Deuteronomy, 9:10

Armed resistance cost lives rather than saved them. As we have
seen in previous chapters, throughout Europe the Nazis introduced
a hostage tally, a set of pre-determined quotas for every German
soldier killed or wounded. In France the quota was 10:1, in eastern Europe it was set at 100:1. If European resisters understandably tended to act cautiously in the light of this deterrent policy,
the same rule applied with much greater intensity as a restraint
upon Jewish armed resistance, where the reprisal rate was 250:1 in
Germany, and often in excess of 1000:1 in eastern Europe. Frequently German reprisals were random and unpredictable. In the
Lvov ghetto in August 1942, after a Jew called Feldman stabbed a
Gestapo official to death, German security police publicly executed
his entire family in front of their houses, and arrested and killed
all Jews registered under the name of Feldman.[33] In Czestochowa
in south-west Poland, the failed attempt to assassinate a German
officer in January 1943 resulted in the arbitrary selection and
execution of 25 Jews, and the further arrest of 300 Jewish men
and women. Most died in concentration camps. In the summer of
1942, a group of German Jewish Communists set fire to an anti-
Soviet propaganda exhibition in Berlin. For this act of sabotage in
which five Germans died, 250 Jews were arrested and shot
immediately, and another 250 were deported to Sachsenhausen concentration camp, where they died soon after. The Berlin Gestapo
chief, Muller, warned that if anything similar happened, 250 Jews
would be killed for every German casualty. According to the Jewish

historian Nora Levin this demonstrated 'the utter futility of physical resistance'.[34]

For every German killed by a Jewish resister in occupied Poland or Russia, over a thousand Jews could be executed as a collective punishment, and usually any captured resisters would be killed by barbaric methods. In the Lublin district, any Jew caught in possession of a gun, or deemed to be committing an act of sabotage, was hung by his scrotum on a hook. The gauleiter of Warthegau burned Jewish resisters at the stake, whilst in Minsk, the SS chief blinded suspected resistance members with hot irons and then returned them to the ghetto as a deterrent warning for future unrest.[35]

Three particularly horrifying incidents reveal the full consequences of armed resistance. On 26 September 1941, in the Kovno ghetto, it was alleged that some Jews had shot at a German police officer. This was used as the official pretext for an 'action' to teach the Jews to keep their place.

> The whole area was surrounded by soldiers and some 1000 Jews were removed from it. . . . The deported did not return.[36]

In Lvov on March 16th 1943, an SS policeman noted for his cruelty was killed by a Jew. The following day 1200 Jews were killed. A rebellion by Jewish fighters who tried to break out of the Bialystok ghetto in August 1943 resulted in the seizure and murder of 1200 Jewish children under the age of 13 as a punishment. The children died in Theresienstadt and at Birkenau, along with 53 adults who volunteered to accompany them.[37]

Collective responsibility drowned Jewish resistance in the blood of the innocent. It was this factor of massive collective punishments – a reprisal ratio of 1200:1 – which more than anything else inhibited, and indeed paralysed, Jewish communities into indecision. Collective responsibility crippled the growth of armed resistance, until the final stages of deportation when there was nothing left to preserve except Jewish honour.

Before that final stage had been reached, it was felt that premature Jewish armed resistance would only precipitate a senseless slaughter of the children, the weak, the infirm and the elderly. They were the first victims, not healthy young workers who might be tempted to take up arms against their fate. Able-bodied Jews who wanted to engage in armed resistance knew that they were putting their family and their ghetto in deadly peril. In January 1943, a group of Jewish partisans visited the Pruzana ghetto, but were surprised by an unexpected visit by the local Gestapo. A Jewish watchman was killed, and some Jewish Council members were wounded in the ensuing escape. The Gestapo then gave the Judenrat a short period in which to complete the impossible task of delivering the partisans, who had vanished. As a result, the entire population of the ghetto was murdered.[38] In the small town of Wawolnica in the Lublin district, an ethnic German was killed, probably by Polish resisters. The Germans used this as a pretext for massacring the whole community of Jews.

While resisters could determine their own fate, the fate of their Jewish brethren, the young and the old, the infant and the infirm, hinged upon their decisions. They could save themselves by escaping, but only by abandoning their neighbours to their fate. Resisters had to weigh up the consequences and repercussions of rebellion, not just for themselves, but for family and friends, and the wider community. Was it right to kill a German soldier, or an SS official, if as a result a thousand innocent men, women and children would perish immediately? It was impossible to disregard the terrible collective vengeance of the Nazis.

Lawrence Langer cites the testimony of a Holocaust survivor called Luna K. She articulates the chronic state of fear engineered by the Nazis, and the need to de-romanticize resistance:

> When you talk about rebellion and resistance . . . every single individual who . . . wanted to perform an act of resistance was an individual who had to make a conscious choice right then and there, that he not only will commit the rebellious act, but he along with himself will take with him scores of people. So it was not a question of . . . 'You can shoot me' but it was . . . 'You can shoot me and another hundred people' and who wanted this kind of responsibility? You know . . . it's very easy to say, 'All right I will be the victim and I will go to the forefront so that you can be free . . . it was far more troublesome to say I will go to the forefront, therefore I am condemning you to death together with me. And that kind of responsibility was a very, very difficult thing to face.[39]

In a similar vein, Yitzak Zuckerman, one of the founders of the Jewish resistance movement in the Warsaw Ghetto, pinpointed the main difficulty in organizing Jewish resistance:

by applying the principle of collective responsibility they sought to destroy all opposition.[40]

So, as we have seen in relation to European resistance as a whole, German security policy was built around the simple, but effective psychological strategy of exploiting the moral confusion of those under their control. The grave issues raised by collective responsibility caused torments of conscience for Jewish resisters. In his diary entry for 17 June 1942, Emmanuel Ringelblum agonized over the dilemma of whether Jews should escape to the forests in order to resist:

> This question bothers us all, but there is no answer, for everybody knows that resistance, even if it causes the death of a single German, is liable to bring about the slaughter of the whole community, even many communities. The first victims are the aged, the weak, the children, who are unable to offer any resistance. The strong ones, the workers – these for the time being are allowed to stay where they are, for they are still needed. . . . The instinct to stay alive is very strong among the workers and those who are fortunate enough to possess the J-card [work permit]. It is stronger than the will to fight and the urge to defend the community. . . . There is also another important factor – complete moral disintegration, erosion of the will to resist as a result of the unprecedented terror being applied to the Jews for three years . . . which is now reaching its height in the deportations. As a result . . . just when we should be displaying some kind of resistance, we are completely defenceless, and the enemy is doing with us whatever he wishes.[41]

The most serious moral dilemma that Jewish resisters had to wrestle with was whether they had the right to jeopardize the lives of countless innocent fellow Jews because they were prepared to risk their own lives. Under the conditions of collective responsibility Jewish resistance was guaranteed to end in collective suicide. It has been necessary to dwell at length upon this crucial aspect of the problem of collective responsibility in order to see Jewish resistance in proper perspective.

It is also instructive to compare Jewish resistance with other European movements, in order to highlight the important similarities and the vital differences between them. There was a common thread, a discernible pattern which can be traced through all European resistance movements – the problem of finding an answer to German security policy. It is important to bear in mind three important factors:

(1) The Jewish experience was unique in the grim history of Nazi Europe. It was qualitatively different – different in kind – from the persecution of other subject peoples, because the Jews were the only people marked for total extinction. In between resistance and co-operation, other peoples could resort to what the French labelled *attentisme*, lying low and adopting a 'wait-and-see' attitude. This was not possible for Jews. If French or Danish resisters laid down their arms, or if no armed resistance existed, they could reasonably expect their communities to survive, and to look forward to liberation and an Allied victory. For Jews, no strategy for survival worked. If they didn't take up arms, they were doomed to annihilation. If they resorted to armed struggle, this only hastened their extinction. Neither resistance, nor negotiation, nor co-operation, could avert death. There were no moral signposts which pointed to life and the future. Every road led to death.

(2) Jewish resistance was unique in the degree, intensity and severity of punishment meted out for defiance. It was both qualitatively and quantitatively different from other resistance struggles.

(3) Jewish resistance was an 'army without arms'.[42] Jews lacked the most elementary prerequisites for resistance. Jews had no government-in-exile to represent them, no Jewish state to speak on their behalf, no supplies of weapons, equipment, money or training. According to the French historian and resistance veteran, Henri Michel:

> it never occurred to the Allies to give the Jews any role. . . . There was no resistance movement which, from the very outset, was more handicapped.[43]

The British government, via SOE, dropped supplies of arms to the Polish Home Army but did not furnish Jews with weapons. The indispensable condition for a successful partisan movement is the sympathy and tacit approval of the indigenous population, in order to have the freedom of movement to conduct their operations, and the shelter of safe areas. Jewish resistance was conducted mong starving populations condemned to live in isolation in sealed, egregated ghettos, with no escape routes and no retreats or safe avens, and with virtually no contact with the outside world, in ostile areas of eastern Europe which were frequently anti-semitic. 'itzak Zuckerman described how partisans required a hinterland ith the sympathy of the surrounding area. But 'because of the ostile attitude of the population, there was no chance for Jewish artisans to remain alive without any backup . . . there practically asn't a single village that was sympathetic to the Jews. Under uch conditions, a Jewish partisan unit simply couldn't exist'.[44] With eapons and local support Jewish resisters would have faced a uperhuman task; without it, they faced an insuperable one.

Armed resistance required weapons, but collective responsibility nade it difficult for Jewish resisters to obtain and procure weapons rom Polish villagers. After the defeat of the Polish Army in 1939 eapons were hidden outside villages. But the peasants were afraid o give them to partisans:

> because giving weapons to the enemies of the Germans was a death sentence on the whole village since the Germans applied collective responsibility. And there was always somebody who, out of cowardice or obsequiousness, would tell the Germans where the weapons were. The ordinary person didn't keep weapons because that jeopardized himself, his family, and his courtyard. And everyone was afraid his friend or neighbour would denounce him.[45]

The Jewish Fighting Organization in the Warsaw Ghetto instructed ts members not to carry weapons unless they were authorized to carry out a specific operation. Wildcat shootings by individuals had ed to mass punishments. In order to avoid any provocation to the Germans which could lead to catastrophic consequences the Jewish resistance movement banned the use of weapons ahead of time

> so as not to bring collective punishment on an entire courtyard. That was a great responsibility. . . . We concluded that even a small provocation was liable to bring the liquidation of the ghetto.[46]

According to Zuckerman, one incident which led to severe retaliation against innocent Jews

evoked a harsh discussion. I argued that a Jewish Fighting Organization that couldn't protect the lives of the Jews was not authorized to engage in acts that endangered their lives! I felt ashamed
in that sharp discussion. There's no trick to killing one or two
individual Germans . . . I felt that those dead Jews who were killed
in a German retaliatory raid were on the conscience of the Jewish
Fighting Organization.

. . . . the average Jew . . . suddenly found himself paying for
something he hadn't done, didn't know anything about, and therefore of course couldn't have refrained from.[47]

Nevertheless, when it became clear that the Jewish Councils' strategy for survival – 'rescue through work' – had failed, Jews committed themselves to armed resistance. But before that final stage
was reached, resisters had to address the vexed question of when
to endanger the whole community, and where to fight.

Jewish resisters conducted passionate debates on the question of
where to engage the enemy – the ghetto or the forest? This was
not just a technical decision concerning the most appropriate military strategy, but fundamentally an ethical issue. If they fled to the
forests, resisters would have to abandon their families and friends
leaving the ghetto population vulnerable to German reprisals. If
the resisters remained, the ghetto would be turned into a besieged
battle camp. The very presence of a predominantly non-combatant
population of children, the sick and elderly, made the ghetto an
inappropriate place to conduct a pitched battle with the might of
the German security forces.

The preserved minutes of a dramatic debate in the Bialystok ghetto
in February 1943, bring out the full tragedy of this choice:

Isaac: 'What we're really debating is two different kinds of death.
Attack means certain death. The other way means death two or
three days later.'
Enoch: 'No illusions! We have nothing to expect but liquidation
to the last Jew. We have a choice of two kinds of death. The
woods won't save us, and certainly rebellion in the ghetto won't.
There remains for us only to die honourably.'[48]

Jewish resisters had to judge when it became morally acceptable
to jeopardize the last remnants of the ghetto, to determine when
there was no hope left because the community was doomed to extinction.

This question tormented . . . the township of Lenin (near Pinsk). All its young people (over 300) were sent to the labour camp . . . several miles distant. For a long time the prisoners suffered torture from the forced labour and general maltreatment, but out of a sense of responsibility they could not bring themselves to implement the plan for collective escape to the forests for they knew that their escape would only hasten the massacre of their townsfolk. When, however, news reached them the latter had been liquidated, they put their escape plan into effect.[49]

A similar dilemma occurred in many other ghettos when resisters tried to gauge when the situation was hopeless. Chaika Grossman n the Bialystok ghetto wrote:

We did not want to arrogate to ourselves the right, in the smallest degree, to decide on the date of the annihilation of thousands of people. Even though we knew that masses of Jews were destined to die helplessly, we did not want to bring that end closer . . . we did not want to hasten that eventuality. Already in Vilna we had been troubled by the central and responsible question of when to begin the armed resistance. Furthermore, if we fought in Vilna, would that not affect the Jews in Warsaw? On the other hand, we knew that if we did not defend ourselves in time we would not be able to resist at all.[50]

As one of the leading organizers of the Bialystok ghetto revolt, Chaika Grossman again provides first-hand testimony of the importance of collective responsibility as a constraint upon resistance. She recounts how she and her fellow rebels were:

troubled by the complex problem of collective responsibility: should we start when the first Jew was taken, or wait until it became evident that the Germans were liquidating the ghetto? That was a vital question for all of us.[51]

The only thing which could justify risking the inevitable reprisals that followed an armed uprising was the complete extinction of hope for survival. As Michael Marrus has observed: 'resistance was guaranteed to punish Jews rather than assist them'.[52] Thus for Jews in most ghettos, resistance and 'collaboration' (rescue through work) were not genuine alternatives, existing simultaneously. Armed resistance only emerged after all strategies to avert the worst had failed – for example, ZOB, the Jewish Fighting Organization in the Warsaw Ghetto, was only established in October 1942, three years after the city had been occupied by the Germans, and three months *after* the first large deportations to Treblinka.[53] Resistance did not provide an alternative to the policy of the Jewish Councils, it emerged when all the life-saving alternatives had been exhausted, and when all that was left was certain death.

Thus, whereas all other European resistance movements were built upon and sustained by the inestimable psychological conviction of hope for victory, Jewish resistance was invariably a last act of desperation when all hopes of survival had been extinguished. For Jews, the choice was not between life and death, but between two types of death. When the last Jews in the Warsaw Ghetto realized that they were not going to be 'resettled' but exterminated, they fought – with the pitifully few guns and home-made bombs that they had – knowing that armed resistance meant instant death. Raul Hilberg has pointed out that the number of German casualties during the 1943 Warsaw Ghetto uprising was 16 dead and 85 wounded.[54]

Hilberg takes this as clear evidence that Jewish resistance was of no consequence: that it was not militarily effective. But we need to distinguish the worth of resistance from whether it 'worked'. It was not effective, it was purely affective. The symbolic significance of the Warsaw Ghetto rising – its epic quality – far outweighs its military importance. We should also not overlook the fact that this was the first urban rebellion against the Nazis anywhere in Europe, a point not lost on the French resistance historian, Henri Michel:

> Need one recollect that on the day that the Warsaw Ghetto uprising broke out, not one partisan existed yet in France? Tito's guerrilla warfare, as well, had not become a serious factor.[55]

Elie Wiesel observes that the liberation of Paris in 1944 occurred with the Allied armies at the gates of the city, and with the Germans in retreat. Similarly, the Warsaw Uprising of the Polish Home Army in 1944 took place with the Red Army encamped on the other side of the River Vistula. The Jewish uprising in the Warsaw Ghetto took place a full year before these gentile rebellions against German rule, and with no support.[56] This observation should not, however, be used as the occasion for polemical points'-scoring or for an exercise in one-upmanship by defenders of the Jewish legacy.

Rather, the contrast should lead to a deeper understanding of the objective differences in circumstances facing Jewish and non-Jewish resistance. In order to repudiate the myth that Jews did not resist, it should not be forgotten that other resistance movements also had to wrestle with the terrible dilemmas of collective reprisals, and were also constrained by the need to avoid premature revolts which would only result in the needless spilling of innocent blood.

To sum up: by the time that they engaged in armed resistance, Jews were not fighting to rescue themselves from slavery and death. They knew that they had no prospect of victory, and that they were waging a 'war of the doomed'.[57] So Jewish resistance takes on a different meaning from that of the rest of occupied Europe. Resistance acquired a redemptive quality, a spiritual dimension: 'It was an existential act of courage in the face of certain death.'[58] The Jews were not fighting for their lives, but struggling to reassert the human value of their lives, and the need to die with honour and dignity. Jewish youth learned how to die before they had learned how to live. They chose death rather than submit to it. In their utter dejection and hopelessness, they knew that armed resistance was not an alternative to death, but an alternative kind of death. The Nazis denied the Jew the right to live like a man, but could not stop him from dying like one.

In conclusion, the question to ask is not, *Why did the Jews go like sheep to the slaughter?* That is a misplaced, indecent question. The pertinent question is: *Why, given the appalling odds stacked against them, was there any Jewish resistance at all?*

9 SOE and British Moral Responsibility for Resistance

> The moral aspect of what SOE was doing has received scant attention.[1]
>
> Philip Knightley

> The whole concept of secret warfare, embracing espionage, counter-espionage, guerrilla warfare, secret paramilitary operations, was an anathema to some. Such secret activities involved varying degrees of illegal and unethical methods which would violate normal peacetime morality and would not only be improper but often criminal ... acts of violence, mayhem and murder.[2]
>
> Jack Beevor,
> Assistant to Sir Charles Hambro: Chief of SOE

After the fall of Poland, Denmark, Norway, Holland, Belgium and France, London became the resistance capital of Europe. Britain sponsored, stimulated and financed European resistance movements. The Special Operations Executive (SOE) was created in July 1940 by Winston Churchill with the instruction to 'Set Europe Ablaze'. Its original objectives were expressed by the first head of SOE, Hugh Dalton, on 2 July 1940:

> We have got to organise movements in enemy-occupied territory comparable to the Sinn Fein movement in Ireland ... to the Spanish Irregulars who played a notable part in Wellington's campaign. ... This 'democratic international' must use many different methods, including industrial and military sabotage, labour agitation and strikes, continuous propaganda, terrorist acts against traitors and German leaders, boycotts and riots.[3]

SOE's charter gave official sanction to a policy of undisguised terrorism. However, it did not anticipate the unbridled state terrorism of German security policy. Because of this SOE was a house built on sand. Its foundation stone rested on false assumptions about the Nazi regime, and romantic illusions about the revolutionary preparedness of the people who lived under German occupation to rebel against the 'master race'. Europe was portrayed as a continent seething with democratic and nationalist discontent, and ripe for rebellion. The conquered people of Hitler's Europe would be the Achilles' heel of the Nazi empire. With some prompting in the wings from Britain, in the form of arms and other supplies, Europeans would revolt against their oppressors and throw them off the stage of world history. It was anticipated that the collapse of the Third Reich would be brought about in early 1941 by the combination of the bomber offensive, the Royal Navy's economic blockade of continental Europe, and mass subversion by the peoples of Europe.

Incredible as it may seem now, Hugh Dalton, on the eve of Dunkirk, predicted that within six months Nazi Germany would be on the verge of defeat, and that the occupation of Europe would prove to be a liability, not an asset. Germany was perceived to be economically vulnerable. The optimistic folly of the First World War was about to be repeated: it would 'all be over by Christmas', and Dalton predicted that Europe would be faced by:

> famine, starvation and revolt, most of all in the slave lands which Germany had overrun.
>
> Nazidom will be like a dark pall over all Europe, but, after only a few months, it may dissolve like the snow in spring.[4]

In the First World War the Allies had used the instrument of the food blockade as a major weapon to defeat the Kaiser's Germany, and in a war of attrition it was successful in fomenting internal discontent and anarchy within Germany in 1918. Therefore the politics of hunger could be used again to ensure that, as one widely-circulated leaflet phrased it: 'in due course Field Marshall Famine may knock at Hitler's door'.[5] Food shortages would lead to lower morale within Germany. Deprivation would stimulate resistance in the occupied territories. Hunger would add to the existing nationalist animosity towards the occupiers, lead to discontent, mass subversion, and the eventual formation of a massive fifth column of resisters throughout Hitler's Europe. This combination would expose all the flaws and vulnerability inherent in the Nazi Empire with its 'vaulting ambition which o'er leaps itself'.[6] The British premise was that German manpower and resources were stretched to the limit, and that the

New Order would rapidly collapse from within, under the sheer weight of its own internal contradictions. What Churchill called a 'gigantic guerrilla' engaged in systematic subversion and sabotage, would be capable of bringing an emaciated Third Reich to its knees, without the need for some future D-Day mass land invasion. The politics of hunger was intimately bound up with the politics of the People's War. SOE's original aim was to mobilize the people of Europe into a democratic crusade against Fascism. Its ethos was summed up in the title of a *Left Book Club* pamphlet written in the summer of 1940 by Richard Crossman and Kingsley Martin: 'A Hundred Million Allies If We Choose'. Dalton envisaged strikes, boycotts and demonstrations as a prelude to a general insurrection. 'We should be able overnight to produce the anarchy of Ireland in 1920'.[7] Dalton's strategy overlooked the fact that the Irish Sinn Fein movement was answered by an official and an unofficial British policy of reprisals, and the unleashing of the Black and Tans. If even the 'civilized' British responded to Irish provocation with methods of barbarism, what was to be expected of the uncivilized Nazis?

The original conception of SOE was based upon two false assumptions.

> The British underestimated the effectiveness of German control of the occupied countries, and over-estimated the ability of the Europeans to resist.[8]

It was an impossible task to ignite the flames of patriotism and to set Europe ablaze in the climate of 1940 when it was raining hard, and when SOE only had a few damp matches and hardly any kindling wood. As Dalton's biographer has observed, 'Today it is hard not to see it as a romantic absurdity'.[9] The breathtaking naivety and innocence of the initial aim of SOE was rooted in traditional British insularity, and bore no relation to European reality. The sheltered conditions of British life helped to foster a wholly unrealistic conception of German power and ruthlessness, and ignorance and incomprehension of the techniques of totalitarian control. The long history of isolation and freedom from invasion was immensely beneficial for the development of Britain's internal political tradition. But it exacted a heavy price in terms of trying to understand the circumstances and dilemmas of those who lived under the jackboot. Because Britain had had no experience of even the mildest form of foreign occupation, it was ill-prepared to comprehend the sheer might of the German army, and the grim realities of Nazi security measures. The accumulated habits of national life all stood between British government policy and some genuine understanding of occupied Europe. Phillip Knightley argues that self-delusion underpinned the original charter and aims of SOE:

> Not only were many of SOE's agents politically illiterate as far as knowledge of Europe was concerned, but they had a dangerously romantic conception of what they were about.[10]

Given the necessity of ordinary 'everyday collaboration' with a brutal conqueror prepared to resort to stunning reprisals and exemplary punishment for acts of defiance, it is not surprising that, as Dutch resister Louis De Jong put it:

> The fires that kept blazing were those of Europe's steel mills.[11]

Dalton's optimistic vision of European rebellion was eventually replaced by a more sober appraisal of the realities of life in Hitler's Europe. It should also be noted that SOE was the poor relation of Britain's armed forces; it was constantly operating under financial constraints; it was economically dependent especially upon the RAF, and had to go around with a begging bowl to secure resources for its missions. The RAF was reluctant to release aircraft for secret missions of doubtful value. All of this meant that 'ambitions had accordingly to be scaled down'.[12] As the school of experience taught its bitter lessons, a new realism crept into SOE. Churchill's and Dalton's revolutionary vision of spontaneous combustion and wholesale arson was superseded by a revised strategy, 'the detonator concept', which was an 'important milestone in the history of SOE'.[13] The underground armies were to engage in more discriminate and carefully targeted acts of sabotage and subversion, and to:

> ignite a carefully controlled fire whose embers would be dampened and fanned into flames only when desired by Britain.[14]

With the entry of the United States and the Soviet Union into the war, SOE's function became even more marginal, a side-show, because the Allied invasion could occur, if need be, without assistance from the resistance:

From now on, secret armies were regarded as a bonus rather than an essential prerequisite for Allied landing in Europe.[15]

In-between the demise of Dalton's revolutionary romanticism and the D-Day landings, SOE had to do something. The question was what, and at what human cost to the peoples of occupied Europe? A key question which must be addressed is whether SOE showed sufficient concern for the peoples of Europe who had to pay the price of its operations. When we examine most works on SOE, including official histories, what is striking is how little is said on this matter: it is either omitted altogether, or at best mentioned briefly in passing. It is very difficult to find any detailed, accurate information about civilian casualties, and the number of people executed in reprisal for SOE operations.

SOE AND NON-COMBATANT IMMUNITY

By concentrating on the detail surrounding particular SOE operations, it is very easy to overlook the fact that the very existence of SOE, and its main purpose – to organize sabotage and guerrilla warfare – was such as to undermine non-combatant immunity. The principle of non-combatant immunity is central to the just war tradition: civilized warfare is limited to combatants. The separation of soldier and civilian has played an incalculable role in mitigating the evils of war, and is one of the great triumphs of the international laws of war. In a calculated manner, SOE chose to ignore or override the elementary protection afforded to non-combatants. The uniform of the regular soldier is the identification mark which classifies him as a combatant, and which thus procures for non-combatants the immunity which belligerents accord to civilians. By discarding the uniform and fostering irregular-guerrilla war, SOE enabled the Germans to claim that because the laws of war had not been adhered to, they were not bound to discriminate between soldiers and civilians. By encouraging sabotage, and by inciting the civilian population to take up arms and to kill Germans, SOE was striking at the roots of the laws of war, which protect civilians as long as they remain non-combatants. SOE activities raised important moral questions because sabotage and assassination inevitably brought severe reprisals. Because war was no longer confined to clearly-identifiable combatants, SOE and the British authorities bore grave responsibility for inciting forms of resistance which put the lives of innocent civilians at risk.

A more general moral and philosophical issue emerges at this point. If the concern to avoid innocent civilian casualties is always the overriding moral consideration, then carried to its logical conclusion this would have entailed a much more limited range of resistance activities, restricted to intelligence-gathering and organizing escape lines. It would also entail submission to German terrorism. A morally absolutist view that it is intrinsically wrong to engage in acts which endanger civilians could lead to the conclusion that there was no justification for violent resistance at all. If non-combatant immunity is regarded as an absolute, unbreakable commandment, then the side which adheres scrupulously to this rule clearly puts itself at a military disadvantage against an unscrupulous enemy which threatens to resort to hostage-taking, reprisal killings and the use of 'human shields' in order to protect itself against sabotage. Many resisters regarded the principle of non-combatant immunity as a very strong *prima facie* rule, with a built-in presumption against the taking, or endangering of innocent life, aiming to give civilians protection as far as possible, and to minimize casualties. But it was a rule which could be overridden in extreme emergencies, and if the gravity of the case required it. Sometimes the object of the sabotage was so important that it had to take precedence over the principle of non-combatant immunity. Where the good achieved decisively outweighed the harm, the risk of civilian casualties was licit. Each case had to be judged on its merits, according to its importance to the war effort. This was essentially the position that Colonel J.S. Wilson, Head of the Norwegian Section of SOE, spelled out in a report to the British War Cabinet:

> The threat of reprisals by the Nazis cannot be permitted to justify the cessation of all activities of an aggressive nature. But there is this much to be said in relation to the problem. The use by the enemy of reprisals as a weapon demands that the utmost care be taken in the preparation and planning of every operation that is undertaken, particularly the thorough training of all personnel.[16]

Whether this prudent advice was always taken is a debatable point. Did SOE always live up to this general ground-rule? At times SOE's encouragement of small-scale sabotage and routine assassination resulted in gratuitous friendly casualties – for acts of no strategic importance which had no bearing upon the outcome of the war. At other times a great deal of hard thinking went into weighing up the necessity of a given act of subversion.

Britain also needed the co-operation of the governments-in-exile. SOE could only achieve the desired results if it had the confidence and support of the exiled Europeans, who often proved to be the best SOE agents in the field. They showed a deep concern over civilian casualties and the dangers of exposing their fellow country men to reprisals. This created tensions, because British interest often conflicted with the national interests of the occupied countries.

Was SOE concerned with the human cost of its actions, or was Europe to be set ablaze irrespective of the price in European blood? Starting from first principles: if the overriding objective of SOE was to create mayhem in Nazi-occupied Europe, then it is axiomatic that this could only be achieved at the expense of, and with fore knowledge of, heavy civilian casualties. Thus M.R.D. Foot writes:

> Churchill and SOE were both aware from the beginning of the danger that sabotage might trigger off savage reprisals, if too much of it was done too soon.[17]

If, however, great care was taken from the outset to minimize civilian casualties (and some authors, including Foot and Stafford do clearly state this to be the case) then SOE cannot have been wholeheartedly committed to the achievement of its original aim and *raison d'être*. The logical corollary of 'setting Europe ablaze' was to commit acts which would necessarily incur a German backlash, resulting in the homes and villages of Europeans being set ablaze, and the execution of their inhabitants. M.R.D. Foot concedes that

> reprisals could help resistance even more than hinder it . . . for every Frenchman . . . that reprisal . . . executions frightened into acquiescence, a score more were shocked into opposition . . . and so became ripe for recruiting.[18]

Both Foot and Stafford stress the caution which guided SOE policy and the need to avoid actions which would only result in the slaughter of the civilian population. Thus Stafford:

it was British policy to avoid premature uprisings in Europe and to discourage resistance activity which would lead to massive reprisals against the civilian population.[19]

Two of the main keynotes of SOE policy towards European resistance had been the avoidance of premature risings and the minimisation of the risk of civilian reprisals.[20]

Again, in similar vein Foot writes:

There was some tendency in Europe to think that the unoccupied Allies were inclined to order ... resistance activity for irrelevant or even frivolous reasons without due regard for the reprisals casualties that were sure to follow. ... There was nothing in this: on the contrary, the British and American high command was painfully sensitive about reprisals, and very senior officers ... were known to forbid proposed irregular operations on the ground that the danger to the civilian population in the raided area would be too great.[21]

These passages seem clear and unequivocal. They convey the impression that London acted as a brake and a restraint upon eager and impetuous young hot-heads who wanted to prove their militant resistance credentials by acts of bravado. But the reality was more complicated, and we need to recognize the tension between SOE's long-term strategy of building secret armies towards some distant D-Day, and its short-term tactics of creating as much havoc as possibly by sabotage and subversion. Sir Colin Gubbins, the Director of Operations for SOE, and later its Executive Director from September 1943, admits that SOE carried out:

two broad tasks simultaneously which were themselves hardly compatible, that is action, day by day and week after week, in specific attacks against selected targets ... and at the same time, the creation of secret armies.[22]

It is at this point that inconsistencies creep into the analysis of Foot and Stafford, reflecting the incompatible long-term objectives and short-term goals that SOE pursued. At times Foot and Stafford want to have it both ways. Thus Stafford writes that 'sabotage as a task for SOE remained unchanged'.[23] But sabotage inevitably brought German reprisals, and in some cases, a scorched-earth policy.

Sabotage was incompatible with the protective, paternalistic atti
tude of minimizing casualties. The clearest evidence of the ten
sions and inconsistencies emerges in Stafford's account of SOE policy
in Denmark. Because the German occupation in the 'model pro
tectorate' was mild, there was very little resistance:

> The best way to create a growing and nation-wide resistance
> movement was to provoke the Germans into repressive action
> and force them to take over executive power. To this objective
> SOE applied itself in the early months of 1943, with total
> success. . . .
> . . . the imposition of direct rule by the German army and the
> resignation of the Danish government . . . was an outcome for
> which SOE had assiduously worked.[24]

Again, Foot contradicts himself in his description of SOE objectives in the Balkans:

> SOE pursued its usual policy of arming whichever party provided
> the most satisfactory proof that it was killing Germans; irrespec-
> tive of longer-term political consequences.[25]

And, one is tempted to add, irrespective of the human consequences. For killing Germans meant that Germans would kill civilians at a reprisal ratio of 100:1. The result of this policy in the
Balkans was the setting ablaze of villages such as Kalavryta and
Kragujevac, and the massacre of the civilian population. The cynical European interpretation was to view SOE activity as an expression of British self-interest, with the subordination of the interests
and lives of continental Europeans to 'Perfidious Albion'. The old
perception of Perfidious Albion had deep roots in European history, and suspicions of English treachery were widespread throughout
occupied Europe. After Munich and the abandonment of Czechoslovakia, Dunkirk, and the Royal Navy's sinking of the French Fleet
at Mers-el-Kabir with the loss of 1200 French sailors' lives in July
1940, there was an understandable scepticism or bitterness about
English motives. For many continentals these events merely confirmed the cynical jibe that the English were prepared to fight to
the last Frenchman or European.

The British authorities did not encourage the Channel Islanders to engage in active resistance, on the grounds that it would be suicidal on such small islands. A comparable policy was not adhered to on Crete, where Britain supported violent resistance, despite the high casualties. After a misguided uprising in August 1944, the Germans killed over 1000 victims and burned 30 villages. The 'V for Victory' campaign was promoted throughout occupied Europe; it was conspicuous by its absence in the Channel Islands.[26]

Setting Europe ablaze was a fine rhetorical phrase when uttered in the relative safety of London. As seen from Paris, Prague, Brussels or Belgrade, the British willingness to put Europe to the torch and to support those who killed Germans could be interpreted as a frivolous indifference to the value of European lives, and at no personal risk to the bowler-hatted city gents and merchant bankers who headed SOE. After all, were these not 'far-away countries of which we knew little?' The physical and psychological distance between the London clubland of St James' and Piccadilly, and the killing fields of Televaag, Lidice and Lezaky raises the question of moral distance, and the inability to comprehend what reprisals entailed in practice. It is not possible in the limited space available to provide an exhaustive account of this complex issue. In order to illustrate the tensions in SOE's activities, and the complex and contradictory nature of the evidence. I intend to examine two case studies: (1) SOE and Norway; (2) the assassination of Reinhard Heydrich.

SOE and Norway

British operations in Norway created deep suspicion of SOE by the Norwegian government-in-exile and bitter resentment and mistrust of British motives by the Norwegian resistance movement, Milorg. The first 'hit and run' commando raid in the Sognefjord area provoked German reprisals against the local civilian population in December 1940. This was followed by the melodramatic 'Operation Claymore', an attack upon the Lofoten islands near Narvik in March 1941, in which 11 German and Norwegian ships were destroyed and four fish-oil factories blown up. 213 Germans and 12 Norwegian quisling collaborators were captured and brought back to Britain as prisoners. SOE chiefs regarded the raid as an unqualified success, but the Norwegian resistance condemned such 'hazardous sabotage actions' in militarily and strategically unimportant areas, because the Gestapo replied with mass arrests, the killing of several hostages, and the burning of more than 100 homes on the islands. A large number of men and women were taken to a concentration camp outside Oslo, where they were held as hostages to deter further unrest. The German authorities also arrested the parents of anyone who fled to Britain on the 'Shetland Bus' – the fishing boats which carried the exodus of Norwegians. At Alesund alone, 74 parents were arrested as hostages. The destruction primarily of Norwegian rather than German property – the factories provided 50 per cent of Norway's production of fish-oil – led to destitution in an area which was largely dependent upon the fishing industry for its livelihood. The raids had a more adverse effect upon the Norwegian people, whom SOE were trying to liberate, than upon the enemy. Milorg's cautious and prudent desire to avoid futile sacrifices was made clear in a letter to King Haakon and the government-in-exile in London. The indigenous resistance expressed its fear of German reprisals as a result of British coastal raids, and pointed out that the Norwegian people were 'not yet immunized against German threats and Gestapo terror' and insisted that 'every action should be carefully thought out, with our co-operation.'[27] The Norwegian Communist Party criticized Milorg for its 'passivity'.

The tensions between SOE and the Norwegian resistance were fully exposed in the Televaag raid in April 1942. Two SOE agents on a sabotage mission were discovered at Televaag. While attempting to escape they killed two German policemen. Reichscommissioner Terboven ordered the complete destruction of the village, and all 344 buildings were laid waste. All animals were killed or confiscated, all fishing boats were sunk, 260 men between 16–65 were sent to German concentration camps, of whom 76 perished at Sachsenhausen. The remainder of the population – women, children, the elderly – were put in internment camps. The Norwegian SOE agents were tortured and then executed. An additional 18 young men who had been arrested previously in Alesund were executed as hostages, despite the fact that they had no links with the resistance. Televaag was Norway's Oradour or Lidice: wiped off the map as a reprisal, and as a deterrent against further underground activity. The tragedy caused even greater mistrust among ordinary Norwegians and members of the Norwegian resistance who argued that the price paid in the loss of innocent civilian lives was far too high for the meagre results of SOE operations. The slogan 'No More Televaag!' was a powerful emotive weapon employed

by the Norwegian government-in-exile and by Milorg against further SOE raids.[28] The Germans publicly warned that complete lists
of hostages had been prepared for all towns and localities in the
event of future resistance. These British-led raids stand in sharp
contrast to SOE operations controlled by exiled Norwegians who
went to inordinate lengths to protect their fellow countrymen.

The Vemork Raid

The Vemork raid illustrates the strengths of the humanitarian considerations which underpin the just war criteria for the justifiable
use of violence, but also the breaking-point of its central principle
of non-combatant immunity. When the Germans occupied Norway,
they seized the Norsk Hydro Works at Vemork, which produced
'heavy water' (water enriched with deuterium). The Germans soon
started to manufacture large quantities of heavy water needed for
their early experiments to make an atomic bomb. The first attack
upon German production occurred in February 1943, when a group
of Norwegian saboteurs, trained by SOE, blew up the tanks containing heavy water. The saboteurs were discovered by two Norwegian guards. If the guards had tried to alert the Germans the
saboteurs would have been forced to kill them. The guards remained
silent. They later informed the Germans that the sabotage was a
British operation, but were not believed, and were sent to a German concentration camp. This incident illustrates the moral perils
inherent in even the most legitimate of resistance actions.

It took several minutes for the Germans to realize what had
happened. This allowed the saboteurs to escape. The easiest escape route would have been across a suspension bridge, but this
would have required the killing of the German sentries. One member of the SOE team was a local man from the nearest town of
Ryukan. He ruled out the attack upon the German guards, even
though this increased the team's personal danger.

> Even if we're able to kill them without suffering any casualties
> on our side, there will be severe reprisals against innocent people
> in Ryukan.[29]

The attack on the Vemork factory was carried out by Norwegian
exiles wearing British commando uniforms. Commandos found behind
German lines were not granted prisoner-of-war status like normal

troops, but shot on sight as a result of Hitler's notorious *Commando Order* of 18 October 1942. Even unarmed or injured men were subject to summary execution. A British machine gun was deliberately left in a conspicuous position, along with other equipment stamped 'Made in Britain,' in order to deflect German hostility from the local population, and to avert civilian reprisals.

German security investigations included the arrest of ten of Ryukan's most prominent citizens. The local Gestapo chief threatened to kill them the next day, and also arrested fifty workers from the heavy water plant. It was only the timely intervention of General Von Falkenhorst – the Supreme Military Commander in Norway – that prevented the execution of the threatened hostages. He 'realised' immediately that the sabotage had been carried out by British soldiers in uniform, and was therefore a legitimate military operation and not a 'terrorist' act by the local resistance. He ordered the release of the hostages, and stipulated that no further reprisals were to be taken against the population of Ryukan.

Jomar Brun, whose parents had been interrogated and searched following his disappearance [as a worker from the Vemork plant four months earlier], later expressed deep appreciation of this action on the part of Falkenhorst. 'I would like to pay tribute to the German General in command of Norway. . . . who, against the will of the Nazi authorities, decided that the action must be considered a military operation, and that accordingly no steps of reprisal should be taken against the local population.[30]

Although the sabotage operation was successful, British scientific intelligence had seriously miscalculated the amount of time needed to resume heavy-water production. The British had estimated that the Germans had been set back by two years in their experiments to make an atomic bomb. In fact, within two months production had re-started, and heavy-water supplies were being sent to Germany by late June 1943. By August, production levels had reached a new peak – with the equivalent of an annual output of three tons – in excess of Germany's requirements.

General Leslie Groves, the Head of 'the Manhattan Project' America's atomic programme, was so concerned about production levels at Vemork that he recommended that the Allies bomb the plant as a top priority. A mass bombing raid took place in November, with the loss of 22 Norwegian civilians, mostly women and children, killed by stray bombs, although the Vemork plant itself escaped without damage.

This raid led to further tension between the Allied governments and the Norwegian government-in-exile, which had not been consulted on the raid, or given advance notice of an attack upon its territory. The Norwegians argued that the saturation bombing:

> seems out of proportion to the objective sought. Furthermore, the Norwegian authorities have always done everything possible to furnish the Allies with the most detailed and precise information on factories and installations in Norway.... If the aim of this bombing was to stop production ... of heavy water, better results could have been achieved by specialised methods of attack than by overall bombing of the factories.[31]

Although this air raid failed, it forced the German authorities to consider the likelihood of further attacks, or possible internal sabotage. Therefore, they decided to move their supplies of heavy-water to the relative safety of Germany. In early February 1944, 70 giant container drums were to be taken by rail to Lake Tinnsjo, then for a short journey across the lake and onto southern Norway by train, before being taken by ship across the Baltic to Germany. The British Cabinet regarded an attack upon these supplies as top priority, and the Cabinet secretary informed Colonel J.S. Wilson, Head of SOE Scandinavian Section: 'The P.M. says the delivery must, repeat must, be stopped at all costs.'[32] On being informed of the gravity of the situation, the Norwegian government-in-exile agreed that whatever was required to stop the Germans gaining access to weapons which might give them a decisive victory was of overriding importance. The action had to be carried out without regard to the certainty of reprisals against the civilian population, and irrespective of the human cost to innocent people. Nevertheless, this was easier to authorize in the comparative safety of London, far from the consequences of German security measures, than to implement on the ground.

The agents in the field who had to carry out the operation were SOE-trained Norwegian exiles, and local men. They wanted to minimize the risk of innocent casualties within the framework of successfully completing their task. This is an important point to emphasize: it illustrates the deep concern that these battle-hardened resisters had for human life. Their subsequent actions show that they were clearly opposed to the frivolous disregard for human life, or any callous indifference to the human cost of their actions. The leader of the group was Knut Haukelid, whose sabotage team had previously blown up the heavy-water containers at the Vemork plant. Haukelid had calculated that an attack upon the train carrying the heavy-water, before it reached the ferry, was out of the question. The route was heavily guarded by specially-selected SS troops spaced at every tenth sleeper on the railway track. A pilot engine ran ahead of the train to detonate any dynamite on the line. The Germans placed the heavy-water freight on an ordinary passenger train of workers, in order to deter any attacks. In addition, 40 hostages were detained in a Gestapo prison to guarantee the safety of the train.

Haukelid saw the ferry as the Achilles' heel in German security and planned to sink it at the deepest part of Lake Tinnsjo, where the cargo would be irretrievably lost. However, because of the inevitable civilian casualties – both on the ferry and in reprisal killings – Haukelid was understandably reluctant to commit an act that would lead to the death of innocent people. He telegraphed London to seek permission to sink the ferry, and spelled out the consequences: 'We must count on reprisals in the case of both civilian and of military action.'[33] Haukelid wanted to be absolutely certain that the action was essential to the Allied war effort, and so he sent a further message to London to confirm the necessity of the operation:

> Our contacts at Ryukan .... doubt if result of operation is worth reprisals. We ourselves cannot decide how important the operations are. Please reply this evening if possible.

London's reply was immediate:

> Matter has been considered. It is thought very important that the heavy water shall be destroyed. Hope it can be done without too disastrous results.[34]

The message from London also recommended that the saboteurs should leave behind British uniforms at a suitable place in order to minimize attacks upon the local population, and to draw German attention away from the indigenous resistance movement.

SOE made contingency plans in case Haukelid's plan failed

Without telling him, they had assembled 'Chaffinch', another team of saboteurs to blow up the next train south of Lake Tinnsjo. The Germans intended to use passengers as a 'human shield' to protect the train. The train's cargo included tanks of ammonia, and if these exploded, then nobody would survive. RAF Bomber Command was also on stand-by to bomb the ship in the Baltic if both sabotage attempts failed. 'London was taking no chances.'[35]

Once committed to the necessity of sinking the ferry, Haukelid arranged a plan with his contacts in the Vemork plant, to minimize the loss of life. His memoirs testify to the importance of moral considerations:

> It is always hard to take a decision about actions which involve the loss of human lives. An officer has often to take such decisions in wartime, but in regular warfare it is easier; for then the officer is a small part of an organised apparatus, and his decisions as a rule have consequences only for soldiers, or at most for an enemy population. In this case an act of war was to be carried out which must endanger the lives of a number of our own people – who were not soldiers.[36]

The Norwegian resisters were guided by considerations of conscience and concern for the lives of their fellow countrymen. Kjell Nielsen, the technical engineer in charge of siphoning off the heavy-water at the Vemork plant, was a secret resistance informer, in constant contact with Haukelid. He delayed the timing of the train's departure so that it would connect with the earliest sailing of the ferry on Lake Tinnsjo on a Sunday morning, when the number of civilian passengers, and especially schoolchildren, could be expected to be at a minimum. Haukelid arranged for Nielsen to be taken into Ryukan hospital to have an 'emergency' operation to remove his healthy appendix. Nielsen would have been the obvious suspect for the German security police, and Haukelid's action ensured that he would have a ready alibi to present to the Gestapo.

> Co-operative surgeons at the hospital performed the operation without enquiring too deeply. They understood it was an emergency, even if not in the usual medical sense of the word.[37]

Haukelid also arranged for the chief engineer at the Vemork plant, Alf Larsen, to be sent to Sweden before the ferry was sabotaged. Although he had not been involved in the sabotage, he would be a prime suspect for Gestapo interrogation. His disappearance would also provide the Germans with a scapegoat.

On the night before the ferry was due to sail, Haukelid and two other members of the sabotage team sneaked on board the craft, which incredibly had no armed guards. They were discovered by the ferry's night-watchman, but they played upon his patriotism by telling him that they were on the run from the Gestapo, and needed a place to hide. The local Ryukan man engaged the watchman in inconsequential conversation, while the other two pretended to go to sleep below deck. They placed timed explosives below the bow of the vessel so that it would sink rapidly. This was necessary to prevent the transfer of the cargo if the ferry was only damaged. The operation went exactly as planned: the explosives went off as the ferry reached the deepest part of the lake. At the depth of 1300 feet the cargo could not be salvaged.

The ferry contained 53 people, including her Norwegian crew, passengers and German guards. Twenty-six people drowned, including women and children – two brothers aged 14 and 15 perished – but they could not have been forewarned without arousing the Germans' suspicions. Everything had to appear normal. The force of the explosion necessary to sink the ferry quickly meant that the crew had little time to save lives. The explosion ended any hopes that the Germans entertained about building atomic bombs in order to achieve victory.

It transpired after the war that Germany's atomic plans were not as well advanced as had been thought at the time. They were on the wrong track with their experiments, and could not have developed the atomic bomb, even if their heavy-water supplies had not been destroyed. But this was not known at the time, and the fear that Hitler would gain a monopoly of atomic weapons and use them without hesitation (as he did with the VI and VII rockets) was regarded as a sufficient justification for those who had to make this awesome decision to sacrifice the innocent lives of their fellow countrymen.

The painstaking efforts that Haukelid made to save lives, wherever possible, demonstrates the extent to which he was tormented by the human costs of even necessary resistance. Haukelid felt guilt over his treatment of the night-watchman:

When I left the watchman I was not clear in my mind as to what

I ought to do. He had shown himself to be a good and useful Norwegian. It was very probable that he was just the person whom the Germans would interrogate after the ferry was sunk, and I should have liked to warn him and get him out of the danger zone. I was tempted, too, to take him with us and try to bring him into safety. I remembered the fate of the two Norwegian guards at Vemork, who had been sent to a German concentration camp after the attack there. I did not want to hand over a Norwegian to the Germans. But if the watchman disappeared, there was danger of the Germans' suspicions being aroused next morning.[38]

In a later account, Haukelid wrote:

That man is still the man on my conscience. . . . I felt like Judas as I shook hands and thanked him. But what could I do?. . . . his absence would have raised the alarm and the whole operation would have been wrecked.[39]

What emerges clearly from this examination of the Vemork raid is that moral considerations – rooted in the just war tradition – were always a major factor in restricting the means of subversive warfare employed by Haukelid's team. Although they had to make decisions which resulted directly in the loss of innocent lives, Haukelid's team first explored all other possibilities in order to ensure that the death of non-combatants was a desperate last resort, and not something to be accepted lightly or casually as a normal practice. They did not merely pay lip service to the doctrine of the just war by offering ritual expressions or gestures of regret. Rather, they engaged in acts which maximized the risk to themselves while attempting to minimize the risk to their fellow countrymen. Their behaviour, in trying strenuously to avoid actions which would result in reprisals, was a model of how to fight a just war by just methods against an unscrupulous enemy, in the most trying of circumstances. Haukelid realized that his plan inevitably involved the loss of civilian lives. But he also wrote of his fear that a mistake by his team would lead to the uncovering of the identities of his helpers, and would bring destruction to that entire region of Norway. This 'had been a heavy burden on us; for the Germans would have shown no mercy if they found out who our helpers were'.[40]

Haukelid's team of saboteurs faced the very real dilemmas of military necessity, and did so with honesty – knowingly and openly breaking the absolute rule which prohibits attacks which result directly in civilian deaths, and accepting their moral responsibility and guilt. The agonizing reluctance and self-doubt of Haukelid is evidence of his moral authenticity and his abhorrence of killing. Haukelid's sadness at the pity of war, his detestation of war and violence ensured that he retained his sense of compassion and essential humanity even while engaged in justifiable acts of necessary violence under conditions of military necessity.

The Assassination of Heydrich: 'Operation Anthropoid'

Reinhard Heydrich was Himmler's deputy, Hitler's 'favourite son' and probable heir apparent. The physical embodiment of the ideal Aryan man, Heydrich was one of the most feared and ruthless men in the Nazi hierarchy. When the assassination attempt took place, on 27 May 1942 in Prague, the 38-year-old Heydrich was Chief of the Reich Central Security Office (RHSA.) which meant that he controlled all security functions, including the police and the Gestapo, in the occupied territories; he was also the co-ordinator, and one of the main architects of, the Final Solution of the Jewish Question. In addition, Heydrich was the Reich Protector of Bohemia and Moravia.

Why was Heydrich assassinated? Why was he singled out for special treatment rather than Himmler, or some other leading Nazi figure? Some authors speculate that Heydrich was closing in on important British agents who were working for the *Abwehr*, German Military Counter-intelligence – and that the killing of Heydrich was ordered by the British Secret Service in order to protect its leading double agent, Paul Thummel. However, Thummel had been arrested for the second and final time by the Gestapo before Heydrich's assassination.

A more plausible explanation was given by Colonel František Moravec, the former Chief of Czechoslovak Intelligence, and thus a leading person within the exiled Czech resistance movement. As a central figure in the assassination plot, Moravec briefed the men who carried out the execution, which was requested by President Beneš, the leader of the Czech government-in-exile, and also by the British Intelligence Service.

At that time there were patriotic reasons enough to justify such an action, but I will be frank and say that political considerations did predominate. President Beneš and his provisional government in London were hardly recognised by the Foreign Office. . . . the crux of the matter. . . . lay in the unwillingness of the British Foreign Office to furnish him with a formal declaration that the Munich Agreement was no longer valid. . . .

The British and the Poles never ceased to reproach us with passivity under the German occupation. It was, alas, partly true. The Germans had not behaved in Czechoslovakia with the same ferocity and cruelty as in Poland, in Greece and in Soviet Russia . . . a solid resistance movement was yet to be created and when Heydrich was appointed Protector, Beneš hoped that a hardening of the German attitude could be met with a stiffening of Czechoslovak resistance. The opposite happened. . . . Heydrich was a ruthless butcher, but he displayed a spectacular personality and seemed an acceptable figure to the workers and the peasants at the same time as he increased the severity of his treatment of the intellectual and ruling classes.[41]

The British had mixed feelings about the Czech people under German occupation. According to Sir William Strang, inside the Foreign Office Czechoslovakia was known as 'the Eldorado of the occupied territories'[42] because of its high level of industrial production for the German war effort. It was the only country in occupied Europe where food rations were increased.

Heydrich carefully courted the Czech industrial workers and peasants with material benefits in order to guarantee even higher production levels. He increased wages and food rations, took severe measures against unpopular profiteers and black marketeers, instituted a new social insurance policy, and requisitioned luxury hotels for use as holiday homes for labourers. This policy of wooing the workers through their wallets and their stomachs paid dividends in increased output among agricultural workers, and especially in the vitally important Škoda armaments factory. Heydrich's subtle policy of 'the carrot and the stick'[43] succeeded in pacifying or neutralizing the workers while simultaneously instituting severe repressive measures against the intelligentsia, whom he saw as the backbone of the resistance. Heydrich succeeded in driving a wedge between the workers and the resistance movement. 'The rape of the Czechs began to turn into a seduction.'[44]

Heydrich was assassinated by two Czech agents working for the Czech government-in-exile under Benes. They were trained, equipped and transported by SOE, and parachuted into Czechoslovakia in order to execute 'Operation Anthropoid'. It is important to stress that the mission was conceived and initiated by the Czech government-in-exile, which wanted to establish its resistance credentials in London, and also to eradicate the shame and stigma of widespread collaboration by the Czech people. Compared to the French, Serbs and Dutch, the Czechs were regarded as having a poor resistance record.

With the inevitability of massive reprisals that would follow the assassination, the German occupation would be seen in its true light. Thus inherent in the planned assassination of Heydrich was a calculated measure designed to provoke a brutal wave of German terror in order to shake the Czech people out of their mood of extensive collaboration, and to demonstrate to the world that the Czechs were not passively obedient subjects of the Third Reich. This point was made explicitly by Ronald Paget, Counsel for the Defence of Field Marshall Von Manstein:

> Partisans often deliberately provoke reprisals in order that hatred of the occupier may be intensified and more people may be induced to resist. That was our general idea when we flew in a party to murder Heydrich in Czechoslovakia.[45]

Resistance was to be artificially stimulated by a massive act of provocation to the Germans. This interpretation was confirmed by Colonel Moravec, the man who trained the assassins:

> An abominable calculation without a doubt, but we weighed up for a long time the immense propaganda advantages abroad of such an action against the obvious suffering that would ensue for the Czech population.... Alas.... I must say that at that time we had not imagined the tragedy of Lidice.[46]

In Britain the immediate public reaction to the news of the assassination was a mood of elation. The consequences were, however, predictable. Only the *Manchester Guardian* in its edition of 29 May 1942 had the foresight to see that the attack was 'bad news for it provides another occasion for savage reprisals'. On hearing of the assassination attempt, Hitler flew into a rage and demanded vengeance and exemplary punishment, in the form of the immediate execution of 30 000 Czechs. This figure was moderated by Heydrich's successor, Karl Hermann Frank, who persuaded the Führer that such wholesale terror would alienate the entire population, and would have an adverse effect upon Czech economic productivity. Hitler amended his order and instead demanded the arrest of 10 000 hostages, and Himmler supplemented this with a demand to shoot 100 members of the intelligentsia. This was carried out on the night of Heydrich's assassination. On the day of the assassination attempt, 150 Berlin Jews were killed as a reprisal, and Goebbels ordered the arrest of an additional 500 Berlin Jews as hostages. The leaders of the Jewish community were warned that any 'assassination attempt by Jews would result in the shooting of 150 Jewish hostages. Large numbers of convicted Jewish criminals were shot in Sachsenhausen.

In the following weeks, Frank pursued a policy of selective, graduated terror. Over 3000 people were arrested, and 1350 death sentences were pronounced at special courts-martial in Prague and Brno. 3000 Czech Jews were transferred from the so-called model camp at Theresienstadt to Treblinka, Belzec and Sobibor, where they were gassed. The SS dedicated their deaths to the beloved memory of Heydrich: the beginning of 'Operation Reinhard'. Heydrich's assassination also provided the incentive for medical experiments upon human guinea-pigs with sulphonamides at Ravensbrück. After Heydrich's death the executions continued at an accelerated pace. At Pankrac prison in Prague 1700 Czechs were killed, and in Brno 1300 people were executed at a college which had been converted into a prison. The executions received massive publicity in order to instil yet greater terror and subservience. Deliberate rumours were spread that every tenth Czech would be killed. During the remainder of the occupation, 305 000 Czechs were deported to concentration camps. Only 75 000 returned alive at the end of the war. In April 1944 Frank boasted that one hundred Czechs were sentenced to death each month.[47]

Lidice and Lezaky

On the day after Heydrich's funeral, Hitler ordered Frank to 'carry out a special reprisal action to teach the Czechs a lesson of subservience and humility'. In one of the most notorious war crimes in the Second World War, the 500-year old village of Lidice, situated 12 miles north west of Prague, was destroyed, razed to the ground, and the site bulldozed and ploughed in order to erase any trace of the former village. Lidice was literally wiped off the map – the act which, more than any, epitomizes the destructive nihilism that was at the centre of Nazi philosophy. According to SS records, 199 men (over the age of 16) were murdered; 174 men were killed in the village; the remaining 25 men from the village who were working in the neighbouring region, were taken to Prague and shot; 198 women were sent to Ravensbrück concentration camp, where 42 died of ill-treatment; 7 were gassed; 35 of the older women were sent to the medical block at Auschwitz where they died undergoing Nazi racial medical experiments. Four pregnant women were allowed to give birth to their babies. The babies were then murdered by having their throats slit, and the mothers sent to Ravensbrück. Of the 99 children, eight under the age of one year were 'Germanized' – that is, adopted and reared as Germans under the 'Lebensborn' programme. Nine other children were eventually deemed suitable for Germanization. The 82 remaining children were deemed to be racially unsuitable to live, and on Adolf Eichmann's instructions, were gassed at Chelmno concentration camp. A similar fate befell the smaller village of Lezaky, which was burned to the ground and the entire adult population of 33 people were murdered. The only survivors were two young girls considered to be racially pure. The rest disappeared.

One of the captured parachutists revealed under torture that the assassination squad had some contacts in Lidice. Furthermore, the Germans knew that two men from the village were serving in the Czech Brigade in Britain. One of the radio operators had been seized in Lezaky. Because the Protectorate Ministry of the Interior had what it described as 'impeccable evidence' that the people of Lidice and Lezaky had 'aided and abetted'[48] the assassins, the villagers were punished under the principle of collective responsibility.

In September 1942, as a deterrent against further Czech unrest, 4000 people – the relatives of exiles and resistance leaders – were detained as hostages, under the principle of collective family responsibility. In the event of further resistance activity they would be executed. Anyone who concealed information about Heydrich's assassination, or who had hidden or assisted the assassins, would be shot alongside their entire family.

Callum MacDonald in his excellent detailed study of Heydrich's assassination observes:

The Czechs paid a heavy price in blood for the death of the tyrant, with over 5000 victims of Nazi reprisals. In the light of this casualty list, the majority innocent civilians, the inevitable question must be asked – despite the heroism of the parachutists and their helpers, was anything achieved by the assassination?[49]

That Heydrich deserved to die for crimes against humanity is indisputable. But was the assassination worth the reprisals it provoked? And to whom? To the British and SOE? To the Czech government-in-exile? To the Czechoslovakian population still under German control?

The Lidice massacre attracted massive international publicity, and sent waves of revulsion around the world. The American Secretary of the Navy, Frank Knox, said on 13 June 1942: 'If future generations ask us what we were fighting for in this war we shall tell them the story of Lidice.'[50] In a display of human solidarity and sympathy, numerous towns throughout the world – including Stern Park Garden in Illinois – were renamed Lidice. One historian argues that the propaganda value of goading the Germans into the destruction of Lidice was a major consideration in the Allies' minds, for the small village became synonymous with Nazi barbarism.

> Perhaps . . . because the Allied architects of the assassination had taken into account, or even expected and hoped for, something like this act of destruction.[51]

M.R.D. Foot points out that the impact of the world-wide publicity devoted to Lidice was 'a superb gift to Allied propaganda services: it showed what Nazi domination actually meant'.[52] But was this propaganda benefit really necessary, given the Nazis' proven track record of atrocities? Was it commensurate with the human sacrifice? Anyone who studies the hauntingly normal photograph of the assembled schoolchildren of Lidice knows that the question answers itself.

Serious questions need to be asked about Britain's involvement, and the role of SOE in the assassination plan:

(1) Although the Czech government-in-exile bears the ultimate responsibility, why did London let the mission proceed in the first place when the intended target became clear? On previous

occasions SOE had overruled proposed ventures by governments-in-exile.

(2) One of the leading collaborationists, Emmanuel Moravec, the Minister of Public Education, calculated the arithmetic of Heydrich's death in a radio broadcast to the Czech nation:

> do not know whether you are aware what happened in France a year ago in a certain place where a German NCO was murdered, and it proved impossible to discover the murderer. Ten French civilians were shot as hostages and as a warning. What could the criminal have thought who committed this outrage against the highest representative of the Greater German Reich in these Czech lands? Meditate for a moment what would happen to the Czech people if the criminals were not discovered.[53]

As headmaster to the Czech nation, Moravec set his pupils a simple mathematical problem to solve for their homework. If ten people were killed for the death of an 'ordinary' German soldier, how many would perish for the assassination of the Reich Protector? The lesson was to school the nation in the realities of the occupation, and the need to inform upon those who broke the rules.

Given the publicly-declared German policy of operating a hostage quota of 100 civilian deaths for the life of every 'ordinary' German soldier in Eastern Europe, then SOE and the British government must have known, and indeed expected, that the scale and savagery of reprisals would be much greater in the case of a high-ranking Nazi, and Hitler's intended successor. The murder of one of the most powerful men in Germany was certain to provoke mass retaliation against the Czech people. Either they didn't realize that this was the inevitable consequence, in which case SOE was guilty of amateurism and negligence, or they did know, in which case, people in Prague might be forgiven for thinking that 'Perfidious Albion' was prepared to fight to the last Czech. The Czech historian, V. Mastny, argues that after the consequences became clear, there was an unwillingness to acknowledge responsibility, but:

> despite the exiles' reluctance to claim full credit, the plot against Heydrich seems to have been an overwhelmingly Czech undertaking.[54]

Nevertheless, SOE provided the training and logistical support. Given the intended target and the inevitable reprisals, it could have vetoed the operation at an early stage. And even after the agents had landed in Czechoslovakia, it was still possible to pull the plug on the mission. When the internal Czech Resistance leaders discovered the identity of the intended target, they were totally opposed to the plan and urgently contacted London because they had been unable to dissuade the assassins. The message they sent to SOE read:

> This assassination would not be of the least value to the Allies, and for our nation it would have unforeseeable consequences. It would threaten not only hostages and political prisoners, but also thousands of other lives. The nation would be the subject of unheard-of-reprisals. At the same time, it would wipe out the last remainders of any organisation. It would then be impossible for the resistance to be useful to the Allies. Therefore we beg you to give the order. . . . for the assassination not to take place. Danger in delay, give the order at once.[55]

Colonel Moravec showed the message to President Beneš and to the Chief of the British Secret Service: 'I learned after the war that the British not only did not cancel the operation, but continued to insist on it being carried out'.[56] The indigenous Czech resistance had little doubt that the British authorities had put very heavy pressure on Beneš, and that the attempt to abandon the assassination plan was overruled. After an agonizing delay Benes sent a categorical order:

> In the interests of the Western Allies the attack must be carried out as planned.[57]

Thus the desperate plea from the resistance movement inside Czechoslovakia, registering its disapproval of the planned assassination, was rejected. It accurately predicted precisely what would happen. Far from stimulating resistance, Heydrich's assassination had the opposite effect. One very important result of the German security dragnet was the virtual elimination of the Czech Resistance movement. A Foreign Office report in November 1942 indicated the success of German terrorism in pacifying the civilian population, and SOE concluded that 'the spirit of "open resistance" in the Protectorate had been broken'.[58] When the Russians asked the Czech Resistance to destroy the Škoda armaments works in the spring of 1943, this request was rejected because of the fear of a new round of reprisals.[59]

Heydrich's assassination was a massive blow to the Nazis' self-esteem. The Czech government-in-exile had shown a preparedness to sacrifice the lives of its own citizens in order to be taken seriously as an ally. The assassination of Heydrich guaranteed Czechoslovakia a seat at any post-war conference table as a fully independent state. In August 1942, the British government repudiated its commitment to the Munich Treaty of 1938 signed by Neville Chamberlain. The Munich pact was null and void, and the chapter of British appeasement over Munich was closed. The disputed Sudetanland was returned to Czechoslovakia in 1945, and the German minority was forcibly evicted and transferred to Germany. One of the leaders of the assassination plot, Colonel Moravec, remained unrepentant, despite the human costs:

> Given the circumstances in which we were placed at the time, it was a good try. . . . it is a good page in the history of Czechoslovakia in the Second World War. The Czech people should be proud of it. I am.[60]

A diametrically opposite conclusion was drawn by Colonel Frank Spooner, the Head of SOE's training school which organised the assassination plan.

> After the war, Spooner confessed that he wished he had not organized the assassination and that SOE tended to pay too little regard to the possibility of reprisals being taken against civilians.[61]

SOE's involvement in the assassination of Heydrich stands in sharp contrast to the care and effort that guided the Vermork raid. It remains a serious query against SOE's reputation, and Lidice is an indelible stain on Britain's conduct in the 'shadow war'. It is difficult to avoid the conclusion that the lives of the people of Lidice were deliberately hazarded. When future generations are told 'the story of Lidice' they must be told the whole story.

CONCLUSION

> Criminal means once tolerated are soon preferred.[62]
>
> Edmund Burke

> We but teach
> Bloody instructions, which being taught, return
> To plague the inventor: this even-handed justice
> Commends the ingredients of our poisoned chalice
> To our lips.
>
> Macbeth, Act I, Scene 7

A number of professional military men felt an in-bred distaste for SOE's methods of subversion and assassination. They regarded partisan war as a breach of the code of orthodox warfare between states. Worse still, London became the headquarters of this unprecedented body dedicated to terrorist methods. The Ministry of Economic Warfare was widely known in military circles as the 'Ministry of Ungentlemanly Warfare', and Sir Arthur Harris, the Commander in Chief of Bomber Command, described it as 'amateurish, ignorant, irresponsible and mendacious'.[63] SOE was regarded, in M.R.D. Foot's words, as 'the British dirty tricks department'.[64] The military historian Captain Basil Liddell Hart questioned both the effectiveness and the morality of SOE. Liddell Hart argued that although armed resistance 'undoubtedly imposed a considerable strain on the Germans', nevertheless it was 'rarely more than a nuisance', and was less effective than widespread non-violent resistance. Moreover, violent resistance 'provoked reprisals much severer than the injury inflicted on the enemy'.[65] But for Liddell Hart, the 'heaviest handicap, and the most lasting one, was of a moral kind. . . . its widespread amoral effect on the younger generation'.[66] Involvement in the underground often, of necessity, led to contacts with the criminal underworld in order to obtain essential goods and materials. Resistance quartermasters organized bank raids and burglaries from warehouses, shops and farms, to feed and clothe their men on the run. In many areas, living off the land was a euphemism for pillage and plunder. Forced requisitioning caused tensions with peasant farmers in various parts of occupied Europe, and in places resistance verged on banditry and criminality. Britain's policy of fanning the flames of violent resistance was unwise because the legacy of disorder far outweighed the contribution

SOE made to victory. The Germans have a saying: 'Beware the first step'. Britain's sponsorship of assassination and partisan warfare set a dangerous precedent: creating a climate of lawlessness, the coarsening and erosion of moral values, and also giving comfort to those who support terrorism. According to military historian John Keegan, the strongest and most important reason for condemning SOE is that 'it dirtied the British government's hands'. Britain's response to contemporary terrorism 'is compromised by what we did through SOE'. In Keegan's strongly-worded critique:

> Means besmirch ends. SOE besmirched Britain.[67]

Thus the example that SOE set was a role-model for people fighting for self-determination against foreign occupation. The long-term consequence of SOE's existence was the breeding of terrorism in the post-war world.

This is a weighty consideration which should not be lightly dismissed. There is some evidence to support the claim. Desperate temporary measures of last resort have a tendency to become a normal, settled method of action, or a method of first resort. So is there a connection between the forms of militant, violent resistance practised during World War II and modern terrorist groups who also see themselves as 'freedom fighters'? Is this a case of SOE's chickens coming home to roost? The glamorization of resistance in highly-romanticized films and novels in the post-war period contributed to the lure of violence, and the cult of the outlaw. Various contemporary terrorist groups have pointed to wartime resistance as a model to emulate, and as a justification for their own actions. They also employ the *tu quoque* argument ('You did it too') in defence of their own violence, citing Allied terror bombing and resistance assassinations as a justification for violence, and in order to deflect criticism – the technique of 'guilt transfer'. Thus, when the ANC was criticized for killing civilians in bomb attacks upon shopping centres in South Africa in 1985, Oliver Tambo, the deputy leader of the ANC replied:

> How many children were killed when the RAF was bombing Germany? After all, we are fighting a Fascist Nazi State too.[68]

Similarly, the Irish nationalist Eddie McAteer wrote in 1948:

Our attitude must be the attitude of the French to the Germans while France was under German occupation.[69]

Père Lazarbal, a Catholic priest and leading spokesman for the Basque separatist group ETA, claimed:

We are not terrorists. We are liberators. . . . This Baque country of ours is under foreign occupation, just as France was under the Germans. This is a war too, like World War II. Well, then, in any war, do you kill or don't you?[70]

The widespread killing of informers and 'collaborators' during the Palestinian *Intifada*, necklace killings in black South African townships and the widespread adoption of head-shaving as a form of humiliation for those who have engaged in 'horizontal collaboration' and sleeping with the enemy – all testify to the power of imitation and the romance of the resistance gunman. Because of SOE, British governments are open to the charge of hypocrisy and double-standards, and are morally compromised in their condemnation of terrorism. Nevertheless, while there is a grain of truth in this allegation, the criticism overlooks the crucial difference that many modern sub-state terrorists use terrorism as a first, not a last resort, and they abuse the freedoms of relatively open societies, and wage war against constitutional states where the right to protest, demonstrate and dissent are legally enshrined in the rule of law. By contrast, resisters in Occupied Europe were struggling against one of the most ruthless police states in history. There is a very real difference between making urgent choices in extraordinary conditions, and appealing to them as a normal means of recourse and a settled policy. Even if one questions the wisdom of particular resistance operations, it still remains true that the difference in circumstances between wartime resistance and modern terrorism is profoundly important. Blanket criticism of SOE's terrorism also ignores the moral circumspection and painstaking efforts of resisters like Knut Haukelid to avoid civilian casualties, in comparison with many modern terrorists who deliberately cause the deaths of innocent people in order to publicize their cause.

A more telling criticism of SOE lies in the need to distinguish between its encouragement of sabotage, which was useful to the war effort, and its casual support for the routine assassination of German personnel, which resulted in civilian casualties which far outweighed any benefit. Some acts of sabotage had strategic importance, and were an important component in the Allied war of attrition – attacks on armaments' factories such as Le Creusot in France, the blowing up of vital rail and communications' links such as the Gorgopotamos Viaduct in Greece, or attacks upon oil supplies for U-boats. What SOE's critics overlook is that the Vemork raid, which deprived the Germans of any chance to make atomic weapons, on its own was sufficient to justify SOE's existence.

In Western Europe the gravity of the moral issues surrounding SOE's sponsorship of sabotage – which led to reprisals – was compounded by the further dilemma that if the local resistance did not attack vital targets then the RAF would attempt to bomb them, with the likelihood of far higher friendly civilian casualties. What tilted the moral balance in favour of sabotage was the negative utilitarian consideration of minimizing casualties. So the arguments which were employed against sabotage because it provoked reprisals, could also lead to reluctant approval of sabotage as a lesser evil than clumsy saturation bombing by the RAF. Resistance sabotage was a more accurate form of warfare than indiscriminate aerial bombardment, and more economical and frugal in human lives. This helped to ease the doubts which afflicted many resisters, but still left residual guilt, because choosing the lesser of evils still left the deaths of large numbers of innocent reprisal victims on their consciences. The serious moral question for SOE is how much control it exerted over less important acts of minor sabotage which had a negligible military effect, but which resulted in routine reprisals. Given that London provided the logistical support for resistance, did SOE caution against, or did it turn a blind eye to measures which were unwarranted and unjustified in military terms? Under the conditions of collective responsibility, if it was not militarily necessary to engage in an act, it was morally necessary not to engage in that act.

10 Conclusion

In America, and in this country too, there is an enormous defect of imagination about the Third Reich. . . . It's a defect with some honourable, decent roots in societies which have never known occupation, dictatorship or modern revolution.[1]

Neal Ascherson

If a man would understand the love of England he must do what hardly anyone would dare to do: that is he must clearly envisage England defeated in a final war and ask himself, 'What should I do then?'[2]

Hilaire Belloc

Just as great art and literature holds up a mirror in which we see ugly truths and the hideous reflection of ourselves – our blemishes, flaws, weaknesses and confusions – so too the Nazi occupation of Europe probes disturbing truths, and forces us to contemplate things that we would rather not look at. It reflects profound questions about individual responsibility, the cracks, the breaking-point in our values and beliefs. Hence the intriguing question: what if Britain had been invaded? If it had happened to us, would we have acted and responded in the same way as the French, the Belgians, the Serbs? We can identify ourselves in them. How would we have behaved in similar circumstances? The history of the occupation has much to teach us. In her excellent, thought-provoking analysis of the Channel Islands under German rule, Madeleine Bunting reminds us that 'islanders compromised, collaborated and fraternized just as people did throughout occupied Europe'.[3]

The occupation of the Channel Islands presents a challenge because it does not fit neatly into the British collective memory of the Second World War, in which this happy breed of men did not compromise, and alone retained an unblemished record of defiance of Nazi Germany. The notion that we were made of sterner stuff and would not have collaborated, was not put to the test, thanks largely to the defensive moat of the English Channel and RAF Fighter Command. Nevertheless, as Bunting points out:

The islands' experience flatly contradicted Britain's dearest and most complacent assumptions about the distinctness of the British from the rest of Europe. Under occupation, the British behaved exactly like the French, the Dutch or the Danish.[4]

The islands' traditional authorities – the Bailiffs of Jersey and Guernsey – remained in office, and civil governors and civil servants co-operated with the invaders. The police enforced a mixture of British law and German orders. Eventually the authorities over-stepped the fine line between passive co-operation and collaboration. At a time when the British government, through the BBC and SOE, was encouraging the 'V for Victory' propaganda campaign throughout occupied Europe, the Bailiff of Guernsey, Victor Carey, offered a reward of twenty-five pounds (the equivalent of three months' wages) for information leading to the arrest of anyone painting 'V' signs. The Guernsey police passed on the name of one farm labourer to the Germans for committing such an offence. He was sentenced to one year's imprisonment.[5]

The civil service agreed to compile a register containing details of place of birth and religion. This helped to isolate British-born islanders, who were eventually held hostage, and also Jews. British officials – civil servants and policemen – co-operated in tracking down and deporting the small number of Jews on the islands. Many islanders informed on their neighbours. Louisa Gould and her brother, Harold Le Druillenec, sheltered an escaped Russian slave labourer. In her words:

I had to do something for another mother's son.[6]

Informers caused her arrest, and this unsung heroine died in Ravensbrück. Her brother was one of the few British prisoners to survive Belsen. Another forgotten war heroine, Marie Ozanne, was tortured, and subsequently died, for protesting about the harsh conditions for the slave labourers on the islands.[7]

If in our flights of fantasy we would like to see ourselves in the role of heroic resister, do we not feel uncomfortable in the realization that it is more likely that we would have engaged in many of the inevitable, unavoidable but shabby compromises of everyday life under brutal enemy occupation? How many of us would have resigned our teaching posts in protest at the imposition of a Nazi-inspired racialist national curriculum? Who would have spoken out at the disappearance of Jewish students from our classes? How many civil servants would have refused to be party to the compilation of a racial census, a registration aimed at isolating minority group victims? How many policemen would have refused to participate in the round-up and deportation of unwanted Jewish aliens, or to assist the German army of occupation in taking civilian hostages? How many prison officers would have refused to detain their innocent fellow countrymen in a hostage camp? How many railwaymen would have declined to staff the deportation rosters? How many industrialists would have turned down lucrative contracts to supply the German war effort in its international crusade against Bolshevism? After years of unemployment and neglect, how many factory workers would have refused to turn out equipment for the German war machine? How many actors, musicians, artists, would have declined to compromise their art by not performing in front of a German audience? How many journalists and writers would have refused to sully their hands? Writing for a newspaper from which Jews had been banned could be seen as providing moral assistance to the occupiers, in confirming the legitimacy of Nazi racial policy. Authors would have had to submit their work to a German committee of 'aesthetics' officials who exercised the power to grant or withhold permission for artistic 'licence'. At some point, self-expression would inevitably collide with self-censorship. How many cinema owners, managers, projectionists, would have refused to show the notorious anti-semitic films of the new cinema? (The Gaumont in Guernsey was used for such propaganda movies. Would the Ritz in Rochdale, or the Savoy in Stockport have done the same?) How many printers would have refused to print anti-semitic propaganda posters, or warnings of reprisal action and lists of named hostage detainees? Which managers of garments' factories would have refused to supply large quantities of the badge of shame, the Yellow Star?

British Jewry too would have faced the same dilemmas as its European counterparts. Industrial Lodz was known as the Manchester of Poland. Would a Mancunian Rumkowski have emerged from the Cheetham Hill ghetto? In London, would a Czerniakow figure have presided over the steady reduction of the Bethnal Green ghetto? Would the Board of Deputies of British Jews have been placed in the same compromising position as the UGIF in France – or in the role of the *Joodse Raad* (Jewish Council) in Amsterdam – protecting British Jews at the expense of foreign Jews? Finally, how many of us would have put our family first, rather than risk the uncertain consequences (possibly the loss of the wage earner, perhaps deportation) of protesting or resigning on an issue of principle? These questions illustrate the way in which the complicities of 'ordinary collaboration' spread their tentacles into every aspect of life. The point of raising these questions is not to indulge in easy moral indignation, or to sit in judgement, or to generate feelings of guilt by proxy. Nor is it to bathe in the comforting thought that as life was riddled with complicity, we are all guilty in general, but that nobody is guilty in particular. Rather, the purpose is to show the moral complexity of the choices that people did have to face throughout Hitler's Europe, and the price of resistance, and to illustrate the all-embracing grip of the system of collective responsibility. Nazi security policy succeeded with satanic meticulousness in turning decency and humane feelings into a theatre of psychological warfare by attacking the uneasy, equivocal conscience. In their sub-Nietzschean contempt for compassion and pity, the Nazis grasped that the conquered peoples were most vulnerable, and most squeamish, at this point. Collective and family responsibility sapped the moral strength and incapacitated the resistance potential of the enemy. The primary purpose of collective responsibility was to shatter the adversary's capacity to resist, and to bring about a crisis of confidence, a moral collapse. All the muddy compromises, the unwitting complicities stemmed from the imperceptible merging of good intentions with the fear of evil consequences.

Imagine yourself living under Nazi occupation. Consider which resistance action you would agree to if you knew that in consequence, your son, your brother, your husband or father, was to be rounded-up and executed as a hostage:

(1) the killing of an 'ordinary' soldier in the German army of occupation?
(2) the assassination of a high-ranking Nazi official?
(3) the assassination of a known informer/collaborator ... and members of his family?
(4) a minor act of sabotage?
(5) a major act of sabotage on vital equipment?
(6) the rescue or shelter of refugees?

These questions are asked, *not* because your relatives are more important than your unknown fellow citizens, but because there are *no unimportant people* whose death warrant can be signed without consideration of their rights and interests. We should not ask or expect more from others than we are prepared to accept for ourselves. Which standards would we want to have applied to ourselves? Perhaps the measure of the importance and necessity of various acts of resistance is what we would be prepared to countenance, knowing that all that we hold dear may be the sacrifice – the blood price – that has to be paid. If you would not be prepared to support any of the above actions in which your own family may be the victims, by what authority do you claim the right to sacrifice the lives of innocent strangers? This is the very question that ghetto Jews put to Jewish partisans in the fevered debates concerning the appropriate means of resisting the Nazis. These are nagging, conscience-stabbing questions, with cruel choices. How many of us would have given hospitality to the shivering, despised Jew who had just knocked on our door? Who would have done so at the risk of endangering their own children? Yisrael Gutman, who participated in the Warsaw Ghetto uprising, observes:

> there is no moral imperative which demands that a normal mortal should risk his life and that of his family to save his neighbour. Are we capable of imagining the agony of fear of an individual, a family, which selflessly and voluntarily, only due to an inner human impulse, bring into their home someone threatened with death?[8]

How many of us would have harboured resistance 'terrorists' if we knew that the consequence of discovery would be the massacre of the population and the levelling of our village?

> One former SOE Commander, detailed to plan guerrilla defence in East Anglia in the event of a German invasion, was told by a senior regional official, William Spens, the Master of Corpus Christi College, Cambridge, that if the enemy landed, he would have the SOE man shot rather than risk German reprisals against innocent civilians in the area.[9]

High-sounding phrases such as 'the true purpose of resistance is to save a nation's soul'[10] must be set against the enormous cost in human suffering. How much blood-letting of the civilian body was necessary to save the nation's soul? How many mutilated villages like Oradour, Lidice, Marzabotto, Kragujevac, was it acceptable to endure? The Germans destroyed 90% of Warsaw after the 1944 Uprising. Could London have expected less?

It is difficult for us, looking back, to appreciate the extent to which many resisters were tormented and bedevilled by this kind of question. It is only by trying to put ourselves in the shoes of the potential resister, only by attempting empathically to understand the high cost of resistance – and the high cost of non-resistance – that we can begin to grasp, let alone pass judgement on their decisions and actions. My aim has been to clarify what were the ultimate issues at stake in the fateful, possibly fatal, choice between resistance and 'collaboration'. Madeleine Bunting aptly describes how the Channel Islands' experience was:

> informed by the moral complexity of war. Unlike the British, those who had been occupied could never view the war in quite the same terms of moral absolutes: of good against evil, the Allies against the Nazis.[11]

WAS RESISTANCE WORTHWHILE?

> I soon realized that a guerrilla army . . . was capable only of slowing down the offensive of a regular army. This means, as a rule, the necessity of evading enemy attacks.[12]
>
> Milovan Djilas

The question of whether European resistance was worthwhile will remain a contentious, unresolved issue because of the incommensurability of the factors being weighed. How can one measure the honour of one's country against the lives of one's countrymen? How does one weigh the lives of Frenchmen against the freedom of France? Was it right to sacrifice the people of Poland for the idea of Poland?

> There is no answer to such a question. Some people believed that any sacrifice was worthwhile if it disrupted the German war effort, however slightly. Others would take a more relative view, but would find themselves floundering in some impossible conundrum: how many innocent hostages to be shot for the death of a German soldier; how many streets burned and blasted to cripple one tank.[13]

This is an unavoidable question to ask, an impossible question to answer definitively. My own sceptical answer may be inferred from the text. Briefly it may be summarized.

It is difficult to draw up an over-all balance sheet of European resistance, partly because of the sheer scale of such an assessment, and the need to take into account the varied conditions of German occupation policy in different countries. Also, resistance was not all of one piece. Resistance took many forms, which can be broadly divided into violent and non-violent resistance, and then sub-divided into the various types of violent and non-violent actions. But whatever form resistance took, there were real yet limited achievements. While the courageous non-violent rescue action of pacifists saved individuals from the death camps, it could not destroy the foundation of the death camp system, nor could it threaten the very existence of Nazism. But neither could violent resistance be decisive in itself in overthrowing the Nazi empire. Resistance did not, and could not, win the war by itself. Honest resisters who 'did their bit' for the war effort had enough modesty to recognize this. Jean-Paul Sartre wrote shortly after the liberation:

Resistance was only an individual solution and we always knew it: without it England would have won the war, with it they would have lost if they were going to lose. Its value in our eyes was above all symbolic.[14]

The alternatives were not a national uprising or perpetual national submission. Armed resistance was totally dependent upon Allied finance, weapons, training and support, and ultimately upon an Allied invasion. Its military value prior to invasion was regarded as negligible by the Germans themselves. One may recall Albert Speer's impatient answer to an enquiry about the economic effectiveness of the French resistance: 'What French Resistance?'[15] French Resistance veteran Henri Michel conceded that:

Nowhere ... did the guerrillas score a decisive success.... The vast majority of German units never came into direct contact with the guerrillas ...
without Allied assistance, the partisans, however heroic ... must inevitably succumb to enemy superiority.[16]

After extensive research, Professor Alan Milward concluded that because a great deal of resistance was isolated, unplanned and unco-ordinated, it had little economic effect. Most resistance was 'entirely unimportant compared to the co-ordinated and controlled actions of real armed forces'[17] in affecting the ultimate outcome of the war. Nevertheless, against this must be set the view of the Supreme Commander of the Allied Forces, General Eisenhower, who paid tribute to the 'inestimable value' of the French resistance, and especially the Brittany resistance, saying that:

> without their great assistance, the liberation of France and the defeat of the enemy in Western Europe would have consumed a much longer time and mean greater losses to ourselves.[18]

Eisenhower put a figure on French resistance, saying that their support had been worth fifteen regular army divisions, and had shortened the war by two months. Allowing for the element of political diplomacy in Eisenhower's fulsome praise, and the way in which it would help to heal France's wounded pride after four years of humiliation, such an assessment cannot be lightly ignored. Thus the timing of resistance is important in assessing its morality as well as its strategic worth. Only the most fervent nationalist or communist could argue that resistance should be waged whatever the cost. Only a committed pacifist could claim that the price should never be paid.

Defenders of the resistance legacy also point to Yugoslavia, where Churchill frequently claimed that Tito's partisans were holding down twenty-four German divisions. Recent historians have shown that Churchill's figures were exaggerated, and that in 1943, German troop strength in Yugoslavia never exceeded eight divisions, and that these were supplemented by Axis forces from Italy, Bulgaria and Croatia. They bore the brunt of the fighting, with Germany only ever employing two divisions in anti-guerrilla operations, even in 1944. David Martin questions whether Tito's partisans were really tying down German troops.[19] Yugoslavia had virtually no industry, and was of little economic importance in itself to the Nazis. Even without any armed resistance, and the uncivil war which raged within the country, Germany had to garrison troops in order to protect its consignments of raw materials and its communication lines to Greece and North Africa. In addition, top priority was given to securing the coastline in order to avert the possibility of an Allied invasion of Europe, via Yugoslavia. The Allies had used the cover plan of a Balkan landing in order to stretch German resources. Outside of these security zones, the Germans ceded large areas of non-strategic territory within Yugoslavia. When military operations dictated, these areas were flooded with troops. It would be a mistake to believe that Tito's partisans 'liberated' these areas from the Wehrmacht in open battle. Rather, the German Army relinquished them.

Often the most spectacular forms of resistance were the least effective, and the least spectacular were the most effective. Information gathering was more useful to the Allied war effort than the assassination of troops. Rescue activities contributed more to humanity than paramilitary action. Armed resistance had a nuisance value in harrassing, disrupting and temporarily immobilizing the enemy. The cumulative weight of this should not be ignored or denigrated, nor should the enormous bravery of resisters be minimized, or their reputations tarnished. But violent resistance must be placed in proper perspective. It was a supplement, and not an alternative, to conventional war. It played a minor supporting role in the great drama of clashing armies. What should never be forgotten is that after June 1941, the Red Army had to contend with never less than three-quarters of the German Army, and for long periods, nine-tenths of the Wehrmacht was locked into the life-and-death struggle in the eastern theatre, which, above all others, determined the outcome of the war. Violent resistance raised other questions concerning the human and moral costs of opposing the Nazis.

The Dehumanizing Effects of Nazism

Whoever fights monsters should see to it that in the process he does not become a monster. And when you look long into an abyss, the abyss also looks into you.[20]

Nietzsche

Perhaps the last and most long-lived victory of Hitlerism is to be found in the shameful scars made on the hearts of those who fought Hitlerism most vigorously. How could it be otherwise? . . . this world has been subjected to an unparalleled outbreak of hatred. . . .[21]

Albert Camus

During the war I learned that the cruellest thing about cruelty is that it dehumanizes its victims before it destroys them. And the hardest of struggles is to remain human in inhuman conditions.[2]

Janina Bauman

The war against Nazi Germany was not just a military conflict, but a battle of ideas, and a struggle for elementary human dignity and decency. At its best the spirit of resistance was a fight for a world in which as Albert Camus put it, there would be neither victims nor executioners. But before the 'army of the shadows' could emerge from the shadow of the Swastika and into light, resisters had to wrestle with their troubled consciences. Resisters had to calculate their own contribution to the human costs of defeating Nazism and

the conscious acceptance of guilt in the necessary murder.[23]

Even clearly justifiable acts of resistance, such as the Vemork raid to ruin Germany's atomic bomb programme, or the blowing-up of the strategically important Gorgopotamos viaduct in Greece, or the rescue of Jews, carried a heavy blood price in innocent hostage lives. Under the terms dictated by the Nazis' system of collective responsibility, it was impossible to remain pure, free from the defilements incurred by responsible action. But what of the unnecessary murder, the symbolic gesture of defiance which resulted in gratuitous suffering upon the civilian population? Resistance often provoked reprisals much more severe than any injury inflicted on the enemy. In many cases the suffering to the resisters' own people was so disproportionate that it far outweighed any material damage to the Germans. Frequently resisters committed reckless acts of sabotage or provocation that cost lives but achieved little or nothing. The military benefits of resistance were won at great human cost, and also at a high moral price to the resistance's own ideals. For all its heroism, much paramilitary resistance was fruitless, and there was a disparity between the exorbitant level of bloodletting and the modest achievements. Many acts of resistance were of dubious value, and arguably did more harm than good. Many needlessly endangered the civilian population and put innocent lives at risk. Apart from undermining non-combatant immunity, such acts fell way short of the just war principle of proportionality. In any assessment of resistance it is important to ask: how many hostages died in vain? How many civilian reprisal victims were sacrificed unnecessarily, for no discernible military benefits?

Some partisan units attempted to minimize civilian casualties by operating in sparsely populated areas. The Osoppo Brigade of Italian partisans kept up a barrage of sneak attacks on convoys of German troops, and moved from place to place in order to avoid German reprisals on innocent villagers. Their leader, Don Ascanio, insisted on strictly disciplined units, and was determined that his men should not kill unnecessarily.[24] One young Dutch resister recalls the success of railway sabotage in her area of Holland near Driebergen, and the need to halt such operations out of fear of German reprisals:

> Local men were forced to patrol the line which of course hampered our operations because *we could not put these men at risk by blowing up the line anywhere near them.*[25]

Similarly, in Greece, Bill Jordan, on guerrilla operations with the non-communist EDES partisans, records:

> ... we feared reprisals on the civilian population and Colonel Pantiledes deliberately chose a stretch of line as far away from villages as possible.[26]

Other resistance groups, however, ran the risk of being tainted by the very evil that they were fighting against. Partisans could resort to morally indefensible and barbaric methods by deliberately provoking reprisals against their own people, by intimidation and terrorist methods against their compatriots, and by reducing the civilian population to expendable pawns:

> If ... the partisans wished to destroy a bridge, they would send a long column of old men, women and children towards it; the German guards, presuming them to be refugees, took no action. But behind the column crept the guerrillas, who opened fire when the leading civilians had reached the bridge, killed the sentries and pinned down any further resistance until the charges had been placed on the target. The civilians had to look after themselves as best they could.[27]

After a decade of forced collectivization, most Soviet peasants were hostile to the Communist cause. Villages were raided and large numbers of peasants were compelled to join the partisans. Anyone who refused was shot as a German agent. Their house would be burned as a punishment for the whole family. Unreliable recruits were dealt with sternly, being sent on assignment to dangerous missions as cannon-fodder. Desertion was regarded as the greatest crime, and the Soviet authorities, like the Nazis, practised collective family responsibility: 'If a recruit managed to desert, his family were immediately killed.'[28] A Greek resister, Nikiforos, who participated in the destruction of the Gorgopotamos viaduct, became disillusioned with Communist methods of warfare, but was counselled by SOE agents to stay with Aris' notorious group:

> If Nikiforos left him, Aris would seek him out and murder him. If he could not get him, then he would take reprisals against Nikiforos' family. To leave the Communists was desertion, and desertion was punishable by death.[29]

The same threat hung over other resisters who joined Communist Front paramilitary organisations.

While making every allowance for the unprecedented conditions of warfare dictated by Hitler's war of extermination on the eastern front, it still remains true that ignoble means perverted good ends. The evil of the Nazi regime is no reason for ignoring the crimes perpetrated by the resistance, or for attempting to justify its own inhumanity. The Russian partisans repaid the Nazis in their own barbaric coinage. In one incident a German hospital train carrying wounded soldiers was derailed, and the injured men were burned to death with paraffin. In another, an army barracks had its water supply poisoned.[30] German soldiers were prosecuted as war criminals at Nuremberg for comparable atrocities. The principles affirmed at Nuremberg are sound, but they must be applied in an even-handed way in order to repudiate the problem of victor's justice. Telford Taylor, Chief Counsel of the American Prosecution at Nuremberg, declared: 'We must not forget that to kill a defenceless prisoner-of-war is not only a violation of the rules of war. It is murder.'[31] Similarly, the Chief French Prosecutor, François de Menthon – a former resistance member – declared that all killing of hostages was 'contrary to Article 50 of the Hague Convention'.[32] Also, 'the killing of prisoners of war, of hostages . . . falls, in French law, under Articles 295 and following of the Penal Code which define murder and assassination'.[33] In May 1942, leading Soviet propagandist Ilya Ehrenburg, set an exacting standard for the assessment of partisan conduct:

> We hate Fascism because we love people . . . because we love life.
> The Soviet people will never be like the Fascists: they will never torture . . . or torment the wounded . . . only justice is capable of mitigating our suffering. . . . If the German soldier lays down his rifle and gives himself up, we will not lay a finger on him and he will remain alive.[34]

While undoubtedly admirable, these declarations were not consistently applied to the condemnation of Allied, as opposed to Axis, war crimes. Massacres pervaded the partisan war on both sides. Many of the practices of resistance were hardly less abhorrent than those of the Nazis. Victory alone could not justify the terrible means which some resisters used to obtain it. Guerrillas committed atrocious crimes. Torture of captured Germans was widespread. Enemy prisoners were treated abominably. In areas of partisan activity the ambush, capture, mutilation and torture of German troops was common practice; intended to weaken the morale and to terrorize all German security forces. Did resistance atrocities and violations of the laws of war serve only to excuse Nazi war crimes? A directive from the Central Committee of the White [Belorussian] Russian Communist Party, July 1st 1941, read:

> The enemy was to be destroyed anywhere he could be found, and put to death by any means that was to hand – axe, scythe, crowbar, pitchfork, knife. . . . In the destruction of the enemy, one must not shrink from using any means: strangulation, hacking to pieces, burning, poisoning.[35]

The methods recommended are identical to those employed by the Croatian Fascist Ustaše against Serbs. Captured Russian partisans revealed that they had been given instructions for German soldiers, including the wounded, to be tortured by mutilation prior to death.[36] When Soviet guerrillas overran German field hospitals, wounded men were usually mutilated and murdered, and Red Cross nurses killed.

In August 1941 a partisan group ambushed a German bus properly marked with a red cross, and carrying 19 German wounded.

Driver, staff, and all wounded were killed, a number of them . . . mutilated.[37]

There was growing hostility towards the enemy among German medical orderlies and doctors, 'who were sickened by the repeated occurrences of deliberate mutilations inflicted on German soldiers'.[38] In one notorious incident in December 1941, 160 injured German soldiers were killed at a convalescent hospital in Feodosia on the Crimean coast. Some had been carried to the beach, drenched with seawater and left to freeze to death. A Russian male nurse who escaped testified, 'two of the Russian hospital personnel were shot because they had treated the German wounded'.[39]

The use of torture and mutilation was not confined to the war in the Soviet Union. On Crete a Wehrmacht commission investigating allegations of war crimes and atrocities reported:

> On corpses of German soldiers countless mutilations have been established; some had their genitals amputated, eyes put out, ears and noses cut off . . . hands chopped off. The majority of these mutilations were probably defilement of the dead bodies; only in a few cases does the evidence indicate that the victim was maltreated and tortured to death.[40]

The Wehrmacht War Crimes Bureau took numerous legal depositions, concluding that the mutilation of corpses and the maltreatment of soldiers was committed almost exclusively by Cretan civilians and resisters, and not by British military personnel. Similar abominations can be recounted from other theatres of resistance, but one final example from France will suffice to illustrate the widespread nature of partisan atrocities. A senior Wehrmacht doctor reported that:

> A single group of forty bodies had been discovered, horribly mutilated. Their faces had been stove in, and their testicles cut off and stuffed in their mouths.[41]

Apart from its intrinsic barbarism, we should remember that the calculated purpose behind the practice of mutilation and torture was to provoke German reprisals. After their farms and villages had been burned, and their families destroyed, survivors would swell the ranks of the Communist partisans. Perhaps guerrilla warfare was an inescapable part of resistance to German occupation policies in eastern Europe and the Balkans. There were extenuating circumstances in the unequal struggle against a ruthless and uncompromising enemy. Partisan atrocities were not on the systematic scale of Nazi war crimes. In that sense no equation can be made between the oppression of the aggressor and the resistance of the victim. But let us not blind ourselves to the morally corrosive qualities of this form of war, or close our eyes to what it entailed in practice. Although the level of Nazi state terrorism overshadows the sub-state terrorism of the Resistance, to be equitable and morally credible we must condemn with equal force the violations of the laws of war by the partisans. One cannot have it both ways: either anything goes in war, or there are limits for both sides. If a practice is condemned as a moral outrage if the Germans perpetrated it, then it cannot be excused if resisters carried it out.

Just as one is heartened to come across examples of humanity and decency in the enemy – German soldiers like Rommel who protested against illegal orders and prevented war crimes, or heroic examples of ordinary conscripts who refused to be a party to the violation of the rules of war in shooting innocent civilian hostages, and were subsequently charged with treason and executed alongside the hostages – so one is jolted by examples of resistance excesses, and the infliction of gratuitous violence. As we have seen, resistance was capable of degenerating into acts of savagery and bestiality which dehumanized the enemy, reducing German soldiers to the level of 'things', and which also dehumanized the resisters' own civilian population. Any form of resistance which degraded or cheapened the value of human life, diminished the very cause it was fighting for. It provided a posthumous victory for Nazism, for as Goebbels noted:

Even if we lose, we shall win, for our ideals will have penetrated to the hearts of our enemies.[42]

The worst damage that the Nazis inflicted was to make their enemies resemble them, and for resisters to act in violation of their own declared principles. The uncomfortable truth in Goebbels' words came back to haunt the French with the publication of the book, 'The Question' by the Algerian Communist Henri Alleg. Although originally banned by the French government, it was eventually published in 1958. The book caused an outcry, and then self-examination, because it exposed the fact that Alleg's captors – the state servants who were the heirs to the French Resistance tradition, and to the 'Rights of Man' – were systematically using torture in Algeria. One of Alleg's torturers had been tortured himself while in the Resistance. The victims of the Gestapo were now using Gestapo methods. We have noted French resister Marguerite Duras' admission of personal involvement in torturing suspected collaborators. This caused her inner torment and remorse, but it also took her to the edge of the abyss of nihilism into which the Nazis forced their opponents to stare, for as Jean Paul Sartre observed, the torturer: 'has in a single victim, symbolically gratified his hatred of all mankind'.[43]

These examples expose the heart of darkness within all of us, that we are all capable of descending to the Nazi level. In fighting against Nazism, it was not always possible to be innoculated against its evil force and powers of moral contamination. This should give cause for introspection and a more self-critical appraisal of the resistance legacy. Is it implausible to see a connection between the evil means employed by resistance movements during the Second World War, and the subsequent adoption of similar methods after 1945? Guerrilla warfare in World War II could be seen as a dress rehearsal for post-war liberation struggles. The nemesis effect of resistance lay in the dangerous precedent that it set for others to emulate. If it was legitimate for European resistance to use any means against foreign occupation – including not only political assassination and the execution of collaborators, but also methods of barbarism: mutilation and torture – why was it not equally permissible for resistance to European colonial occupation to resort to identical means? In the Second World War, guerrillas failed to wage war in accordance with the principles of international law. Guerrillas undermined the laws of war by clear violations of the prisoner-of-war convention, and the rules governing the protection of civilians. The principle that anything was permitted against the enemy was not only morally flawed, but corrupting in its long-term consequences. Did resistance methods poison the peace by legitimizing the ready resort to political violence to solve political disputes? Furthermore, was the violence employed by the Resistance habit-forming? On the day that the war ended in Europe, VE Day, 8 May 1945, French troops massacred at least 15 000 (according to some accounts as many as 45 000) Algerians at Setif, as a reprisal for the murder of French settlers. On the most modest calculation this was a reprisal ratio of 10:1. Alistair Horne writes that:

the Army repression must have been carried out on orders from de Gaulle's government... and it must equally have been fully aware of the extent of the ensuing bloodbath... Communist ministers shared responsibility without a murmur.[44]

This was an administration comprised of leading resistance figures, and which derived its authority from the Resistance ideal. Jacques Verges, the defence lawyer for Klaus Barbie, asked the pointed question about the skeletons in the Setif closet: 'How many Oradours can you get into that?'[45] In August 1955 another 1200 Algerians were massacred by French army troops in reprisal for the slaughter of French colonists at Philippeville. The subsequent resort to torture against Algerian suspects served to emphasize the contrast between the profession of resistance ideals and the imitation of Nazi methods. Not only did the end not justify the means, but rather the use of evil means corrupted the end. 'Men who had risked their lives in the Resistance found themselves compared to their former tormentors.'[46] France's experience of occupation and resistance provided critics of the Algerian war with a powerful propaganda weapon, for memories of the Gestapo, 'impassioned the debate over the army's methods. Politicians who had resisted the Nazis found themselves identified with them'.[47]

The whole purpose of resistance was to prevent the Germans from nazifying them; to fight for a vision of humanity and the future which valued every single human life. Precisely because they wanted to remove the inhuman philosophy of Nazism, resisters had to come to terms with dehumanization and a growing callousness in their own conduct. The moral problems posed by torture concerned the irredeemable damage to the human dignity of the victim, but also the brutalization of the torturer, and the negation of the prospect of brotherhood that resisters proclaimed as their goal. The Resistance cause was dishonoured by 'conduct unbecoming'. Torture had been explicitly abolished during the French Revolution. The use of torture by resisters betrayed the standards and traditions that the Resistance defended. It threatened to undermine their own ethical foundations. Resisters could not attempt to justify the resort to torture without betraying their own sense of justice. In treating enemy human beings as less than human, they became less human themselves, a mirror image of the enemy. We become what we hate. As Holocaust victim Etty Hillesum observed:

If we allow our hatred to turn us into savage beasts like them then there is no hope for anyone.[48]

J. Glenn Gray, an American soldier in World War II, articulated this problem, recognizing the symptoms in himself:

The enemy was cruel, it was clear, yet this did not trouble me as deeply as did our own cruelty. Indeed their brutality made fighting the Germans much easier whereas ours weakened the will and confused the intellect.[49]

It was not possible to defeat Nazism without contributing to the deaths of many innocent people. At times it was not possible to disavow the use of evil means without capitulating to a ruthless foe who had no such moral qualms. This gave rise to the philosophical and moral problem for resistance of how to meet the challenge posed by Nazism while remaining true to its own ideals: how to defend civilized values without at the same time using uncivilized methods which undermined the very principles that resisters were defending. It was not possible to act without becoming tainted by guilt. This tells us something about the remorseless momentum of total war, and the catastrophic consequences of unrestrained conflict.

Much of this book has been concerned with unjust war waged against defenceless civilians by German security forces, and the problem of how to counter that threat. Perhaps the most depressing aspect of the resistance struggle lies in the imitation of Nazi methods: the resort to hostage-taking by the victims, and the use or threat of collective responsibility and collective reprisal measures against Germany and its collaborators. As we have seen, the Jewish Council in the Lodz ghetto authorized its police force to take the families of fugitive Jews hostage. Various partisan groups used captured German prisoners as exchange hostages for resisters caught by the Germans. During the liberation of Paris the FFI occupied a military hospital under German control. The 250 wounded Germans were treated not as prisoners-of-war but as hostages, with the threat that if resistance demands were not met, the soldiers would be killed. In fact they were exchanged for French people in German hands. One Communist historian has written that 'the threat of reprisals against German hospitals alone may have saved Paris from blanket-bombing'.[50] In Genoa in April 1945, partisans who participated in the City's uprising, threatened to kill 1000 German soldiers if the German Army bombed their positions in the City. In effect, the German prisoners-of-war became human shields.

The French Resistance also invoked the notion of collective family responsibility at times. The murder of the entire family of the Milice chief Jourdan at Voiron has already been discussed. In a premature suicidal attempt to liberate the town of Saint-Amand-Montrond in central France, immediately after D-Day, the local Maquis kidnapped the wife of the leading Milice official and held her hostage alongside six other women whose relatives were suspected of collaborationist sympathies. Guilt by association is but another version of collective responsibility. In addition, a number of militiamen were also taken prisoner. SS troops organized a counter-raid on the town, killing 10 men, destroying some shops and houses, and threatening to raze the town. The Milice and their German allies selected 64 suspected resistance sympathisers and members of their families as a counter-reprisal. Although there was an eventual exchange of the female hostages for the townspeople, 13 militiamen were hanged by the Resistance because they feared that if their captives were released, they would betray the location of the maquis hiding place. As we have seen, the mobile nature of guerrilla warfare precludes the provision of permanent prisons. Transporting their captives would hinder the guerrillas' own freedom of movement. And so the militiamen were executed, and transformed from prisoners-of-war into expendable hostages. In retaliation, the Germans and their French collaborators rounded up and killed 70 Jews from the locality.[51] Hostage-taking by the resistance was never on the same scale as the planned and routine hostage quota system. Nevertheless, the very adoption of the concept of collective responsibility and collective guilt was an important moral milestone and an uncomfortable reminder of just how far the resistance had emulated Nazi methods. In a radio broadcast on 1 March 1941, the President of the Polish government-in-exile, Mr Racziewicz, described collective responsibility as a 'monstrous principle' and referred to it as 'one of the most terrible devices of National-Socialist "culture"'.[52] By June 1942 General Sikorski, the Polish Prime Minister, was asking the leaders of the Allied governments to consider reprisals against German civilians in retaliation for German terror policies in the occupied territories:

Only by the announcement of retribution and the application of reprisals wherever possible can a stop be put to the rising tide of madness of these German assassins.[53]

In addition to the recommendation that the RAF should bomb civilian targets, Sikorski suggested that 'drastic measures' be taken against German civilians living in Allied countries. The Polish underground press reiterated these views:

> On July 22, 1942 'Glos Polski' recommended that Britain and the United States turn over German nationals living in their countries to the Polish government-in-exile. For every Pole killed, 100 of those Germans would be eliminated.[54]

This theme was taken up by Jews in the Warsaw Ghetto, who echoed the demand for reprisals. A message from Dr Feiner, the Jewish Bund representative to the Polish National Council in London stated

> We know that no political action, no protests or proclamations of punishment after the war will help. None of this will make any impression on the Germans. The only thing that will make an impression, and perhaps even save the remnant of the Jews who are still alive is to execute a number of Germans abroad and state publicly that if the Germans do not stop the slaughter of Polish Jewry, large numbers of Germans will be shot in public.[55]

The most extreme example of the adoption of collective responsibility occurred in the power struggle between Communist and noncommunist resistance groups for control in Greece. Before it withdrew from Athens in January 1945, ELAS, the military wing of the Communist resistance, carried out mass executions of middle-class Athenians, who were subsequently buried in mass graves. It is estimated that OPLA, the Communists' secret police, killed 13 500 Athenians. Up to 35 000 civilians were also taken hostage from Salonika, and when ELAS withdrew from Athens, as a reprisal for the British internment of left-wing suspects. These hostages lived and died under execrable conditions. The harrowing accounts of their suffering, and the calculated, cold-blooded cruelty of some of their captors, make grim reading. Approximately 4000 hostages were executed as 'enemies of the people' or perished on the forced marches in severely cold winter weather. The callous treatment of the hostages created moral revulsion at ELAS's methods:

> more than any other action, the abduction and killing of these hostages ... destroyed much of the moral credibility which EAM ELAS had enjoyed in the eyes of the world until then.[56]

A British soldier summed up the widespread feeling about the Greek Communists' methods of silencing and liquidating their opponents: 'Too much like Nazism for me, sir.'[57] In fact, both sides in the savage Greek civil war engaged in ruthless mass killings, and over half a million people died between 1945 and 1949. In March 1948 the Communist Provisional Government in the regions of northern Greece that it controlled announced over the radio that all children between the ages of three and fourteen would be rounded up and sent to the People's Democracies – USSR, Albania, Bulgaria and Yugoslavia. This policy of 'Pedomasoma' – literally 'the gathering up of children' – was ostensibly a humanitarian move to protect the children from the ravages of civil war. Over 28 000 children were removed by the end of 1948. Many of them never returned.[58] The United Nations condemned the policy of forcible evacuation as kidnapping. The abduction of the children was widely perceived as a form of hostage-taking to guarantee the loyalty of their parents and the villages under Communist control.

This is the forgotten side of resistance, the untold story which is all but ignored in conventional histories of the shadow war. The trouble with many earlier hagiographic studies of resistance is that they present resisters as icons, one-dimensional romantic heroes. Such accounts fail to explore the ugly side of resistance and also the tragic dimension of the underground war, by ignoring the daunting moral dilemmas that resisters faced. The restoration of the unavoidable guilt which was an accompanying part of the opposition to Nazism, provides us with a more accurate picture of the complexities of resistance.

Lawrence Langer relates the testimony of Pierre T, a man who was proud of his resistance work, helping to organize escape lines for Allied airmen who had been shot down over France, and making forged papers for Jews and Communists on the run from the Germans. He was proud until a certain incident made him "vulnerable" to the wider implications of his involvement in resistance activities:

One day a German officer was assassinated in the area where Pierre T lived; Nazi officials announced that unless those responsible turned themselves in, they would execute one hundred hostages chosen at random from 'detainees' in surrounding villages. And in fact this is what happened. Twenty-seven of the hostages were taken from Pierre T's town, Chateaubriand. He remembers following on his bicycle the truck carrying the victims to the execution site, hearing the shots, then creeping up to see the nine posts against which they were killed, three at each one. The observation point becomes a metaphorical knothole through which he 'views' not only the physical evidence of SS brutality, but also the intellectual results of the Resistance work in which he was engaged. . . . The executions unsettled his security.[59]

In terms of the 55 million people who died in the Second World War, these one hundred hostages, and the other victims directly attributable to the cycle of resistance activity and German retaliation, were a tiny number of casualties: a drop of blood in the ocean of human suffering. In the eerie phrase from the Vietnam War, these victims were a small 'body count' to offset against the necessities of resistance. But to be true to its own spirit, resistance had to believe that *every body* counts. Pierre T's experience reminds us that we should never lose sight of the individual hostage tied to the post, facing the firing squad – whom Camus calls 'the man of flesh and blood'.[60] Any purely utilitarian ethic which judges resistance solely by the criterion of whether it contributed to the long-term goal of defeating Nazism, is in danger of ignoring the unsettled conscience of resisters like Pierre T. He came to a realization, through his own involvement, that the death of each innocent hostage killed as a result of resistance action, was an absolute loss, an inexpiable and irreparable evil, and not simply a relative weight to be placed in the scales of history. Pierre T reflected that the worst thing about Nazism was its moral corruption of all who came into contact with it:

> They have made us lose our civilized ways. . . . Gradually, gradually, you become a different person. And you do things that you would *never* think you'd do – and you do it.[61]

We may recall Bill Jordan's assessment of his involvement with the Greek and French resistance movements. He had seen enough brutality in this 'dirty, stinking, treacherous war' to last him a lifetime.

Nobody emerged morally unscathed, or spiritually intact, after contact with Nazism. Lucie Adelsberger was a German Jewish doctor with over 20 years' experience before her imprisonment in Auschwitz. She had rejected the offer of a prestigious post at Harvard in 1932 because she could not obtain a visa for her mother, who was paralysed after a stroke. Adelsberger had witnessed the humiliating conditions which elderly Berlin Jews had to endure, especially after their children – their caring support system – had been deported. She faced an agonizing moral choice of abandoning her mother to her fate, or administering a dose of poison to save her mother from the clutches of the Gestapo.

> The mere thought of it drove me half mad. Was I, who had spent her whole life struggling to save each and every human life, was I supposed to kill my mother, the person most dear to me in all the world?[62]

She prayed for her mother's death:

> And I wasn't the only one ... many sons and daughters did the same. We all knew but one prayer: the death of our parents. [the Nazis had] transformed this most sacred bond into a death wish.[63]

This inversion of moral values continued when Adelsberger reached Auschwitz.

> Every Jewish child automatically condemned his mother to death. ...
> Every woman who had a child in tow ... was marked for death. Old, experienced prisoners frequently tried to shift children from their mothers to their grandmothers as soon as they got off the train; after all, the grandmother was already doomed because of her age.[64]

Adelsberger administered poison to new-born babies. 'The child had to die so that the life of the mother might be saved.'[65] Olga Lengyel was also a prisoner doctor at Auschwitz. She too faced the reversal of ethical standards. She had taken an irrevocable oath that bound her to the preservation of life, and yet was driven to kill babies in order to save the lives of their mothers. Her words capture the full tragedy of complicity and the wounded conscience of the resister:

> I marvel to what depths these Germans made us descend. ...
> The Germans succeeded in making murderers of even us.[66]

These haunting words show how long and lingering were the shadows cast by the Swastika.

Notes

1 INTRODUCTION

1. H. Krausnick & M. Broszat, *The Anatomy of the SS State* (London: Paladin, 1968), p. 15.
2. J. Hanson, *The Civilian Population and the Warsaw Uprising* (Cambridge: Cambridge University Press, 1982), p. 17.
3. R. Landau, *The Nazi Holocaust* (London: I.B. Taurus, 1992), pp. x–xi
4. G. Wright, 'Reflections on the French Resistance (1940–1944)', *Political Science Quarterly*, 1962, Vol. 23, part 3, p. 376.
5. E. Kogon, quoted in G. Schoenberner, *The Yellow Star* (London: Corgi 1978), p. 193.
6. J.-P. Sartre, *What is Literature?* (London: Methuen 1967), p. 167.
7. J. Miller, *One, by One, by One* (London: Weidenfeld & Nicholson 1990), p. 286.
8. See H. Michel, *The Shadow War* (London: History Book Club (by arrangement with André Deutsch Ltd), 1972), p. 259.
9. Joseph Kessel, *Army of the Shadows* (London: Cresset Press, 1944) p. 159.
10. Anny Latour, *The Jewish Resistance in France (1940–1944)* (New York Holocaust Library, 1981), p. 118.
11. Y. Zuckerman, *A Surplus of Memory* (Los Angeles: University of California Press, 1993), p. 678.
12. In B. Magee (ed.), *Modern British Philosophy* (St Albans: Paladin, 1971) p. 191.
13. R.M. Hare, *Freedom and Reason* (Oxford: Oxford University Press 1963), pp. 182–3.
14. Judy Chicago, *Holocaust Project* (New York: Viking, 1993), p. 22.
15. Cited in J. Fraser, *Violence in the Arts* (Cambridge: Cambridge University Press, 1973), p. 29.
16. Review of Niall Ferguson, 'Virtual History', *Daily Telegraph*, 26 April 1997
17. A. Gilbert, *Britain Invaded: Hitler's Plans for Britain, A Documentary Reconstruction* (London: Century 1990), pp. 102–3; p. 121.
18. M. Bunting, *The Model Occupation: The Channel Islands under German Rule, 1940–1945* (London: Harper Collins, 1995), p. 3.
19. Sonia Hillsdon, *Jersey: Occupation Remembered* (Norwich: Jarrold, 1986) p. 112.
20. John McCarthy and Jill Morrell, *Some Other Rainbow* (London: Corgi 1994), p. 75; p. 87.
21. *Ibid.*, p. 476; p. 464.
22. *Ibid.*, p. 573.
23. Rupert Brook, *1914 Part IV, The Dead.*
24. M. Walzer, sub-title of *Just and Unjust Wars* (London: Allen Lane 1978).

25. *Ibid.*, p. xvii.
26. U. Von Hassell, *The Von Hassell Diaries 1938–1944* (London: Hamish Hamilton, 1948), p. 188.
27. J. Glenn Gray, *The Warriors* (New York: Harper & Row, 1967), pp. 185–6.
28. A.V. Dicey, *Introduction to the Study of Law of the Constitution*, tenth edn (London: Macmillan, 1959), p. 303

2   MYTHS AND REALITIES OF RESISTANCE

1. G. Kren & L. Rappoport, *The Holocaust & The Crisis of Human Behaviour* (New York: Holmes & Meier, 1994), p. 111.
2. R.L. Rubenstein & J.K. Roth, *Approaches to Auschwitz* (London: SCM, 1987), p. 174.
3. D. Littlejohn, *The Patriotic Traitors* (London: Heinemann, 1972), pp. 336–7.
4. In S. Hawes & R. White, *Resistance in Europe 1939–1945* (London: Allen Lane, 1975), p. 26.
5. Quoted in Judith Miller, *One by One by One*, p. 141.
6. Henry Rousso, *The Vichy Syndrome* (Massachusetts: Harvard University Press, 1994), p. 16.
7. Roderick Kedward, *Occupied France* (Oxford: Blackwell, 1985), p. 54.
8. R. Cobb, *French and Germans, Germans and French* (New England, MD: Brandeis, 1983), p. 103.
9. See W. Thornton, *The Liberation of Paris* (London: Rupert Hart-Davis, 1963), pp. 189–90.
10. Roderick Kedward, *In Search of The Maquis* (Oxford University Press, 1993), p. 228.
11. H. Rousso, *op. cit.*, p. 18.
12. Michael Walzer, *Just and Unjust Wars*, p. XVI.
13. Jon Bridgman, *The End of the Holocaust The Liberation of the Camps* (London: Batsford, 1990), p. 110.
14. *Ibid.*, p. 118.
15. S. Hawes & R. White, *Resistance in Europe 1939–1945*, p. 227.
16. M.R.D. Foot, *What Good Did Resistance Do?*, In S. Hawes and R. White eds, *Resistance in Europe 1939–1945*, p. 219.
17. M.R.D. Foot, *Resistance* (London: Eyre Methuen, 1976), p. 319.
18. *Ibid.*, p. 6.
19. Quoted in H. Michel, *The Shadow War*, p. 247.
20. S. Hawes & R. White, *Resistance in Europe 1939–1945*, pp. 19, 21.
21. Henry Rousso, *The Vichy Syndrome*, p. 225.
22. Jean–Pierre Azema, *From Munich to The Liberation 1938–1944* (Cambridge University Press, 1984), p. 104.
23. See G. Best, *Humanity in War* (London: Methuen, 1983), pp. 241–2.
24. David George, *Terrorists or Freedom Fighters*, in M Warner and R. Crisp, *Terrorism, Protest and Power* (Aldershot: Edward Elgar, 1990), pp. 63–5.
25. Milovan Djilas, *Wartime* (London: Secker & Warburg, 1977), p. 75.
26. *Ibid.*, p. 227.

27. Werner Rings, *Life With The Enemy* (London: Weidenfeld & Nicholson, 1982), p. 201.
28. *Ibid.*, p. 202.
29. *Ibid.*
30. J.K. Zawodny, *Nothing But Honour: The Story of the Warsaw Uprising, 1944* (London: Macmillan, 1978), p. 158.
31. Norman Davies, *God's Playground: A History of Poland* (Oxford University Press, 1981), Vol. 2, p. 474.
32. *Ibid.*
33. *Ibid.*, p. 475.
34. Commander Stephen King-Hall, *Defence in a Nuclear Age* (London: Gollancz, 1958), p. 184.
35. Alexander Werth, *Russia at War* (London: Pan, 1965), p. 652.
36. John Keegan, *The Battle For History* (London: Hutchinson, 1995), p. 63.
37. M. Djilas, *Wartime*, p. 149.
38. *Ibid.*, p. 147.
39. *Ibid.*, p. 155.
40. *Ibid.*
41. Story quoted in Phillipe de Vomecourt, *Who Lived to See The Day. France in Arms, 1940–45* (London: Hutchinson, 1961), pp. 247–8.
42. R. Lamb, *War in Italy* (London: Constable, 1970), p. 262.
43. *Ibid.*, p. 264.

3   THE MORAL GREY ZONE: COLLABORATION

1. Stanley Milgram, *Obedience to Authority* (London: Tavistock, 1974), p. 6
2. Richard Cobb, *French and Germans, Germans and French*, p. 145.
3. *Ibid.*, p. 150.
4. Alexander Werth, *France 1940–1955* (London: Robert Hale, 1957), p. 119.
5. R. Cobb, *op. cit.*, p. 63.
6. M. Marrus & J. Paxton, *Vichy France and the Jews* (New York: Basic Books, 1981), p. xii.
7. J. Presser, *Ashes in the Wind* (London: Souvenir Press, 1968), p. 200
8. *Ibid.*, p. 19.
9. G. Block & M. Drucker, *Rescuers: Portraits of Moral Courage in the Holocaust* (New York: Holmes & Meier, 1992), p. 20.
10. A. Martens, *The Silent War* (London: Hodder & Stoughton, 1961), pp. 102–3.
11. D. Pryce-Jones, 'Paris during the German Occupation', in G. Hirschfeld & P. Marsh, *Collaboration in France* (Oxford: Berg, 1989), p. 25.
12. M. Buckmaster, *They Fought Alone* (London: Popular Book Club, 1958), p. 40.
13. R .Kedward & R. Austin (eds), *Vichy France and the Resistance* (London: Croom Helm, 1985), p. 244.
14. M. O'Shaughnessy, 'La Bataille du Rail', in R. Kedward & N. Wood (eds), *The Liberation of France* (Oxford: Berg, 1995), p. 22.

15. See W. Rings, *Life With the Enemy*, p. 80.
16. W. Warmbrunn, *The Dutch under German Occupation* (California: Stanford University Press, 1963), p. 140.
17. J. Presser, *Ashes in the Wind*, p. 147.
18. W. Rings, *Life with the Enemy*, p. 79.
19. G. Lewy, *The Catholic Church and Nazi Germany* (London: Weidenfeld & Nicholson, 1964), p. 293.
20. John Sweets, *Choices in Vichy France* (Oxford University Press, 1986), pp. 111–2.
21. Cited in A. Martens, *The Silent War*, p. 181.
22. Gerhard Hirschfeld, *Nazi Rule and Dutch Collaboration* (Oxford: Berg, 1988), p. 173.
23. *Ibid.*, p. 175.
24. See J. Miller, *One by One by One*, p. 97.
25. Quoted in Hirschfeld, *op. cit.*, p. 173.
26. Quoted in D. Caute, *The Fellow Travellers* (London: Quartet, 1977), p. 193.
27. Quoted in frontispiece to M. Marrus & R. Paxton, *Vichy France & The Jews*.
28. In J. Smart & B. Williams, *Utilitarianism: For & Against* (Cambridge University Press, 1973), pp. 98–9.
29. B. Paskins & B. Dockrill, *The Ethics of War* (London: Duckworth, 1979), p. 152.
30. J. Roy, *The Trial of Marshal Pétain* (London: Faber & Faber, 1968), p. 18.
31. P. Laval, *The Unpublished Diary of Pierre Laval* (London: Falcon Press, 1948), p. 127.
32. Quoted in A. Werth, *France 1940–1955*, p. 16.
33. Marcel Ophuls, *The Sorrow and the Pity* (St Albans: Paladin, 1975), p. 40.
34. Gabolde's deposition in *France during the German Occupation – 1940–1944* (Stanford University, Hoover Institution, 1957), Vol. 2, p. 595.
35. *Ibid.*, p. 596.
36. P. Novick, *The Resistance versus Vichy* (London: Chatto & Windus, 1968), p. 85.
37. Quoted in A. Werth, *France 1940–1955*, p. 192.
38. Cited in A. Werth, *op. cit.*, p. 113.
39. J. Delarue, *The Gestapo* (New York: William Morrow, 1964), p. 221.
40. *Ibid.*, p. 292.
41. *Ibid.*, p. 293.
42. Quoted in G.W. Fortune, *Hitler Divided France* (London: Macmillan, 1943), p. 53.
43. M. Marrus & R. Paxton, *Vichy France & The Jews*, p. 12.
44. *Ibid.*, p. XIII.
45. *Ibid.*, p. 346.
46. How Far Did Vichy France 'Sabotage' The Imperatives Of Wannsee? in D. Cesarani (ed.), *The Final Solution* (London: Routledge, 1994), p. 198.
47. Cited in R. Griffiths, *Marshal Pétain*, p. 304.

48. *Ibid.*, p. 204.
49. See G. Warner, *Pierre Laval and the Eclipse of France* (New York: Macmillan, 1968), pp. 372–3.
50. *Ibid.*, p. 306.
51. How Far Did Vichy France 'Sabotage' The Imperatives of Wannsee? in D. Cesarani (ed.), *The Final Solution*, p. 207.
52. *Ibid.*
53. R. Paxton, *Vichy France* (New York: Columbia University Press, 1972), p. 372.
54. How Far Did Vichy France 'Sabotage' the Imperatives of Wannsee, in D. Cesarani (ed.), *The Final Solution*, p. 194.
55. Collaborationism in France during World War II, in *Journal of Modern History*, Sept 1968, p. 375.
56. Introduction to Marcel Ophuls, *The Sorrow and The Pity*, p. X.
57. Vichy Revisited, *Virginia Quarterly Review*, USA, Vol. 34, 1958, pp. 513–4.
58. *Daily Telegraph*, 24 March 1994.
59. Henri Rousso, *The Vichy Syndrome*, p. 159.

4 MORAL CHOICES IN OCCUPIED EUROPE

1. T. Morgan, *An Uncertain Hour* (New York: William Morrow, 1990), p. 67.
2. F. Harris, *Encounters with Darkness* (Oxford University Press, 1983), p. 213.
3. H. Rousso, *The Vichy Syndrome*, p. 58.
4. H. Frenay, *The Night Will End* (London: Coronet, 1977), pp. 99–100.
5. J. Fest, *Hitler* (London: Weidenfeld & Nicholson, 1974), p. 963.
6. Madeleine Bunting, *The Model Occupation*, p. 50.
7. J.-P. Sartre, quoted in F Harris, *Encounters with Darkness*, p. 196.
8. Livia E. Bitton Jackson, *Elli* (London: Granada, 1984), pp. 163–4.
9. E. Wiesel, *Night* (Harmondsworth: Penguin, 1987), p. 80.
10. Emil Fackenheim, 'The Spectrum of Resistance during the Holocaust' in *Modern Judaism*, Vol. 2, 1982, p. 124.
11. See Lawrence Langer, *Holocaust Testimonies*, p. 70 for details.
12. In J. Schoenfeld, *Holocaust Memoirs*, p. 258.
13. D. Bonhoeffer, *Letters and Papers from Prison* (London: SCM, 1973), pp. 6–7.
14. In Renate Wind, *A Spoke in the Wheel: The Life of Dietrich Bonhoeffer* (London: SCM, 1991), p. 81.
15. J.W. Allen, *A History of Political Thought in the XVII Century* (London: Methuen, 1957), p. 132.
16. N. Tec, *When Light Pierced the Darkness, Christian Rescue of Jews in Nazi Occupied Poland* (Oxford University Press, 1986), p. 64.
17. Quoted in G. Block & M. Drucker, *Rescuers* (New York: Holmes & Meier, 1992), pp. 36–7.
18. A. Miller, 'Is Everything Permitted', *The Student World*, Vol. XXXVIII, Part 4, 1945, p. 288.

19. *Ibid.*, p. 289.
20. W. Bartoszewski, *The Warsaw Ghetto: A Christian's Testimony* (London: Lamp Press, 1989), p. 87.
21. *Ibid.*, p. 88.
22. Phillip Hallie, *Lest Innocent Blood be Shed* (London: Michael Joseph, 1979), pp. 125–6.
23. J. Schoenfeld, *Holocaust Memoirs*, p. 107.
24. In A. Polonsky (ed.), *My Brother's Keeper: Recent Polish Debates on the Holocaust* (London: Routledge, 1990), p. 203.
25. P. Hallie, *op. cit.*, p. 121.
26. Zui Weigler, 'Two Polish Villages Razed For Extending Help To Jews' *Yad Vashem Bulletin*, Part 1, 1957, p. 20.
27. N. Tec, *op. cit.*, p. 76.
28. Interview in H.J. Cargas, *Voices from the Holocaust* (University Press of Kentucky, 1993), pp. 87–8.
29. Lawrence Langer, *op. cit.*, p. 130.
30. *Ibid.*, p. 131.
31. W.S. Gilbert, *My Dream*.
32. P. De Vomecourt, *Who Lived to see the Day: France in Arms 1940–1945* (London: Hutchinson, 1961), pp. 81–2.
33. W. Niederland, 'Psychiatric Disorders among Persecution Victims', *Journal of Nervous & Mental Disease (USA)*, Vol. 139, 1964, p. 468.
34. Primo Levi, *The Drowned and the Saved* (London: Michael Joseph, 1988), p. 33.
35. R. Vrba & A. Bestic, *I Cannot Forgive* (New York: Bantam, 1964), p. 164.
36. L. Langer, *op. cit.*, p. 21.
37. J. Garliński, *Fighting Auschwitz* (London: Julian Friedmann, 1975), p. 139.
38. *Ibid.*, p. 141.
39. J. Presser, *Ashes in the Wind: The Destruction of Dutch Jewry* (London: Souvenir Press, 1968), p. 108.
40. R.J. Lifton, *The Nazi Doctors* (London: Macmillan, 1986), p. 224.
41. W. Poller, *Medical Block Buchenwald* (London: Souvenir Press, 1961), p. 97.
42. O. Lengyel, *Five Chimneys* (London: Granada, 1983), p. 110.
43. *Ibid.*, p. 111.
44. E. Lingens-Reiner, *Prisoners of Fear* (London: Gollancz, 1948), pp. 61–2.
45. S. Nomberg Przytyk, *Auschwitz: True Tales from a Grotesque Land* (University of North Carolina, 1985), p. 69.
46. *Ibid.*, p. 70.
47. J. Sternberg Newman, *In the Hell of Auschwitz* (New York: Exposition Press, 1963), pp. 42–3.
48. A. Blady Szwajger, *I Remember Nothing More* (London: Collins, 1990), p. 57.
49. A. Lewin, *A Cup of Tears,* (London: Fontana, 1990), p. 165.
50. A. Malraux, *Anti Memoirs* (London: Hamish Hamilton, 1975), p. 412.
51. T. Des Pres, *The Survivor* (Oxford University Press, 1976), pp. 129–30.

52. S. Nomberg Przytyk, *op. cit.*, p. 29.
53. O. Lengyel, *op. cit.*, p. 111.
54. L. Langer, 'The Dilemma of Choice in the Death Camps', in J.K. Roth & M. Berenbaum (eds), *Holocaust: Religious and Philosophical Implications* (New York: Paragon House, 1989), p. 224.
55. L. Langer, *Holocaust Testimonies*, p. 125.
56. *Ibid.*, p. 162; p. 105.
57. See F.W. Deakin, *The Embattled Mountain* (Oxford University Press, 1971), p. 30. Deakin adds, 'a child's cradle has remained in the cave since that day'.
58. R. Kirschner, *Rabbinic Responses of the Holocaust Era* (New York: 1980), p. 118.
59. E. Hillesum, *Etty: A Diary 1941–43* (London: Triad Grafton, 1985), p. 191.
60. Y. Zuckerman, *A Surplus of Memory*, p. 266.
61. Livia E. Bitton Jackson, *Elli*, pp. 116–7.
62. Quoted in Nechama Tec, *In the Lion's Den: The Life of Oswald Rufeisen* (Oxford University Press, 1990), p. 116. This fascinating book recounts the extraordinary life of Rufeisen in vivid detail, and is thoroughly recommended for its portrait of humane people caught up in an inhumane world.
63. *Ibid.*, p. 117.
64. D. Bonhoeffer, *Letter and Papers from Prison*, p. 135.
65. T. Des Pres, *The Survivor*, p. 46.
66. E. Kogon, *The Theory and Practice of Hell*, p. 274.

5 GERMAN SECURITY POLICY AND THE MORAL DILEMMAS OF RESISTANCE

1. Franklin D. Roosevelt, US President, *New York Times*, 26 October 1941.
2. *Nuremberg Trials*, Vol. XXXVIII, p. 88.
3. *The Prince*, Ch. 16.
4. Quoted in N. Levin, *The Holocaust*, p. 46.
5. Hitler, quoted in H. Michel, *The Shadow War*, p. 21.
6. M.R.D. Foot, *Resistance*, p. 49.
7. N. Chomsky, *Pirates and Emperors* (New York: Black Rose Books, 1987), p. 85.
8. *Nuremberg Trials*, Vol. X, p. 539.
9. *Nuremberg Trials*, Vol. XI, p. 809.
10. Richard Fattig, *Reprisal: The German Army and the Execution of Hostages During the Second World War*, University of California, PhD Thesis, 1980, p. 159.
11. *Ibid.*, p. 64. See *Nuremberg Trials*, Vol. X, pp. 617–21.
12. Quoted in Alan Clark, *Barbarossa* (Harmondsworth: Penguin, 1966), p. 185.
13. Arnie Brun Lie, *Night and Fog* (New York: Berkeley Books, 1992), p. 151.
14. W. Jordan, *Conquest Without Victory, A New Zealander's Experiences*

in the Resistance Movements in Greece and France (London: Catholic Book Club, 1970), p. 82.

15. The German New Order in Poland, p. 92.
16. *Nuremberg Trials*, Vol. X, p. 645.
17. Quoted in R. Hilberg, *The Destruction of the European Jews* (New York: Holmes & Meier, 1985), Vol. II, p. 690.
18. Quoted in Lord Russell of Liverpool, *The Scourge of the Swastika* (London: Cassell, 1954), pp. 116–7.
19. Quoted in *ibid.*, pp. 117–8.
20. E.H. Cookridge, *Inside SOE* (London: Arthur Barker, 1966), p. 341.
21. Max Hastings, *Das Reich*, p. 246.
22. *Ibid.*, p. 247.
23. Details from Mark Mazower, *Inside Hitler's Greece* (New Haven: Yale University Press, 1993), p. 191.
24. *Nuremberg Trials*, Vol. XI, p. 831.
25. Alexander Werth, *Russia at War 1941–1945* (London: Pan, 1964), p. 650.
26. R. Lucas, *The Forgotten Holocaust: The Poles under German Occupation 1939–1944* (University Press of Kentucky, 1986), p. 37.
27. Cited in K. Sosnowski, *The Tragedy of Children under Nazi Rule* (Poznan: Zachodnia Agencja, 1962), p. 86.
28. See Christopher R. Browning, *Wehrmacht Reprisal Policy and the Mass Murder of Jews in Serbia*, Militargeschichliche Mitteilungen 1983, Part 1, p. 33.
29. *Nuremberg Trials*, Vol. XI, p. 801.
30. Browning, *op. cit.*, p. 37.
31. *Ibid.*, p. 39.
32. *Nuremberg Trials*, Vol. VI, pp. 121–2.
33. Lawrence Langer, *Holocaust Testimonies*, p. 182.
34. *Nuremberg Trials*, Vol. X, p. 645.
35. *Ibid.*, p. 644.
36. *Ibid.*, p. 647.
37. R. Fattig, *op. cit.*, p. 96.
38. W. Jordan, *Conquest Without Victory*, p. 245.
39. Quoted in K. Sosnowski, *The Tragedy of Children Under Nazi Rule*, p. 68.
40. E. Hillesum, *Letters from Westerbork* (London: Jonathan Cape, 1987), p. 61.
41. *Ibid.*, p. 118.
42. M. Buckmaster, *They Fought Alone* (London: Popular Book Club, 1958), p. 182.
43. *Ibid.*, p. 183.
44. *Ibid.*, p. 184.
45. W. Jordan, *Conquest Without Victory*, p. 72.
46. Elsa Caspers, *To Save a Life* (London: Deidre McDonald, 1995), p. 38.
47. Lawrence Langer, *Holocaust Testimonies*, p. 1183.
48. See T. Des Pres, *The Survivor* (Oxford University Press, 1976), p. 130.
49. J. Garlínski, *Fighting Auschwitz*, p. 65.

50. Quoted in *ibid.*, p. 66.
51. Eugen Kogon, *The Theory and Practice of Hell*, pp. 278–9.
52. Leon Wells, *The Death Brigade* (New York: Holocaust Library, 1978), p. 165.
53. Etty Hillesum, *Etty A Diary 1941–1943* (London: Triad Grafton, 1985), p. 265.
54. *Ibid.*
55. *Ibid.*, p. 275.
56. Primo Levi, *If This is a Man* (London: New English Library, 1969), p. 6.
57. Quoted in L. Tushnet, *The Pavement of Hell* (New York: St Martins Press, 1972), p. 174.
58. Quoted in G. Hausner, *Justice in Jerusalem* (London: Nelson, 1967), p. 176.
59. Lawrence Langer, *Holocaust Testimonies*, p. 187.
60. Elli Friedmann, *Elli: Coming of Age in the Holocaust*, p. 111.
61. *Ibid.*, p. 114.
62. Lawrence Langer, Holocaust Testimonies, p. 187.
63. Elie Wiesel, *A Jew Today* (New York: Vintage, 1979), pp. 221–2.
64. Tadeusz Borowski, *This Way For The Gas, Ladies and Gentlemen* (Harmondsworth: Penguin, 1976), p. 84.
65. Primo Levi, *If This is a Man*, p. 11.
66. G. Wright, *The Ordeal of Total War 1939–45* (New York: Harper, 1968), p. 125.
67. Quoted in M. Ceadel, *Pacifism in Britain 1914–1945* (Oxford University Press, 1980), p. 251.
68. *Peace News*, 27 March 1937.
69. B. Russell, *Justice in Wartime* (Nottingham: Spokesman, 1972 reprint), p. 45.
70. M. Walzer, *Just and Unjust Wars*, pp. 332–4.
71. In R. Harries, *Christianity and War in a Nuclear Age* (Oxford: Mowbray, 1986), p. 44.
72. Russell, *op. cit.*, pp. 45–6.
73. See R. Lukas, *The Forgotten Holocaust*, p. 35.
74. Quoted in H. Krausnick & M. Broszat, *The Anatomy of the SS State*, pp. 82–3.
75. J. Presser, *Ashes in the Wind*, p. 57.
76. See J. Haestrup, *European Resistance Movements 1939–45*, p. 94; p. 96.

6 COLLECTIVE RESPONSIBILITY AND THE RESPONSIBILITY OF THE RESISTANCE

1. Michael Elkins, *Forged in Fury* (London: Piatkus, 1982), pp. 29–30.
2. Quoted in Edward Mortimer, *The Rise of the French Communist Party 1920–1947* (London: Faber & Faber, 1984), p. 309.
3. Quoted in Milton Dank, *The French Against The French* (London: Cassell, 1978), p. 110.

4. Quoted in *ibid.*, p. 112.
5. Quoted in W. Thornton, *The Liberation of Paris* (London: Hart-Davis, 1963), p. 88.
6. R. Kedward, *In Search of the Maquis*, p. 243.
7. *Ibid.*, p. 250.
8. *Ibid.*, p. 265.
9. Details taken from Michael Padev, *Marshal Tito* (London: Frederick Muller, 1944), pp. 34–5.
10. See Roderick Kedward, *Resistance in Vichy France* (Oxford University Press, 1978), p. 141, footnote 57.
11. Cited in Joseph Fletcher, *Situation Ethics* (London: SCM, 1966), pp. 115–6.
12. Quoted in Henri Michel, *The Shadow War: Resistance in Europe 1939–45*, p. 217. Also see L. Stein, *Beyond Death and Exile: The Spanish Republicans in France 1939–1955* (Harvard University Press, 1979), In the town of Brest To the German announcement that for every Nazi killed ten Frenchmen would be shot, the resister had scrawled the reverse threat on the building walls in the town, p. 144.
13. Henri Michel, *The Shadow War*, p. 223–4.
14. Quoted in Milton Dank, *The French Against The French*, p. 116.
15. See Werner Warmbrunn, *The Dutch Under German Occupation*, p. 208.
16. Henri Frenay, *The Night Will End*, p. 162.
17. R. Katz, *Death in Rome* (London: Jonathan Cape, 1967), p. 214.
18. *Ibid.*, pp. 191–2.
19. *Ibid.*, pp. 242–3
20. Wolfgang Leonard, *New Society*, 27 October 1983, p. 162.
21. M. Djilas, *Wartime*, p. 84.
22. *Ibid.*, p. 341.
23. *Ibid.*, p. 341.
24. *Ibid.*, p. 168.
25. *Ibid.*
26. Quoted in Nicholas Vakar, *Belorussia* (Harvard University Press 1956), p. 193.
27. *Ibid.*, p. 197.
28. G. Gordon, *Soviet Partisan Warfare 1941–1944: The German Perspective* (Iowa University PhD thesis 1972), pp. 30–1.
29. See M. Cooper, *The Phantom War* (London: Macdonald & Jane s, 1979), pp. 45–6, for details.
30. See O. Bartov, *Hitler's Army* (Oxford University Press, 1992), p. 90.
31. M. Djilas, *Wartime*, p. 146.
32. M. Djilas, *Wartime*, p. 155.
33. *Ibid.*
34. *Ibid.*, p. 155.
35. *Ibid.*, p. 168.
36. Quoted in Nora Beloff, *Tito's Flawed Legacy* (London: Victor Gollancz, 1985), pp. 75–6.
37. David Martin, *The Web of Disinformation: Churchill's Yugoslav Blunder* (New York: Harcourt Brace Jovanovich, 1990), p. 39. It is pertinent

to add here that Mihailović had been distressed by the murder of 35 000 Serb hostages as a result of guerrilla activity in the First World War, and his overriding concern was to avoid a repetition of such massacres of the innocent.

38. Djilas, *op. cit.*, p. 73.
39. Quoted in Geoffrey Best, *Humanity in Warfare*, pp. 243–4.
40. *Nuremberg Trials*, Green Series, Vol. XI, p. 846.
41. *Ibid.*, pp. 847–8.
42. *Ibid.*, pp. 1035–6.
43. M. Mazower, *Inside Hitler's Greece*, p. 343, woodcut of hooded figure.
44. See Werner Rings, *Life With The Enemy*, p. 201.
45. *Ibid.*, p. 197.
46. Quoted in Peter Novick, *The Resistance Versus Vichy* (London: Chatto & Windus, 1968), p. 26.
47. Quoted in M. Dank, *The French Against the French*, p. 255.
48. C.H. Lottmann, *The People's Anger* (London: Hutchinson, 1986), p. 127.
49. Quoted in P. Novick, *The Resistance versus Vichy*, p. 29.
50. Quoted in K. Macksey, *The Partisans of Europe* (London: Granada, 1985), p. 82.
51. Martin Gilbert, *The Holocaust* (London: Collins, 1986), p. 500.
52. Nechama Tec, *Defiance: The Bielski Partisans* (New York: Oxford University Press, 1993), p. 78.
53. *Ibid.*
54. Marguerite Duras, *La Douleur* (London: Flamingo, 1986), pp. 133–4.
55. *Ibid.*, p. 115.
56. William Jordan, *Conquest Without Victory*, pp. 229–30.
57. *Ibid.*, pp. 239–40. Significantly, leading SOE figure C.M. Woodhouse wrote a foreword to Jordan's book describing it as 'a healthily frank and utterly authentic account of a grim and fantastic episode of warfare. Much of it may sound incredible . . . but there is not a false note in it.' (p. 9).
58. *Ibid.*, p. 231.
59. *Ibid.*, p. 229; p. 242.
60. *Ibid.*, p. 251.
61. Preface to H. Alleg, *The Question* (London: John Calder, 1958), p. 11.
62. W. Jordan, *Conquest Without Victory*, p. 230.
63. *Nuremberg Trials*, Green Series, Vol. XI, p. 812.
64. *Nuremberg Trials*, Vol. XV, p. 334.
65. R. Hilberg, *The Destruction of the European Jews*, Vol. 1, p. 213.
66. R. Fattig, *op. cit.*, p. 26.
67. *Ibid.*, p. 189.
68. In Mark Mazower, *Inside Hitler's Greece*, p. 178.
69. Quoted in C. Aubrey Dixon & Otto Heilbrunn, *Communist Guerrilla Warfare* (London: Allen & Unwin, 1954), p. 142.
70. *Ibid.*
71. *Ibid.*, p. 143.
72. Quoted in James M Spaight, *War Rights on Land* (London: Macmillan, 1911), p. 466.

73. See David Lampe, *The Savage Canary: The Story of Danish Resistance* (London: Corgi, 1969), p. 170.
74. See Roderick Kedward, *In Search of The Maquis*, pp. 172–3.
75. Quoted in Robert Aron, *The Vichy Regime 1940–44* (London: Putnam, 1958), p. 435.
76. J. Hanson, *The Civilian Population and The Warsaw Rising*, p. 92.
77. Norman Davies, *God's Playground: A History of Poland*, Vol. 2, p. 476.
78. Quoted in Theo Schulte, *The German Army and Nazi Policies in Occupied Russia* (Oxford: Berg, 1989), p. 141.
79. Quoted in *ibid.*, p. 333.
80. Matthew Cooper, *The Phantom War: The German Struggle Against Soviet Partisans 1941–44*, p. 181.
81. *Ibid.*, p. 53.
82. Quoted in Dixon and Heilbrunn, *op. cit.*, p. 14.
83. *Nuremberg Trials, Vol. VI*, pp. 151–2.
84. Alexander Solzhenitsyn, *The Gulag Archipelago* (London: Collins, 1980), Vol. 1, p. 24.
85. *Nuremberg Trials*, Vol. IV, p. 11.
86. See D. Mountfield, *The Partisans* (London: Hamlyn, 1979), p. 179.
87. Alexander Dallin, *German Rule in Russia 1941–1945* (London: Macmillan, 1988), p. 71.
88. Djilas, *Wartime*, p. 84.
89. *Nuremberg Trials*, Green Series, Vol. XI, p. 285
90. N. Vakar, *Belorussia*, p. 200.
91. *Ibid.*, p. 192.
92. *Ibid.*, p. 53.
93. Bill Jordan, *Conquest Without Victory*, p. 52.
94. K. Macksey, *The Partisans of Europe in World War II* (London: Hart-Davis Macgibbon, 1975), p. 233.
95. G. Reitlinger, *The House Built on Sand* (London: Weidenfeld & Nicholson, 1960), p. 231.
96. W. Jordan, *Conquest Without Victory*, pp. 193–4.
97. Marcel Ophuls, *The Sorrow and the Pity*, pp. 113–4.
98. Michael Walzer, *Just and Unjust Wars*, p. 179.
99. *Nuremberg Trials*, Green Series, Vol. XI, p. 1051.
100. R. Fattig, *op. cit.*, p. 218.
101. R. Fattig, *op. cit.*, p. 220.
102. M. Djilas, *Wartime*, p. 113.
103. *Ibid.*, p. 351.
104. *Ibid.*, p. 351.
105. *Ibid.*, p. 207.
106. Quoted in N. Beloff, *Tito's Flawed Legacy*, p. 76.
107. *Ibid.*, p. 338.
108. Jack Olsen, *Silence on Monte Sole* (London: Pan, 1969), p. 50.
109. *Ibid.*, p. 132.
110. *Ibid.*
111. *Ibid.*
112. See F. Veale, *Advance to Barbarism* (London: Mitre Press, 1968), p. 291.

113. See F. Knight, *The French Resistance*, p. 172.
114. See Max Hastings, *Das Reich* (London: Pan, 1983), p. 139.
115. See M. Walzer, *Just and Unjust Wars*, Ch13, for a discussion of this reprisal.
116. D. Arsenijevic, *Voluntary Hostages of the SS* (Geneva: Ferni, 1979), p. 153.
117. W. Jordan, *Conquest Without Victory*, p. 235.
118. G. Orwell, *Notes on Nationalism* in *Collected Essays* (Harmondsworth: Penguin, 1980), Vol. 3, p. 419; p. 430.
119. *Nuremberg Trials*, Vol. XX, p. 373.
120. A Camus, *Resistance, Rebellion and Death* (London: Hamish Hamilton, 1961), p. 60; p. 175.
121. Speech in R. Falk (ed.), *Crimes of War* (New York: Random House, 1971), p. 222.

7   JEWISH RESISTANCE/JEWISH 'COLLABORATION'

1. Emil Fackenheim, *To Mend the World* (Indiana University Press, 1994), pp. 215–6.
2. Elie Wiesel, *Against Silence*, Vol. II (New York: Holocaust Library, 1985), p. 268.
3. Primo Levi, *The Drowned & The Saved* (London: Michael Joseph, 1988), p. 42.
4. Text of speech quoted in L. Dawidowicz, *The Holocaust Reader* (New York: Behrman House, 1976), p. 334ff.
5. Quoted in R. Rubenstein & J.K. Roth, *Approaches to Auschwitz* (London: SCM, 1987), p. 160.
6. Raul Hilberg, *The Destruction of the European Jews* (New York: Holmes and Meier, 1985), Vol. III, p. 1037.
7. *Ibid.*, p. 1030.
8. *Ibid.*, p. 1037.
9. *Ibid.*, p. 1044.
10. *Ibid.*, p. 1039.
11. *Jews, Tradition and Resistance*, in R. Gottlieb (ed.), *Thinking the Unthinkable. Meanings of the Holocaust* (New York: Paulist Press, 1990), pp. 319–20.
12. R. Hilberg, *The Destruction of the European Jews*, Vol. III, p. 1031.
13. Emmanuel Ringelblum, *Notes from the Warsaw Ghetto: The Journal of Emmanuel Ringelblum*, p. 310.
14. See R. Hilberg, *The Destruction of the European Jews*, Vol. II, p. 505.
15. Abraham Lewin, *A Cup of Tears* (London: Fontana, 1990), p. 119.
16. Jenny Robinson, *Emmanuel Ringelblum – Rumour in Ghetto. Poems of the Warsaw Ghetto*, p. 64.
17. *Ibid.*, pp. 98–9.
18. Quoted in Joseph Kermish, *Emmanuel Ringelblum's Notes Hitherto Unpublished, Yad Vashem Studies VII*, 1968, p. 180.
19. *Ibid.*, p. 1035.

20. *Jews, Tradition & Resistance*, in R. Gottlieb, *Thinking the Unthinkable*, p. 320.
21. See Charles Roland, *Courage Under Siege: Starvation, Disease & Death in the Warsaw Ghetto* (New York: Oxford University Press, 1992). For a detailed analysis, pp. 110–2, 175–7.
22. Abraham Lewin, *A Cup of Tears*, pp. 114, 131–2.
23. Chaim A. Kaplan, *The Scroll of Agony* (London: Hamish Hamilton, 1966), pp. 86 and 125–6.
24. *Ibid.*, p. 160.
25. *Ibid.*, p. 222.
26. Quoted in M. Berenbaum, *The World Must Know* (Boston: Little Brown, 1993). See pp. 92–3 for an excellent account of the Jewish chroniclers.
27. Kaplan, *op. cit.*, p. 303.
28. *Ibid.*, p. 313.
29. *Ibid.*, p. 318.
30. Avraham Tory, *Surviving the Holocaust* (London: Pimlico, 1991), pp. 167, 168–9.
31. This moving incident is quoted in Helen Fein, *Accounting for Genocide* (New York: Free Press, 1979), pp. XVII–XVIII. It is poignant that Helen Fein dedicated her book to the sewing-machine writer.
32. Avraham Tory, *Surviving the Holocaust*, p. 114.
33. *Ibid.*, p. 132.
34. Chaim Kaplan, *The Scroll of Agony*, p. 252.
35. *The Resistance Movement in the Vilna Ghetto*, in Y. Suhl (ed.), *They Fought Back* (New York: Schocken, 1975), p. 149.
36. Elie Wiesel, *A Jew Today*, p. 242.
37. This important phrase is used in a number of places – see *The Destruction of the European Jews*, Vol. 1, p. 314; Vol. 3, p. 1030.
38. *Ibid.*, p. 115.
39. *Ibid.*, p. 117.
40. *Ibid.*, p. 125.
41. *Ibid.*, p. 117.
42. Lucy Dawidowicz, *The War Against the Jews 1933–45* (Harmondsworth: Penguin, 1975), pp. 514–5, 522.
43. Lucy Dawidowicz, *The Holocaust and the Historians* (Harvard University Press, 1981), p. 138.
44. *Ibid.*, p. 137.
45. *Ibid.*, p. 137.
46. Quoted in Helen Fein, *Accounting for Genocide*, p. 122.
47. Quoted in Y. Kermiz, *The Judenrat in Warsaw*, in M. Marrus (ed.), *The Nazi Holocaust* (Westport: Meckler, 1989), Part 6, Vol. I, p. 225.
48. A. Finkelkraut, *From the novelistic to memory* in L. Kritman (ed.) *Auschwitz and After* (New York: Routledge, 1995), p. 90.
49. Avraham Tory, *Surviving the Holocaust*, p. 5.
50. See Lucy Dawidowicz, *The War Against the Jews*, pp. 352; 422–3.
51. Quoted in G. Hausner, *Justice in Jerusalem*, p. 198.
52. T. Richmond, *Konin: A Quest* (London: Vintage, 1996), pp. 77–8.
53. Quoted in L. Dawidowicz, *The War Against the Jews*, p. 364.

54. *Ibid.*, p. 418.
55. H. Arendt, *Eichmann in Jerusalem* (Harmondsworth: Penguin, 1979) p. 117.
56. H. Arendt, *The Origins of Totalitarianism* (New York: Harcourt, 1958), pp. 452–3.
57. H. Arendt, *Eichmann in Jerusalem*, p. 115.
58. *Ibid.*, p. 116.
59. R. Hilberg, *The Destruction of the European Jews*, Vol. 2, p. 495.
60. *Ibid.*, p. 842.
61. R. Hilberg, *The Destruction of the European Jews*, Vol. 2, p. 495.
62. Abraham Lewin, *A Cup of Tears*, pp. 145; 150.
63. M. Edelman, *The Ghetto Fights* (London: Bookmarks, 1994), p. 21.
64. H. Arendt, *Eichmann in Jerusalem*, p. 118.
65. Introduction to I. Trunk, *Judenrat* (New York: Macmillan, 1972), p. XXIX.
66. Abraham Tory, *Surviving the Holocaust*, pp. 259–60.
67. *Ibid.*, p. 242.
68. See A. Adelson & R. Lapides (ed.), *Lodz Ghetto* (New York: Viking, 1989), p. 153.
69. H. Arendt, *Eichmann in Jerusalem*, p. 123.
70. R. Hilberg, *The Destruction of the European Jews*, Vol. 2, p. 505.
71. Y. Bauer & N. Rotenstreich (eds), *The Holocaust as Historical Experience* (New York: Holmes & Meier, 1981), p. 224.
72. Quoted in I. Trunk, *Judenrat*, p. 423.
73. See Abraham Lewin, *A Cup of Tears*, p. 181, and See endnote 349, where Anthony Polonsky states that it has not been possible to *authenticate* Lewin's statement about the Judenrat's stand, p. 289.
74. See L. Tushnet, *The Pavement of Hell*, p. 54.
75. *Ibid.*, pp. 169–70.
76. Quoted in I. Trunk, *Judenrat*, p. 421.
77. *Ibid.*, p. 422.
78. The full text of this speech can be found in A. Adelson & R. Lapides (eds), *Lodz Ghetto*, p. 331.
79. See the detailed discussion in Berel Lang, *Act and Idea in the Nazi Genocide* (University of Chicago, 1990), Ch. 3.
80. *Ibid.*, p. 73.
81. Lucy Dawidowicz, *The War Against the Jews 1939–1945*, p. 522.
82. Lawrence Langer, *Admitting the Holocaust* (New York: Oxford University Press, 1995), p. 44.
83. I. Trunk, *Judenrat*, p. 499.
84. *Chronicle of the Lodz Ghetto* (Yale University Press, 1984), p. 449.
85. *Ibid.*, February 13th 1944, p. 450.
86. *Ibid.*, p. 453.
87. I. Trunk, *Judenrat*, p. 507.
88. The full text of *Days of Nightmare* in Lucy Dawidowicz, *The Holocaust Reader*, quotations from pp. 303, 304, 314.
89. In A. Adelson & R. Lapides, *Lodz Ghetto*, p. 341.
90. A. Lewin, *A Cup of Tears*, p. 106.
91. *Ibid.*, p. 157.

92. *Ibid.*, p. 328.
93. *Ibid.*, p. 376.
94. Chaim Kaplan, *Scroll of Agony*, p. 303.
95. *Ibid.*, p. 305.
96. Leonard Tushnet, *The Pavement of Hell*, p. 56.
97. Abraham Tory, *Surviving the Holocaust: The Kovno Ghetto Diary*, p. 52.
98. *Ibid.*, p. 59.
99. In M. Barkai (ed.), *The Fighting Ghettos* (New York: Tower, 1962), p. 23.
100. Y. Zuckerman, *A Surplus of Memory*, p. 208.
101. *Ibid.*, p. 210.
102. *Ibid.*, p. 280.
103. *Ibid.*, p. 300.
104. *Ibid.*, p. 275.
105. *Ibid.*, p. 192.
106. *Ibid.*, p. 258.
107. *Ibid.*, p. 208.
108. *Ibid.*, p. 327.
109. Primo Levi, *The Drowned and the Saved*, p. 50.
110. *Ibid.*, p. 29.
111. I. Trunk, *Judenrat*, p. 562.
112. Quoted in Avraham Tory, *Surviving the Holocaust: The Kovno Ghetto Diary*, p. 383.
113. Elie Wiesel, *A Jew Today*, p. 242.
114. Leonard Tushnet, *The Pavement of Hell*, p. 208.

8 JEWISH RESISTANCE AND THE DILEMMA OF COLLECTIVE RESPONSIBILITY

1. Joachim Schoenfeld, *Holocaust Memoirs* (New Jersey: Ktav, 1985), p. 187.
2. Yitzak Zuckerman, Commander of the Jewish Fighting Organisation in the Warsaw Ghetto, in M. Barkai (ed.), *The Fighting Ghettos* (New York: Tower, 1966), p. 23.
3. Elie Wiesel, *Against Silence*, Vol. 2, p. 267.
4. Harry Gordon, *The Shadow of Death: The Holocaust in Lithuania* (University Press of Kentucky, 1992), p. 44.
5. Avraham Tory, *Surviving the Holocaust: The Kovno Ghetto Diary*, p. 147.
6. Quoted in I. Trunk, *Judenrat*, p. 457.
7. L. Dawidowicz, *The War Against the Jews, 1939–45*, p. 391.
8. Chaika Grossman, *The Underground Army: Fighters of the Bialystok Ghetto* (New York: Holocaust Library, 1987), p. 152.
9. Avraham Tory, *Surviving the Holocaust: The Kovno Ghetto Diary*, p. 207.
10. Leni Yahil, *The Holocaust: The Fate of European Jewry*, pp. 462–3.
11. Abraham Lewin, *A Cup of Tears*, p. 120.
12. *Ibid.*
13. See Martin Gilbert, *The Holocaust*, p. 212, for details.
14. C.A. Kaplan, *Scroll of Agony: The Warsaw Diary of Chaim A Kaplan*, July 3rd 1942, p. 287.
15. *Ibid.*, July 6th 1942, p. 288.

16. See M. Gilbert, *The Holocaust*, p. 590.
17. For details see I. Trunk, *Judenrat*, p. 456, and M. Gilbert, *The Holocaust*, p. 595.
18. Quoted in I. Trunk, *Judenrat*, p. 456.
19. Yitzhak Arad, *Ghetto in Flames* (New York: Holocaust Library, 1982), p. 400.
20. Chaika Grossman, *The Underground Army: Fighters of the Bialystok Ghetto* (New York: Holocaust Library, 1987), pp. 93, 94–5.
21. Quoted in I. Trunk, *Judenrat*, p. 462.
22. In J. Roth & M. Berenbaum (eds), *Holocaust: Religious and Philosophical Implications* (New York: Paragon House, 1989), p. 142.
23. Joseph Schupack, *The Dead Years* (New York: Holocaust Library, 1986), pp. 38–9.
24. Y. Bauer, in *Holocaust*, J. Roth & M. Berenbaum (eds), p. 142.
25. Avraham Tory, *Surviving the Holocaust*, p. 198.
26. Quoted in Leonard Tushnet, *The Pavement of Hell*, p. 190.
27. See Lenni Brenner, *Zionism in the Age of Dictators* (London: Croom Helm, 1983), p. 205.
28. *Ibid.*, p. 204.
29. *Ibid.*, p. 206.
30. Quoted in L. Tushnet, *The Pavement of Hell*, pp. 185–6.
31. Interview in Harry James Cargas, *Voices From the Holocaust* (University Press of Kentucky, 1993), p. 43.
32. Avraham Tory, Kovno Ghetto, September 4th 1943, *Surviving the Holocaust: The Kovno Ghetto Diary*, p. 464.
33. See J. Schoenfeld, *Holocaust Memoirs*, pp. 113–4.
34. N. Levin, *The Holocaust*, p. 494. See also the account in Y. Suhl (ed.), *They Fought Back*, pp. 55–68.
35. See M. Elkins, *Forged in Fury*, p. 28, for details.
36. Avraham Tory, *Surviving the Holocaust*, p. 38.
37. See M. Gilbert, *The Holocaust*, pp. 599–601, for details.
38. See I. Trunk, *Judenrat*, p. 466.
39. Quoted in Lawrence Langer, *Holocaust Testimonies*, pp. 181–2.
40. Speech quoted in Lucy Dawidowicz, *The Holocaust Reader*, p. 365.
41. Quoted in J. Kermish, *Ghetto Revolts in the Struggle Against the Occupier*, in M. Kohn (ed.), *Jewish Resistance During the Holocaust*, Proceedings of the Conference on Manifestations of Jewish Resistance, Jerusalem 1968 (Jerusalem, 1971), pp. 311–2.
42. M. Gilbert, *The Holocaust*, p. 827.
43. Henri Michel, *Jewish Resistance and the European Resistance Movement*, in Yad Vashem Studies, 1968, Part 7, pp. 13, 16.
44. Yitzak Zuckerman, *A Surplus of Memory*, pp. 396–7.
45. *Ibid.*, pp. 252–3.
46. *Ibid.*, p. 300.
47. *Ibid.*, p. 330.
48. The full text of the minutes is reprinted in J. Gladstein *et al.* (ed.), *Anthology of Holocaust Literature* (New York: Atheneum, 1968), pp. 342–4.
49. J. Kernish, *Ghetto Revolts in the Struggle Against the Occupier*, in *Jewish Resistance During the Holocaust*, pp. 17a, 17b, 314.

50. Chaika Grossman, *The Underground Army*, pp. 80–1.
51. *Ibid.*, p. 153.
52. Michael Marrus, *The Holocaust in History* (London: Weidenfeld & Nicholson, 1988), p. 135.
53. See Z. Bar on *Jewish Leadership: Policy and Responsibility*, in *Jewish Resistance During the Holocaust*, p. 233.
54. R. Hilberg, *The Destruction of the European Jews*, Vol. III, p. 1031.
55. H. Michel, *Jewish Resistance & The European Resistance Movement*, in Yad Vashem Studies, 1968, Part 7, p. 14.
56. See Elie Wiesel, *Against Silence*, Vol. 2, p. 268.
57. See S. Krakowski, *The War of the Doomed: Jewish Armed Resistance in Poland 1942–1944* (New York: Ktav, 1984).
58. Michael Berenbaum, *The World Must Know*, p. 176.

9   SOE AND BRITISH MORAL RESPONSIBILITY FOR RESISTANCE

1. Phillip Knightley, *The Second Oldest Profession* (London: Andre Deutsch, 1986), p. 123.
2. Jack Beevor, *SOE: Recollections & Reflections* (Oxford: Bodley Head, 1981), p. 15.
3. Letter to Lord Halifax, quoted in M.R.D. Foot, *SOE: 1940–46* (London: BBC, 1984), p. 19.
4. Quoted in David Stafford, *Britain and European Resistance 1940–1945* (London: Macmillan, 1980), My analysis in this chapter draws heavily upon this excellent work.
5. Quoted in Stafford, *ibid.*
6. *Macbeth*, 1:VII.
7. Quoted in Ben Pimlott, *Hugh Dalton* (London: Macmillan, 1985), p. 315.
8. David Stafford, *op. cit.*, p. 26.
9. Ben Pimlott, *Hugh Dalton*, p. 315.
10. Phillip Knightley, *The Second Oldest Profession*, p. 122.
11. Quoted in Knightley, *ibid.*, p. 110.
12. Stafford, *op. cit.*, p. 33.
13. *Ibid.*, p. 59.
14. *Ibid.*, p. 27.
15. *Ibid.*, p. 81.
16. Quoted in John D. Drummond, *But For These Men* (New York: Award Books, 1965), p. 53.
17. M.R.D. Foot, *SOE in France* (London: HMSO, 1966), p. 12.
18. *Ibid.*, p. 177.
19. David Stafford, *Britain and European Resistance, 1940–1945*, p. 68.
20. *Ibid.*, p. 100.
21. M.R.D. Foot, *Resistance*, p. 50.
22. Introduction to Captain Haukelid, *Skis Against the Atom* (London: Kimber, 1954), p. XXII. This lengthy introductory essay should be consulted by all students curious about SOE.
23. Stafford, *op. cit.*, p. 81.

24. Stafford, *ibid.*, p. 131.
25. M.R.D. Foot, *Resistance*, p. 185.
26. See Madeleine Bunting, *The Model Occupation*, p. 207.
27. Quoted in R. Petrow, *The Bitter Years* (London: Purnell, 1974), p. 124.
28. See E.H. Cookridge, *Inside SOE*, p. 533.
29. Quoted in T. Gallagher, *The Telemark Raid* (London: Corgi, 1976), p. 21.
30. *Ibid.*, p. 169.
31. Quoted in *ibid.*, pp. 211–2.
32. Quoted in J.D. Drummond, *But for These Men*, p. 153.
33. Captain Haukelid, *Skis Against the Atom*, p. 145.
34. *Ibid.*, pp. 148–9.
35. R. Petrow, *The Bitter Years*, p. 238.
36. Haukelid, *Skis Against the Atom*, p. 150.
37. R. Petrow, *op. cit.*, p. 238.
38. Haukelid, *Skis Against the Atom*, p. 156.
39. Quoted in J.D. Drummond, *But For These Men*, p. 171.
40. Haukelid, *Skis Against the Atom*, p. 157.
41. Quoted in Andre Brissaud, *Canaris* (London: Weidenfeld & Nicholson, 1973), p. 272.
42. Quoted in Victor Rothwell, *Britain and the Cold War* (London: Jonathan Cape, 1982), pp. 181–2.
43. See Charles Wighton, *Heydrich: Hitler's Most Evil Henchman* (London: Corgi, 1963), Ch 23, and Gunther Deschner, *Heydrich* (London: Orbis, 1981), Ch 13, for more detailed accounts.
44. Gunther Deschner, *ibid.*, p. 212.
45. R. Paget, *Manstein: His Campaigns and His Trial* (London: Collins, 1951), p. 145.
46. Quoted in A. Brissaud, *Canaris*, p. 272.
47. See R. Luza, *The Transfer of the Sudetan Germans* (London: Routledge, 1964), p. 213.
48. Cited in G. Deschner, *Heydrich*, p. 274.
49. Callum MacDonald, *The Killing of Obergruppenfuhrer Reinhard Heydrich, 27 May 1942* (London: Macmillan, 1989), p. 199.
50. Quoted in R. Luza, *The Transfer of the Sudetan Germans*, p. 236.
51. G. Deschner, *Heydrich*, p. 275.
52. M.R.D. Foot, *Resistance*, p. 207.
53. J.B. Hutak, *With Blood and With Iron: The Lidice Story* (London: Robert Hale, 1957), pp. 108–9.
54. V. Mastny, *The Czechs Under Nazi Rule* (New York: Columbia, 1971), p. 208.
55. Quoted in Callum MacDonald, *op. cit.*, p. 156.
56. Quoted in Brissaud, *Canaris*, p. 273.
57. C. Wighton, *Heydrich*, p. 271.
58. Callum MacDonald *op. cit.*, p. 204.
59. *Ibid.*
60. *Ibid.*, p. 208.
61. Philip Knightley, *The Second Oldest Profession*, p. 124.
62. Edmund Burke, *Reflections on the Revolution in France* (Harmondsworth: Penguin, 1968), p. 176.

63. Quoted in Sir C. Webster & N. Frankland, *The Strategic Air Offensive* (London: HMSO, 1961), Vol. 3, p. 88.
64. In P. Howarth, *Undercover* (London: Arrow, 1980), p. 11.
65. Liddell Hart, *The Defence of the West* (London: Cassell, 1950), pp. 54–5.
66. *Ibid.*
67. *When Britain Turned Terrorist*. Review of Nigel West, *The Secret War*, *Sunday Telegraph*, 9 February 1992.
68. *Observer*, 3 November 1985.
69. Reprinted in *Irish Action* (Atholl Books, Belfast, 1968), p. 54.
70. Quoted in C. Sterling, *The Terror Network* (London: Weidenfeld & Nicholson, 1981), p. 200.

10 CONCLUSION

1. Neal Ascherson, *Games With Shadows* (London: Radius, 1988), p. 169.
2. Quoted in L. Snyder, *The Dynamics of Nationalism* (Princeton: Van Nostrand, 1964), p. 98.
3. Madeleine Bunting, *The Model Occupation*, p. 6.
4. *Ibid.*, p. 316.
5. *Ibid.*, p. 206.
6. Quoted in BBC documentary, *Jackboots, Buckets and Spades*, 21st June 1995.
7. See M. Bunting, *The Model Occupation*, pp. 219, 324.
8. In Polonsky (ed.), *My Brother's Keeper: Recent Polish Debates on the Holocaust*, p. 203.
9. Andrew Roberts, *The Way We Nearly Were*, *Sunday Telegraph*, May 17th 1992.
10. C.M. Woodhouse, quoted in endpiece to D. Mountfield, *The Partisans*.
11. M. Bunting, *The Model Occupation*, p. 319.
12. Djilas, *Wartime*, p. 32.
13. D. Mountfield, *The Partisans*, p. 10.
14. Jean-Paul Sartre, quoted in S. Hawes & R. White, *Resistance in Europe 1939–45*, p. 118.
15. Alan Milward, *The Economic and Strategic Effectiveness of Resistance*, in S. Hawes & R. White, *Resistance in Europe 1939–45*, p. 197.
16. H. Michel, *The Shadow War*, p. 290; p. 329.
17. *Ibid.*, p. 201.
18. General D. Eisenhower, *Crusade in Europe* (New York: Doubleday, 1948), pp. 332–3.
19. See David Martin, *Web of Disinformation: Churchill's Yugoslav Blunder*, p. 88.
20. Nietzsche, *Between Good and Evil* (New York: Vintage, 1966), p. 89.
21. Albert Camus, *Resistance, Rebellion and Death*, pp. 44–5.
22. Janina Bauman, *Winter in Morning: A Young Girl's Life in the Warsaw Ghetto & Beyond* (London: Virago, 1986), p. XVIII.
23. W.H. Auden, poem: *Spain*.
24. See Maria de Blasio Wilhem, *The Other Italy: The Italian Resistance in World War II* (New York: W.W. Norton, 1988), p. 185.

25. Elsa Caspers, *To Save a Life*, p. 34
26. W. Jordan, *Conquest Without Victory*, p. 153.
27. Matthew Cooper, *The Phantom War*, p. 132.
28. *Ibid.*, p. 74.
29. W. Jordan, *Conquest Without Victory*, p. 55.
30. See Alan Clark, *Barbarossa*, p. 186.
31. Quoted in P. Calvocoressi, *Nuremberg* (London: Chatto & Windus 1947), p. 108.
32. *Nuremberg Trials*, Vol. V, p. 399.
33. *Ibid.*, pp. 416–7.
34. I. Ehrenburg, *Russia at War*, pp. 130–1.
35. Quoted in Theo Schulte, *The German Army and Nazi Policies in Occupied Russia*, p. 122.
36. See *ibid.*
37. A. De Zayas, *The Wehrmacht War Crimes Bureau 1939–1945* (University of Nebraska Press, 1989), p. 105.
38. *Ibid.*, pp. 106–7.
39. *Ibid.*, p. 183.
40. Alfred de Zayas, *The Wehrmacht War Crimes Bureau 1939–1945*, p. 156.
41. Max Hastings, *Das Reich*, p. 137.
42. Quoted in George Delf, *Humanizing Hell* (London: Hamish Hamilton, 1985), p. 21.
43. Jean-Paul Sartre, *What is Literature*, p. 161.
44. A. Horne, *A Savage War of Peace: Algeria 1954–1962* (London: Macmillan, 1977), p. 27.
45. Cited in R. Gildea, *France Since 1945* (Oxford University Press, 1997), p. 73.
46. J. Talbott, *The War Without a Name* (London: Faber & Faber, 1981), p. 94.
47. *Ibid.*, p. 247.
48. E. Hillesum, *Etty: A Diary*, p. 188.
49. J. Glenn Gray, *The Warriors*, p. 6.
50. Frieda Knight, *The French Resistance*, p. 201.
51. I have been unable to go into greater detail about this incident because I completed my manuscript prior to receiving an excellent detailed study. See Tzvetan Todorov, *A French Tragedy: Scenes of Civil War, Summer 1944* (Hanover: University Press of New England, 1996).
52. Quoted in *The German New Order in Poland*, p. 91.
53. Quoted in R. Lukas, *The Forgotten Holocaust*, p. 162.
54. R. Lukas, *ibid.*, p. 163.
55. Quoted in I. Gutman, *The Jews of Warsaw 1940–1943* (Indiana University Press, 1989), p. 363.
56. Mark Mazower, *Inside Hitler's Greece*, p. 372.
57. Quoted in E.D. Smith, *Victory of a Sort* (London: Robert Hale, 1988), p. 187.
58. See Nicholas Gage, *Eleni* (London: Fontana, 1983), pp. 366–7.
59. Lawrence Langer, *Holocaust Testimonies*, pp. 85–6.
60. Albert Camus, *The Rebel* (Harmondsworth: Penguin, 1969), p. 268.
61. Lawrence Langer, *Holocaust Testimonies*, p. 86.

62. L. Adelsberger, *Auschwitz: A Doctor's Story* (London: Robson Books, 1996), p. 12.
63. *Ibid.*
64. *Ibid.*, p. 100.
65. *Ibid.*, p. 101
66. Olga Lengyel, *Five Chimneys*, p. 111.

Note: References to the Nuremberg Trials are to the Blue Series *Trial of the Major War Criminals Before the International Military Tribunal*, 42 vols (Nuremberg 1946–49). Green Series refers to *Trial of War Criminals Before the Nuremberg Military Tribunals*, 15 vols (Washington, DC: US Department of the Army, 1948).

Index of Atrocities, Hostage and Reprisal Killings

General Index

315